P9-DGP-495

TO CATCH A MOUSE, *Make a Noise Like a Cheese*

TO CATCH A MOUSE, *Make a Noise Like a Cheese*

Lewis Kornfeld

Prentice-Hall, Inc., Englewood Cliffs, N.J. 07632

Prentice-Hall, International Inc., *London*
Prentice-Hall of Australia, Pty. Ltd., *Sydney*
Prentice-Hall Canada Inc., *Toronto*
Prentice-Hall of India Private Ltd., *New Delhi*
Prentice-Hall of Japan, Inc., *Tokyo*
Prentice-Hall of Southeast Asia Pte. Ltd., *Singapore*
Whitehall Books, Ltd., *Wellington, New Zealand*
Editors Prentice-Hall Do Brasil LTDA., *Rio De Janeiro*

© 1983 by
Lewis Kornfeld

All rights reserved. No part of this book may be reproduced in any form or by any means, without permission in writing from the publisher.

Library of Congress Cataloging in Publication Data

Kornfeld, Lewis F.
To catch a mouse—make a noise like a cheese.

Includes index.
1. Advertising. 2. Selling. I. Title.
HF5821.K66 1983 659.1 82-13320
ISBN 0-13-922930-2
ISBN 0-13-922914-0 {PBK.}

Printed in the United States of America

INVOCATIONS

The first big corporate get-together I attended after Fort Worth's Tandy Corporation acquired Boston's Radio Shack Corporation began, to my great surprise, with an invocation. I had never run into one of those in New England, possibly because up there we had a tendency in business to give thanks rather than request blessing; or possibly because I ran around with the wrong people.

Now that there's a book at hand, a similar choice is presented: the customary dedication (in thanks), or the one chosen, an *invocation* (to conjure up approving spirits, c.f., the nine Muses who preside over matters like arts and sciences). My muses are more than nine, but the number is far from infinite. With their support, this job of work will have succeeded in fact, regardless of its marketing history.

The First Muse is my wife, Ethel Hardy Kornfeld, who has an innate sense of the uses of quality in a world where "the bleeps"—as personified by the evening television and the morning newspaper—are "killing us," to alter slightly an old refrain by Norman Mailer.

The Second Muse is plural: all my associates in buying, selling, engineering, manufacturing, designing, writing, laying out, pasting up, importing, investing, and keeping score at Radio Shack and Tandy, without whom there would be no book—literary, scrap, or bank.

The Third Muse is singular: the late archetypical entrepreneur, Charles David Tandy, father of the modern Radio Shack, of Tandy Corporation (NYSE), of Tandycrafts (NYSE), of Tandy Brands (AMEX), of Color Tile (OTC), and of the twin towers of Tandy Center which sparked a building and commerce renaissance in downtown Fort Worth, Texas. A lot for one man, but he was a lot of man.

Charles Tandy alone among his peers perceived the wisdom of taking over Radio Shack in 1963 and diversifying from leather into electronics merchandising. He endowed The Shack with a new formula for becoming the world's largest consumer electronics company, a simple formula which I was privileged to help make sufficiently complex to succeed.

Early in our association he told me: "Kornfeld, stay with me and I'll make you rich." His credibility became such that even after he'd gone to deal with his Maker, I was still staying with him.

He understood the need for advertising the way a body understands blood. His pungent, Aesopian philosophy about it emerged one day during the fifth hour of the daily nine-hour improvised monologue he thoroughly believed was a typical interactive business conference.

"If you want *to catch a mouse,*" Tandy said when the subject of advertising came up, "you've got to *make a noise like a cheese.*"

Amen.

DISCLAIMERS

In a litigious society such as ours, no book and few products would dare venture outside without a disclaimer or, more precisely perhaps, a disavowal.

> The contents of this book do not necessarily represent the opinions of Tandy Corporation, Radio Shack, their divisions or subsidiaries, or any of their employees or associates—past or present.
>
> Additional disclaimers are included in Chapter 6 of this book.
>
> Any success I may have had in establishing a record high for the number of scrivener caveats is purely coincidental.

TABLE OF CONTENTS

IN THE BEGINNING. . . .

What to do when George Parker, an editor from a large publishing house, writes to compliment you on your writing style and says, "If you happen to be writing a book or thinking about doing so, we'd be interested in publishing it"? What I did was preen my back feathers and start thinking.

"Provided you'd like to explore this further, I'll look forward to hearing from you," his letter concluded. Quite obviously, this book is the love child of that further exploration.

It all began when Mr. Parker's interest in electronics led him to visit a Radio Shack store, then to become a customer, then to be put on the company's mailing list, then to receive its monthly flyer containing my regular column "Flyer-Side Chat."

The latter was my notion of how to present Radio Shack and its merchandise in an intimate and entertaining manner to the cream of its patrons—the over 10 million most recent of 30 million customer names in the corporate computer. Probably George got my message many times before I got his.

"Flyer-Side Chat" columns pleased (and irritated) quite a few people through the years as I continued to demonstrate a pet marketing theory, to wit: 1000 words are often better than one picture. (For samples, see the chapter "The Boss As

Salesman.") Many fans had hoped to see the Chats in book form but, as I told them, they're too tied to contemporary events and products to stand that sort of test of relevancy.

The book that entered my mind, when my mind was opened to receive the notion of writing one, came as a welcome partial answer to a number of questions I'd left dangling. How long, for example, can a man go on buying and selling, worrying over headlines and deadlines, facing shortages and overstocks, keeping up with technical and stylistic product changes, maintaining leadership in small computer marketing against the likes of such well-heeled newcomers as IBM and Japan, Inc.? How long, that is, without losing his marbles? When you've been pounding the same pavement for three decades, what do you do when you can't pound as hard as you used to?

When I asked a now departed friend, Arthur Fiedler, roughly the same question, he said he intended to keep on conducting the Boston Pops until they carried him (or he fell) off the bandstand. "I don't intend to sit on the front porch in a rocking chair waiting for the doctor to come," Arthur told me.

Not too long after that, the flow of this book began to seem more age-appropriate than the ebb of a rocking chair. I point out in the chapter "Future Schlock" that memory seems not to have any mass at all; yet one thing about memory is surer than mortality, inflation, or taxes: it has no lifetime other than the immediate ticking present. If something is worth writing about, DO IT TODAY, as we say in advertising when we remember to include a response coupon.

Still the question persisted—what to write about? Well, there was this: I had participated in growing Radio Shack from a $1,000,000-a-year midget to a $2,000,000,000-a-year colossus. Many marketing and financial people would appreciate even a small inkling of how that was done, particularly in an industry (consumer electronics) more loaded with famous failures than any other I can think of in modern times. I speak of manufacturing and importing, too, and not only of retailing, because The Shack does all three.

Then there was the unique chance to take a few whacks

at the execrable quality of advertising I'd observed over all the years I'd been responsible for spending millions on it. No, I didn't think ours had the "execrable quality"; that was theirs—the guys in the black hats. Advertising that sells, and sells *measurably,* doesn't have to be ashamed if its collar is blue and its prices are blatant. I had at least these two things in mind about advertising:

1. *To talk about it as if I were addressing a group of managers or owners* whose main task was not to do anything more than sign checks for it and okay invoices. As Tandy used to say, "That's wrongWrongWRONG." And as I say, "It's time you got your money's worth." And I try to show you how.

2. *To talk about ways of doing it better*—copy ways, picture ways, media ways, position ways. It's sort of like what I've always tried to tell Pan Am Airlines: if I pay to go first class, I deserve to get my bags off first, too. Any advertising that's paid for should try to come off first.

Another set of appealing book ideas also presented itself when the metaphor "book as podium" came to mind:

1. *Merchandising and Marketing,* my two most important tasks on the highway to the corner office, are black arts no matter what color was assigned to them in antiquity or academia. In a book I could do a little painting by the numbers, particularly by filling in some blanks involving the personal computer business we'd launched so notably in 1977.

2. *Advertising Agencies* and other consultants score something on the order of 9 on my Least-Needed scale of 10. The reasons for this come partly from experience I'd not at all mind sharing, and partly from natural iconoclasm and do-it-yourselfishness that you can take or leave.

3. *The Breath of a Salesman* contains a large number of words, ideas, and occasionally thoughts. Eventually, as in my case, these harden into rules with a capital R. Hence 65 of Kornfeld's Rules of Marketing are built into this book, along with a large number of what I call *ADvisories* (tele-

grams which might have been Rules except that I like the idea of an assortment broader than one stockkeeping unit).

4. *Weak Competition* is attractive to any joint-venturer. Mine may be the one book by someone who has never worked at an ad agency, business school, or consulting group. Most books I've seen on advertising, for example, are authored by professional MadAvers and many are about as entertaining as the text of a forceps catalog. I've resisted reading through more than two or three of them in the fear of getting a bad case of conventional wisdom and infecting those near and dear.

5. *Radio Shack and Tandy Corporation* offered another book idea, having figured rather prominently in the news ever since all non-electronic divisions were spun off and electronics became the only game left. If my dropped anecdotes about them don't amount to a documentary, at least they're supplemental to the data furnished by Standard & Poor's. Interestingly, Charles Tandy believed that whatever type of business was doing worst at the moment—for example, moccasins or wallpaper—would be the one The Street would tag him with and thereby depress his common stock to the low P/E depth that troubled industry had sunk to at the time. And so?—we'd just stay in the one proven winner, consumer electronics. That was 1975. By 1977, now all-electronic, Tandy was roughed up by The Street for being a "CB radio company." And early in 1982 it was spanked a bit for being such a good "small computer company"! (Next . . . too little short-term debt?)

6. *The Charles Tandy Story* is what many people thought I should write were I to enter second childhood as an author and forsake consume-side economics. He died in his prime in 1978 at 60, but his flag still flies higher than most because he stayed on track every day of his life. Even so, I couldn't get interested in doing a bio. His wasn't the universal role of a Calvin, Kelvin, Ghandi, or the eccentric spectacle of a Howard Hughes. But if more Capital Gainers in this country had his brains, humanity, desire to build and perpetuate, America might actually be more like it allegedly

was when it ran on axiom instead of advertising and litigious claim. I've dropped his name and vernacular quite a few times within these pages.

7. *Teaching by On-the-Job Training* is a fine art I've never entirely mastered. Yet all executives are supposed to be teachers first, and only afterwards self-centered swine; one must pretend to think of #1 as secondary! But haven't I always, for example, taught writers such things as eschewing abbreviations in ad copy? If they say 25A, does the A mean amperes, apples, or the pages inserted after #25? Does "amp" mean ample, amps, or amplifiers?—and why do they say "amp" when they really mean "amplifier and tuner (= receiver)"? Well, regardless of how much teaching I do in the next 15 chapters, please understand that this book is not a textbook. It is a case book, a cause book, a casual book, a caustic book, and it is opinionated as hell. Take it on those terms, and if you can forgive 101 one-liners, you will learn something from it. That's a promise.

8. *The Ego Trip* is—unless one writes to earn a living and probably even then—a reason for almost any book ever written for public sale. Your ticket is a pen, a typewriter, or word processor; but if you're a great talker and not a writer, then all you need is a tape recorder and a copier. Whatever your needs, they can all be filled at Radio Shack. That, at least, is the way I've looked at fulfillment since I rented them all ten fingers and craftsmanship for $5000 p/a in 1948.

Advertising the First Person

There was a moment of debate between Steve and George, two of my publisher's people, as to whether I needed to present credentials at the beginning of this book. In Japan there would be no question about it: we *always* exchange business cards in the Far East; it's an endless who's who environment. (I have four feet of name cards—48 solid inches of them—in one of my desk drawers, a selection which grows an inch a year: ½″ in Japan, and ¼″ each in Hongkong and Taiwan.)

ADvisory. Business cards as credentials-advertising are discussed in one of my chapters on the media. Basically, I say try not to be unique or chauvinistic. For example, the big German cards don't fit into my desk drawer; the little French ones get stuck in cracks; the double-pagers get bent or torn.

"If they don't know who Kornfeld is," said Steve suddenly, "why should they want to read his book?"

"They'll find out about him from us," George replied. George is the Prentice-Hall editor who discovered my weakness for putting words together strongly.

"I was born in Swampscott, Massachusetts, and grew up in Brookline," I confided. "How's that for openers?"

Awful. It was quickly decided to furnish a few credentials but to skip everything from Swampscott and Brookline—all 22 years of it—to the years at the University of Denver as editor of its newspaper *The Clarion,* and its first literary magazine *Space,* and as a graduate assistant and instructor in its department of English Literature, while in the process of earning BA and MA degrees. Noteworthy, in this six-year cruise, is a total absence of courses in finance, marketing, art, advertising, or commerce of any kind.

The next six years were unequally divided between reporting for Denver's daily Scripps-Howard newspaper, the *Rocky Mountain News,* and the United States Marine Corps in WWII—an event that has been going on for so long that now, in the 1980s, it often seems we're on the verge of losing it to people who were adversary or friendly during its first period, and sometimes both simultaneously.

Flashback. While writing for the *News,* I worked for the city editor, a bushy-haired gent who brought his lunch to the office in a black tin lunch box and whose wife had written the successful Broadway comedy "Harvey." Her name was Mary, his was Bob (Chase). My first assignment from Mr. Chase was to cover a convention in downtown Denver, and I went to it with Angelo, one of our staff photographers. On returning to the *News* office, I was brought up short by my boss.

"Where's Angelo?" he demanded.

"I don't know. *Should* I know?"

"Kornfeld," said Bob, coldly, "I hope I'm only going to have to tell you this once: ALL PHOTOGRAPHERS ARE CHILDREN. They have to be told where to go, where to go next, and when to come home."

In retrospect, it's too bad Bob Chase didn't include artists in that lecture. They're also children. Nice. But children. Never give the child who's called an Advertising Artist a gold star (if you do, he'll ask for a gold sky).

When I wasn't decoding messages and trying to overcome constipation in the Solomon Islands, I spent the lonely hours wondering what I'd do when the war was over. I eventually perceived five courses of action—which reminds me that feisty, unneurotic tycoon Charles Tandy much later would say: "The executive who can't think of five solutions to any problem is a damn dumb dodo." My five were:

1. Accept my colonel's invitation to remain in the Marine Corps and have a pension before I was 50. "Ha!"
2. Return to the University of Denver or somewhere and again get into the generally vain attempt to deposit English Lit into crania of the First World. "Ho!"
3. Return to the *Rocky Mountain News* or some other daily journal and work my way up to Ernie Pyle. (The pay to try for this was insufficient and probably still is.)
4. Go into writing full time on my own. (My problem was I was too getting too old to risk failure and I was a newlywed with an urgent mission to provide sustenance.)
5. So my thoughts turned to advertising, a business which seemed to hold out good prospects for the exercise of my credentials. I returned to my native Boston in pursuit of a copywriter's job.

Banned in Boston by BBD&O

At that time I'd never heard of a company ad agency, only of "outside" ad agencies, so naturally I started knocking on the latter's door, waving a fistful of by-lined material and college degrees, touting my talents in a cultivated but brisk manner. Surely one of them would discover that I could write selling copy better than the dullards they had. Obviously I would work cheaper.

"Surely" and "obviously" may define today's graduates—particularly the MBA ones—but for war vets, even those with MAs and writerly credentials, it was thanks but no thanks at BBD&O, Sullivan, and the others. If my "banned in Boston" subheadline is too lurid a description of the treatment I got, maybe it's the sort of hyperbole that'll get their attention. And maybe the next untried youngster with a flair for fluid flummery will get a genuine hearing.

A company called Radio Shack had been set up in 1921 in a section of downtown Boston that now is a walking mall leading by the Old State House toward city hall and into Dock Square, just above the exciting new-fashioned Quincy Market district. By 1948, the company had felt the need for a fulltime advertising manager and, as luck would have it, I got the job.

My arrival virtually coincided with the debut on the American retailing scene of things like television sets, hi-fi components, LP records, magnetic phono cartridges, tape and tape recorders. We were all new together. To become an "industry expert" one didn't need a century of experience and recognition; one needed only to be there—in electronics—instead of in such old fogies as the shoe, department store, banking, or publishing business.

Thus I could be among the first to advertise TV sets with the bonus of an outside antenna thrown in free . . . to advertise hi-fi music systems at a group price instead of in separate and somewhat mysterious parts at "each" prices . . . to preside over the publication of what was then (1948) one of a handful of electronic parts catalogs and is now the only one left . . . to spend all I could get of the co-op ad money that was our supplier's typical way of getting his dealers to get off their duffs . . . to keep our mailing list afloat and growing.

In 1954 I was made Radio Shack's VP of advertising, partly, I've always thought, to avoid being given a raise. And by 1958, it having been mutually discovered that I had some talent for selecting and pricing merchandise, and a taste for private branding, I'd become VP of merchandising and advertising. I was in on the company's first trips to Japan. I helped set up our import-export division, A & A Trading Company, headquartered in Tokyo since 1955; and I'd fallen deeply in love with the idea of self-manufacture, an affair that (see the chapter on "Marketing the TRS-80") would have beneficial consequences a light year beyond my imagination, or even Tandy's.

Despite some lean years, my position and title remained VP merchandising/advertising after the 1963 takeover of Radio Shack by Tandy Corporation. Tandy, in the unique person of its late chairman Charles D. Tandy, had an urge to go coast-to-coast with a store system and nothing could satisfy him—nothing, that is, but going. In the spring of 1970, on the condition that I would move our headquarters from Boston to Fort Worth, Texas, Tandy's home town, I was made president of Radio Shack . . . in 1975 elected to Tandy's board of directors . . . in 1978, executive VP of the parent company . . . and in 1980, vice chairman.

During all that time—over 30 years—I had watched our advertising budget grow from a tame 3% of $1,000,000 annual sales to something startlingly like 9% of $2 billion. Startling, that is, to financial types whose logic tells them our rocket would fly just as safely on one-third less fuel.

In the matter of marketing credentials: I've spent about $600,000,000 on advertising and sales promotion, and billions on buying merchandise and getting it distributed and sold.

These are thoroughbred numbers, Podner, even if I am a maverick. Maybe it's smart to try getting some of your kicks from a horse of a different color?

As my credentials began to acquire the thorns and roses of an elder statesman, the following became evident:

It's true: I don't like ad agencies and consultants.

It's a fact: I recommend an in-house ad agency if you have a business that can make a rationale for setting one up.

It's certain: I feel, along with John Wanamaker, that 50¢ of most ad dollars spent are wasted. We differ only in that I offer a number of ways of improving the waste ratio.

To conclude my resumé, consider the LHD degree I was honored to receive in 1981 from Boston University. It's the acronym for Doctor of Humane Letters. You can take the measure of both my humanity and my letters just by turning the page.

ONE

Advertising: Reasons and Definitions

How to Make a Noise Like a Cheese

Making "a noise like a cheese" is implicit in all efforts to attract a potential buyer to whatever the noise-maker wishes to barter; and it's as old as sin. Actually there are many people who think it *is* a sin to woo customers, and others who find it sinful only for specified days or reasons. When Radio Shack first opened its "Tandy" stores in Europe it quickly encountered interesting examples of impiety:

■ In Belgium we couldn't put a sign inside our store window without first getting approval from the post office, even though it was merely a small sign announcing the particulars of our Grand Opening. Additionally, although we could reduce price without official approval, we could *advertise* price reductions in the newspapers only in the months of January and July, the two government-approved "sale" periods.

■ In Germany we couldn't advertise our famous free five-cell flashlight. The authorities made us remove this traditional customer-puller from newspaper ads because it "forced people to come to our stores by psychological inducement." To tout our useful and popular freebie was a nein-by-Rhine. Also a non-by-Seine.

Flashback. Many people have asked me why our overseas stores (England, Australia, EEC, about 1000 in all) are called "Tandy" instead of "Radio Shack." The truth is, it was the result of a battle of great minds. I said, "Radio Shack has the advantage of the universally known word 'radio' in it, and, together with 'Shack,' it's a proven winner." Charles Tandy, then chairman, saw it differently. "Kornfeld," he said, "I can have how much bigger a sign using the five letters of Tandy as against the ten letters of Radio Shack?" (I lost five to ten, but because the management team we exported had an insufficient awareness of advertising, our Tandy signs abroad turned out to be smaller than our Radio Shack signs in North America, and some—due to delicacies of local custom—even substantially smaller.)

The Pheromone Factor

Proof that advertising is as natural as biological existence itself is demonstrated by its relationship to pheromone. Did you know that pheromone is "a substance secreted and released by an animal for detection and response by another of the same species"? Well, neither did my closest and smartest friends, and for that reason I chose as my book title *To Catch a Mouse*—instead of *The Pheromone Factor*.

In a later chapter ("Ad Copy Made Memorable") I show how consideration of the pheromone factor is one of my five basic considerations of written salesmanship. Everything done in the marketing of products and programs should contain the verbal or pictorial essence of that vital substance we all release for *"detection and response by another of the same species."*

When they stop/look/listen—that's detection. When they buy or don't buy—that's response. Pheromone? If more ad agency copy people knew what it was, maybe they'd write less superficially and more magnetically. Or with less hocus and more focus? But don't delay your vacation in the hope that such a miracle will come to pass before gold hits $1000, or until those writers admit that "pure gold" is 24K; what they're pushing as pure gold is one of these: 10K which is

41% pure, 14K which is 58% pure, or 18K which is only 75% pure. Clearly, golden rules and definitions are needed!

My definition for marketing—oversimplified as is my wont and my prerogative—is "the sum of all the processes involved in distribution after production."

Radio Shack's director of public relations, a bearded portly chap by the name of Martin Bradley Winston, has a somewhat more elaborate notion, as expressed in his book *Getting Publicity,* published in 1982 by John Wiley & Sons, Inc. Marty says, "Marketing means influencing the behavior of one or several persons in such a manner that they will make the purchase, cast the vote, or offer the contribution desired from them. This involves convincing an audience, which in turn means communicating a message."

When I queried The Shack's executive VP of marketing, Bernard Appel, about the word, he replied: "Marketing includes three elements: determination of what's needed—product or whatever; location and negotiation of it; and the sale of it." Bernie reminded me that my age-old definition of what a buyer of merchandise must do was locate, negotiate, and sell, proving that if I haven't had too many ideas over time, the ones I've had have roots that go down to my shoes.

Where is advertising in these definitions? It's part and parcel of selling. It's communicating. It's trying to convince. It's the catching of mice by means of making a noise like a cheese.

Many professional and amateur advertisers think of advertising as a sort of maze requiring a compass, a dowser, a guide, a banker, a jester, and a rabbit's foot to get through. Why? Because like so many misguided businessmen, they believe the shortest line to success is not from A to B, but more like from A to C to G to B. When I was in the Marines' officers' school learning where to place weapons on a battle map, I was told: "They go EXACTLY where we tell you to put them. This is not a college exam. We are not trying to trick you." Anywhere but THERE was called "fighting the problem."

ADvisory. Do not "fight the problem" of what to do in

the name of advertising by being tricky, funny, weird, annoying, exotic, naughty or even nice . . . let the product and the desired customer lead you to the selling message.

ADvisory. If your existing advertising is doing a good job for you, why change it? Why change advertising that lives up to the very definition of the word? If Ford can sell a "better idea" with a switched-on light bulb, who needs guck like a "world car" and "a Ford in America's future"?

Kornfeld's 1st Rule of Marketing involves not swapping existing success for novel experimentation. It says:

---

1 Don't fight problems of creating and placing new advertising or product displays if they seem solvable by old answers. Consider repeating, with or without changes, previously used layouts, copy, art, or display material.

What's wrong with using second-hand marketing wares? Not a doggone thing, says Kornfeld. Management gets tired of its advertising long before the customers and prospects do. And nobody gets tireder quicker than advertising professionals; they'd like a new dress for every party, and one in reserve in case something spills. As Denver poet Thomas Hornsby Ferril once said in a poem, the future is a matter of "back seat lovers starting something over." Me, I'm a reformed poet talking of starting something over, with what's on hand and paid for.

ADvisory. Save those tried and true ad-artifacts; there's no commission on born-again pictures, typography, layouts, pasteups, folders, stationery, logos.

What's advertising in the final analysis?— it's marketing shorn of some of its feathers. If I've confused the two terms, it's deliberate. If my 64 remaining Rules of Marketing are really Rules of Advertising . . . do you care? As stated earlier, this is a travelogue, not a text book!

It's a Sin to Tell a Myth

His Divine Grace A. C. Bhaktivedanta Swami Prabhupāda tells us that the third defect of Man is his "cheating propensity." He believes "everyone has the propensity to cheat others," which is pretty sage stuff from a fellow who may not even know where Madison Avenue is or that it's the Mecca of ad agencies, so to speak. And in case you don't know what a propensity is, it's an *innate inclination,* something that comes naturally, like "little white lie"-ing, hyperbole, exaggeration, half truth, full untruth, error in your favor.

Who needs it?—only those who don't know any better, who believe (erroneously) that it's the duty of advertising to sell no matter what sins are committed in its execution, or who have that "innate propensity" to cheat—the same folks who think only simpletons get to B directly from A.

I have a chapter on the result of this propensity; it's Chapter 12, entitled "Advertising's Articulate Anti's." Please read it. See what happens when you put Spandex into your copy . . . so it's stretchable (the truth, that is). If you can't talk a Ford Granada into becoming a low-cost Mercedes Benz, why tempt Providence and the consumerists? That kind of promise doesn't make a BMW "the ultimate driving machine" either, unless—as my friend of the great pauses, radio and TV news commentator Paul Harvey, says—"it . . izzZ!"

Everybody advertises, as it turns out. You advertised when you cleaned up your home or your car before unloading them onto their next owner . . . when you bothered today to select your clothing from an assortment in your closet (the fact you didn't just grab the nearest thing hanging there is the tipoff) . . . when you decided to do something extra about that program you want to peddle to your club or company or to the government—something like improving its appearance, editing, logic, timeliness, something in short, that's just what advertising is all about.

Each time you make an effort that's a form of advertising, you're faced with a serious decision. Should I run the risk of failure and take on the extra expense? Or sit here, letting nature take its course? And you—or at least I—usually opt against nature because, frankly, the lady's too damn slow. To get momentum, you may only have to do one of these four relatively elementary things:

1. *Do it quicker.* Nature, as just noted, won't get that new product or old inventory off the shelves fast enough. For curing a sick inventory or a slumping sales report—or even for starting a brand-new disease—man-made technology is the way to go. I call it advertising, but I don't look down at extra marketeers like spiffs, ad-ons, rebates, and PR.

2. *Make it a valentine instead of a memo* by sweetening the pot. That means you look at changing messages: distribution, advertising, display, graphics, timing, any piece of your sales puzzle that no longer looks like a love letter.

3. *Repackage it.* To get the most out of your display space, you change that krafty look to something slick or colorful, you change that "nothing" shape into one that fits pockets or hands or shelves, you try to go back to One Up on your competition.

4. *Do it bigger.* You consider advertising in larger space, or more frequently, or with added color; you consider slipping in a coupon, mailing out an offer, piggybacking with other advertisers, doing something about radio and TV—hopefully with a vendor rich enough to pay the freight. (If you decide to have a contest, please take me off your mailing list.)

Whatever you decide to do, above all don't leave the decision up to what C. D. Tandy used to call "the Ribbon Clerks." If you do, and if your little project at goosing sales fails, you'll deserve whatever horrors fate has in store for generals who don't lead the charge. Note: at other times Tandy would call the ribbon clerks "Fry Cooks"; but whatever their titular designation, they can't be made into 90-day-wonder executives by your loan to them of a title or a pad of purchase orders, and their possession of a degree or two in something sober such as Advertising Essentials, World Trade, Corporate Finance, Marketing, or Distribution.

I have a chapter on this, too. Called "The Boss As Salesman," it leans pretty hard on honchos who motivate by saying "Go sic 'em" between dates at the bank and the 19th hole and the hallowed halls of the House of Representatives Office Building.

Why give your sales or inventory or advertising problem to a beginner, or even to a rented think tank? Why propagate the myth that advertising is an occult specialty? Why react by giving its execution to outside consultants? Is advertising a black box that's better left to the folks who brought you Pandora? Then why not also dole out your decisions on accounting, personnel, manufacturing, pricing and dealer relations?

> ***ADvisory.*** The Pandora People didn't put you in business and didn't do the strategic planning, the risk-taking, and the advertising that brought you to your present strong position. They're Johnnies-come-after. You came there first!

Solving Wanamaker's Conundrum

One task I laid out for this hopefully thought-provoking book was to help solve what I call Wanamaker's Conundrum. It's believed that John Wanamaker (1838–1922), founder of a Philadelphia department store chain that now sails under the Carter Hawley Hale flag, once said: "I know one-half of every advertising dollar I spend is wasted . . . but I don't know which half."

Ouch! That's the kind of gentle maxim that lets otherwise tough money men off the hook when it comes to approving outlays and invoices for ads.

"If advertising has a 50% guesstimate factor, who the hell am I to question these numbers?" asks our stiff-necked nickel-chaser just two minutes after chewing out a gal who threw away a two-inch pencil.

Anyway, what's more certain than our unanimous agreement that Wanamaker's Conundrum must be solved, that not knowing which is the wasted half of our advertising dollar is an insult to the intelligence of our lenders and investors and would look pretty comical in an Annual Report or a 10-K?

I might buy a ratio like 80% no-waste and 20% possible waste. But if Radio Shack's ad bill is $120,000,000, a 20% waste factor is $24 million down the tube. (A bad buy!)

I dealt with an 80/20 ratio for years in merchandising, where *80% of sales came from 20% of the products.* What? Only a measly 20% of your sales come from the remaining 80% of our stock-keeping units? Yes, Virginia, them's the numbers.

> ***ADvisory.*** The consolation here would be that an 80% wastefree advertising dollar would be 60% better than 50%. Even Wanamaker could have told you that!

Six Problems, Six Solutions

The move to solve the Wanamaker Conundrum has been made, seconded, and passed unanimously. We don't want to waste 50% (or even 20%) of every ad dollar. We don't want stunned silence as to which half is wasted. To get zeroed in on the quandary at hand, consider six reasonable problems and solutions I've developed for your logical mind:

PROBLEM #1: *Boring advertising.* I can show it to you wholesale, and later in this essay I will. If, alas, one of my examples is your own boring ad, I'll show you some that got by me when I looked at the bottom line instead of the headline.

SOLUTION #1: *Make news, don't just fill space.* News is almost never boring. Make news, not jokes. Jokes in ads are almost never funny. Ask for orders, not applause!

PROBLEM #2: *Excessive hyperbole.* I've already walked you through Man's third basic defect, the cheating propensity. Hyperbole in advertising is an invitation to governmental and consumerist interference. The last time I looked, we couldn't even say our hi-fi equipment makes "better sound"—not better than Sony, say, just better, period—without proving it. How can you prove things that are mostly subjective? The last time I looked, we had to say "battery operated" or "batteries not included." Why? Will these be next: "Cars sold without gas or passengers"—"TV set does not include picture shown"—"This ad certified (percent) true" followed by notarized signatures of ad agency and two witnesses?

SOLUTION #2: *Ask for orders instead of applause and credibility.* I know I've said this before, but it deserves repetition. "Taste verdict: Merit. Former higher tar smokers applaud MERIT as 'best-tasting low tar' they've tried." This is a recent cigarette ad headline. Me, I'd almost rather stamp out ad copy like this than stamp out smoking. The solution? Avoid verdicts that don't result in conviction!

PROBLEM #3: *The boss is too busy to sell.* Now that you're quoted in *Fortune* and honored at Sassafras University you haven't got time to fool with such trivia as ad messages, ad productivity, ad measurability. What's that? You personally okayed the bill to send a TV commercial camera crew to Africa to film your tires conquering those safari-edged rocks? Don't you remember when the rocks around Dayton were sharp enough and your P/E was 21 and your employees admired you?

SOLUTION #3: *Get back in your car,* take a small customer out to lunch, use your WATS line for selling instead of talking to your tax lawyer, skip a few interviews. You were always the best salesman you had. Your ads radiated your confidence and didn't have more than 20% fat on them.

PROBLEM #4: *You've stopped believing in your own people* and your advertising reflects it. Once you got to Z-size, you got too big to continue believing what your salesmen were telling you. Because, well, remember they're only talented amateurs that got up into the big league by accident of being on your payroll. How can they have the gray hairs and see the Big Picture? No way! You need a New York agency and a Chicago consultant to tell you if it's really darkest before the dawn, if your advertising is really adequate, if your product needs repositioning or repackaging, and, of course, how to sell it.

SOLUTION #4: *Ask the man who's been there.* At Radio Shack, I had first-hand experience with this problem. Our expansion in the 1957–1960 period led to the introduction of consultants. What began with plans to move to a new, larger location, ended with their grab for (or our surrender of) nearly everything in sight: the amount of inventory, the table of organization, warehouse handling systems, internal politics, and so on. Charles Tandy, much later, would say to me: "Where can I find a better team of men than the team I have?" What he meant was: taken as a team and not man for man, we could be satisfied with what we had, warts and all. I'm sure you don't want (but may need) a recitation of a list of major American corporations who went outside for their costly "free agents" and with what shameful consequences.

Here's the perfect solution for our credibility problem as presented, albeit for a different situation, in 1953 by Radio Shack's first president, Milton Deutschmann: "Think twice and do nothing." (Carried to its extreme, it's a philosophy for keeping someone like Reagan in the White House forever and a brilliant excuse for closing down the F.C.C.)

PROBLEM #5: *You've let your ad agency replace chaos with comfort.* It's all those meetings, all that neat research, all that clean art, all that Starch (i.e., the Starch report showing how well your ad was seen or recalled versus others in the same publication). You also get the fret-free comfort of knowing that your agency, High Yeller, Inc., has some doggone impressive customers aside from you . . . Levitator Cowboy Boots, Hazel's Witch Perfume, Hupmobile, etc. Umumm, good!

SOLUTION #5: Although it's a pleasure to talk sales-building and positional schemes and logos with Strangeloves from beyond your castle walls, hopefully you'll figure out why it's even more delightful to do it at home with that great team we just mentioned. Why? Because you develop in-house skills that free you from endless meetings and debates, because you build your own talent, because you keep your own secrets, and because you save money and time.

PROBLEM #6: *Your advertising has been designed for the medium instead of the message, and you're getting what you deserve—medium advertising.* Believe me: when you abdicate your right to do anything about your advertising and PR except to initial them for payment or publication, you've just guaranteed yourself second best.

SOLUTION #6: Find the door to what's really vital and fragile about your business. Grab the handle. Don't let go!

ADvisory. The conventional wisdom someone is trying to use to convince you that the advertising sector of your marketing plan is (1) not to be edited by you, (2) not to be revised or cancelled by you, (3) not to be approved by you until it's too late for change, (4) not to be otherwise messed around with by you . . . ENDS HERE!

What's in It for Me?

My first solution to the problem of boring ads, if you remember, was to make sure they "make news." News is a benefit; if not precisely the news of the day, then more precisely the news that can honestly tell your potential buyer what he wants to hear. Specifically, that your product or service is available, ready now, cheaper, more prestigious, an item they couldn't get until now, a lesson capable of learning or profiting from, something enhancing.

There are zillions of newsworthy benefits capable of attracting buyers, believers, balloters, boat-owners and even beefeaters. The woods are full of customers united in the desire to be helped in some way: by a savings of time, money and steps; by advice on how to catch them a catch, how to understand the meaning of life and the reality of death; how to live with calamity when they're chin deep in it.

If you don't understand the technique of getting news and other benefits into your marketing program—and how and why to tell her "what's in it for her"—your ads probably will reveal one or more of these easily avoided characteristics:

1. Message unclear due to art or copy clarity.
2. Message unclear due to humor or other non sequitur.
3. Message unclear due to too many specifications and too few facts (i.e., size, color, material, price).
4. Message undeliverable.

ADvisory. If your promotional package lacks the news value, the pheromone factor, the magnetism of built-in benefits, as much as 90% of its cost is a gift to the media; that's 80% worse than Wanamaker's confession that 50% of his advertising cost was wasted and he couldn't figure out which half.

Here's the neat tale of a business friend. When L. J. Sevin pocketed the $350,000,000 he got for the company he co-founded for $250,000 (Mostek Corp.), he decided not to go back to square one by starting a new manufacturing company. Instead, he told *Newsweek,* he'll find and help other would-be Sevins who might do even bigger things. L.J.'s own words are the giveaway: *"Once you've been God, being a prophet is not very interesting."* And once I read that, all I knew was Sevin had found a benefit more urgent than the last one.

What's in it for me? Tell me I can "learn French in ten easy lessons," as Lew Holtz used to offer, "or one hard one!" Where's the benefit of learning French? Think hard. Well . . . I could learn enough to teach, to translate for a publisher; I could better enjoy a trip; I could be more useful working abroad—Radio Shack has stores in Quebec, France, Belgium, places where French is dominant. Possibilities of bull's-eye benefit begin to surface when you point a rifle at the target instead of a shotgun.

Time out for the 2nd Rule of Marketing:

Don't place any advertising lacking consumer news
value or benefits. Force your buyers and admen to
offer you a choice of benefits; select the best.
2 After a few false starts, they'll know you mean it
when you demand benefits. When the well is dry,
seek out and discuss benefits offered by the competition.

When to Sell the Steak

ADvisory. It's one thing to be famous, but in commerce you'd better be successful, too, or you're another Mr. Nobody with a nice tan.

Elmer Wheeler was a famous and successful seller of sales techniques. Wheeler's most distinctive advice was to "sell the sizzle instead of the steak." The sizzle is supposed to be a benefit, thus the steak is the product. But? But there are times when the steak is a bigger benefit.

In an ad headlined CIGARETTES 20¢ A PACK, TONIGHT FROM 8 PM TO MIDNIGHT, forget about lower tar, pleasure, togetherness. Price is the steak and price is what you sell.

In an ad headlined 3-FOR-1 RECORDING TAPE SALE! GET THREE REELS OR CASSETTES FOR THE PRICE OF ONE WHILE THEY LAST, you can overlook glass-smashing high notes and Realistic's latest Supertape hi-fi formulation (sizzle). When you give steak away you can forget the sound it makes on a plate. Think twice and do something: sort out the sizzle from the steak every time you promote; decide which one will sell quicker.

Flashback. One time back in the 1950s when transistor radios were $8 and up, I put one on sale in Boston for $4. My Ad Manager at the time—by now I was VP of merchandising and advertising—was the late Ernie Kallinich. Ever the bull in the china shop, Ernie slipped the copy by me that read "Get Concert Hall Sound" for four bucks.

"Listen, Ernie," I told him the next morning, "even at $8 it didn't have concert hall sound." His look was far from pained; more like pity. (I had lost my perfect pitch, his look said, and my ear for sizzle along with it.)

Flashback. Carl Marcus is a jeweler in Hollywood. We became phone pals when I phoned him to congratulate him on running the best little ad I'd seen recently. He said yes, his sales from the ad were as good as I'd imagined.

This is a successful ad because it's a bundle of benefits and news and illusion; it sells both steak and sizzle at the same time, in the small miracle of a three-word headline that reads "FINE WATCHES DISCOUNTED."

> **FINE WATCHES DISCOUNTED**
>
> Rolex, Cartier, Piaget, Corum, Concord, Audemar, Omega, Patek Phillipe. All models, Super Savings. New & Used. We take trades. All watches fully guaranteed. Shop anywhere. . .choose your model and then call.
> Special this week: Royal Oak 18K $9950, Piaget $10 watch $2750, Piaget Polo $9950, Rolex Pres. diamonds $6950, Rolex quartz 18K $5950
>
> **CARL MARCUS (213) 271-6244**
> **the SOURCE since 1970**
> **9460 Wilshire Blvd.**
> **Beverly Hills, CA 90212**

The ad measures less than two square inches, proving you don't need a haystack if you know where a needle is. It sells a single product, any "fine watch" that may cost 100s or even 1000s of bucks, so you don't really need a picture either.

What's more, the Carl Marcus ad appeals to buyers who don't like to haggle locally; it appeals to people who like discounts when offered, i.e., everyone. It appeals to folks who already own a watch and would like to replace it without a large loss—"We Take Trades," this Marcus says. Do Cartier or Neiman take trades? Do they react kindly to counter offers? It might be, but they could never say it in two inches!

In the end, I did, actually, conclude my research by

sending Carl my old watch plus cash for a Rolex. "I'm not sending you the watch in its original box," said Mr. Marcus, "because you didn't send me yours." Swapping to trade up has its own rules, you see; one of them is never ever to do anything about sales taxes.

Remembering Charles Tandy

You were dead wrong if you were one of those employees, acquaintances, businessmen, bankers, brokers, analysts, who thought Charles D. Tandy was either a lucky Texas industrial wildcatter or an egotistical one-man show. Here's what I said he was, after his death in late 1978, in an editorial written for Radio Shack's company magazine *Intercom:*

"He stood tall in any group of distinguished people, radiating intelligence, class, good will, humor. He was always himself. He was always approachable in person or by telephone, a facet of his personality that astounded people who imagine persons of high rank as being unavailable, distant, secluded, too important to make time for strangers or subordinates. He drove his own car. He answered his own phone. He smoked 30-cent cigars. He served coffee from a thermos jug on his desk, and the cups were plastic."

He would feel right at home here in this chapter on advertising reasons and definitions. It was central to his life that advertising's music be trumpeted to make products dance out of warehouses and onto store shelves, and off shelves into homes. Tandy, at least for the corporation that bears his name, was the Pied Piper of American Commerce.

Hey, what's this—the cult of the personality? Well, can you find me a place that runs on time where the cult of the personality isn't the criterion for leadership? Some say the Lord is a person; yea or nay, His advertising never sets with the sun, and He is looked up to (in all directions).

In my foreword I said that Tandy understood advertising the way a body understands blood. If you need some, don't just stand there—get a transfusion! If your sales curve droops, damn the budget—full speed ahead with more advertising. None of that waiting for a turnaround, none of that paralyzing awe of the already published plan. Que será, será? . . . Tandy's answer to that was always "Not me, Buster!"

Flashback. Once I had a sudden urge to advertise myself. The medium was an automobile vanity plate, available for an extra $10. At that time (1970) we had just acquired Chicago's old Allied Radio Corporation and changed our name—temporarily, as it happened—to Allied Radio Shack. Being president and the #1 guy, I put the acronym ARS-1 on my vanity plate. Soon Tandy saw my car with its ARS-1 plate near our door. "Hell, Kornfeld," he bellowed across the parking lot, "you don't even know how to spell ass!"

"If you can't get it done, I can!" Tandy would say, apropos of anything undone. Good headline for an ad?

"We're not overbought, we're undersold," he'd say, no doubt a maxim that's not original with Tandy. All of us genius merchandisers are often overbought and always undersold—our genius (i.e., saving grace) is knowing how we shall overcome.

Tandy's instinctive reaction to stagnation was to roll out "the advertising machine" and not to wait for the calendar or the Unknown Customer to bail us out. Neither he nor I nor our successors ever lost that urge; if that doesn't totally explain our success, it certainly helps explain those seeming floods and avalanches of Radio Shack advertising!

"Whaddaya mean 'born equal'?" he'd inquire. "No two people are equal five minutes after they're born." Think about that possibility the next time your account executive tells you he knows more about promoting computers than you do because he has been doing it for IBM for seven years.

A perceptive sketch of Tandy was limned for the *New York Post* by Irwin Lainoff, an investment advisor and columnist. "Charles Tandy used to swing through Wall Street with a warmth that set him apart from most businessmen who like to fashion themselves in granite. He'd hold court with style, jaunty cigar-holder aloft, and tempt his audience with an outpouring of statistics. He'd draw alternative financial maneuvers for you (and) before long you'd realize that there was one of the true marketing giants of our age."

Charles Tandy's desire to sell whatever was lying around also extended to the marketing of what he referred to as "his" stock; though it was also your stock and my stock and not even principally "his" stock during the great push of the 60s, 70s, 80s. I have a friend in a similar position in another company who always commented enviously on the constant activity in Tandy Corporation common stock and financial dealings.

Invariably, I'd explain how Tandy thought of "his" stock as if it were merchandise to be advertised and sold.

"That may be, but my stock hasn't moved more than a buck or two in years," my friend would complain.

"Then you'll just have to make your company more interesting," I'd reply. "Imagine what you'd do if your stock actually *was* merchandise . . . you'd try in some way to market it, right?" Although he'd agree, it was clear he'd never plan to do anything about it.

You can do a lot of newsworthy "marketing" things with securities when they're approached as action items instead of problems—splits, reverse splits, buy backs, options—always, of course, within the limits of prudence and law. You can sell bonds, subordinated debentures, real estate, receivables, leases, and make news at the same time; how pro or con the news is will depend on your use of PR. I have more to say about the latter in future chapters.

You can advertise yourself by sponsoring "dog and pony shows," by sending your team around the territory to pitch your dreams to various audiences. This was a game to Charles Tandy, but a serious game involving merchandising, selling, acting, diplomacy, persuasion, and the occasional miracle, using available capital and talent. . . particularly ours at Radio Shack.

No matter what it was, "They'll say anyone could have done it," Tandy said once, "after we've done it."

TWO

Up (and Around) the Agency

A business publication, *High Fidelity Trade News,* on the subject of choosing an ad agency, asks, "Which one is right for you?" Good question! Radio Shack has answered that question with a resounding "NONE!" during most of its green years.

There's a problem in choosing between full-service and limited-service agencies, says HFTN in the article, because "retail work is often delegated to copywriters and artists fresh out of school." Later I prove this with an example from the dream world we sometimes refer to as "real life."

"When should you hire an advertising agency?" asks the magazine, giving a two-part answer: "(1) When you're convinced that advertising is an important part of business management and growth, and (2) when you're convinced you don't have the time or ability to do the job yourself." Sort of like if you're hungry and lazy at the same time, go get someone to feed you?

High Fidelity Trade News also suggests a few cheaper and less complicated routes to getting your advertising done: by production houses and/or freelance people, finally arriving at my own solution for Radio Shack—what they call "the in-house alternative"—but with a severe caveat.

"Generally, the added overhead and frustrations associated with hiring additional employees (for in-house ad jobs) outweigh the advantages—except to the very largest retailers."

When I read that last sentence I knew it was time to saddle up my great horse Boilerplate and ride to the rescue of do-it-yourself advertising. And not only advertising, but also do-it-yourself marketing, sales promotion, public relations, annual reports—everything right on down to the Dumpster. (I can't quite give a hoot who handles that aspect of our business so long as Security tells me the inventory didn't go out with the trash).

Advertising: Agency or In-house?

There is NO NEED to rush right out and get yourself an in-house ad agency today.

Get yourself an in-house ad manager and grow him or her into an agency if that's the way cookies crumble as time goes by.

> ***ADvisory.*** Steel yourself to pay this person like a relative or at least try to make him one of the family, commercially speaking.

Grow yourself an ad *department,* and while you're about it, *grow yourself into it* as at least a fairly full-time participant in its deliberations. You will discover some very interesting things:

1. That you have been "doing advertising" for your enterprise right along. Granted you weren't a professional, you were doing what a pro should and must do, which is to *make sales* by various means, including articulating and demonstrating and planning for the future.
2. That the pros you've met haven't been exceptional people with deep trade secrets and skills; all in all they appeared to be either competent or something less.
3. That advertising didn't have to be "done" outside;

most of it could be "done" anywhere out of the cold, including your premises.

4. That every time you had to tell an outside person or group what you wanted done, you had to educate them and you had to allocate quite a bit of meeting time, and then you had to check back and often rework part or all of the assigned task.
5. And then, if you're at all like me, you asked yourself a question like this: Why should I be afraid of the "added overhead and frustrations associated with hiring aditional employees" for advertising and sales promotion, and NOT be afraid of the overhead and frustration of employees hired to do bookkeeping, warehousing, mailing list maintenance, window dressing, engineering, drafting, manual writing, and so on?

In a word: what makes advertising so special that you have to go outside to get it done?

In reply: nothing except laziness, ignorance and superstition. In fact, a 3rd Rule of Marketing might just as well get pickled in pine right here and now:

---

3 The more you tend to go outside for advice and services in business, the more you tend to lose confidence and control.

Learning by Negative Example

Hired as Radio Shack's advertising manager in 1948, I found things arranged neatly but in total disarray. The mailing list hadn't been attended to for many moons before the full moon before the last. Customer correspondence, including product inquiries, was packed in cobwebbed cartons. The rack for filing manufacturers' product literature was full of dust; most of the received packages of it had been accumulated in tipsy piles arranged in what I call "FILO"—first in, last out. There was no plan for the next flyer or other mailed customer contact. The catalog (1948 issue date, which turned out to be 1949 issue time) was at an ad agency. And the next magazine ads were at an art studio awaiting final details such as knowledge of what products to run 60 days later in the November issues.

Kornfeld did not despair. He was too happy at finding a home to carp at the condition he found it in. And in the farthest long run, all this resulted in an observation that will do nicely for our 4th Rule of Marketing:

---

4 One of the quickest ways of learning what to do in any business situation is first to be able to observe it done incorrectly.

Do you laugh? Better not to. I am deadly serious. When you come across my small collection of genuine published ads in later pages of this MS, you'll note I dwell more upon bad ads than upon good ones. There's method in this. If I show you why I think something is bad—actually just "not good enough"—you'll see first-hand what I mean. And you'll be able to avoid it yourself . . . something like feeling fire instead of merely being told fire is hot and painful.

I am a firm believer in *learning by negative example.* What happens, for example, if I use "Xmas" in an ad headline in a newspaper in Boston? I get letters from Catholics and other fine people saying Xmas is not an abbreviation or proper substitute for Christmas. You'll have to try it to believe it.

What happens if you advertise the thrill of having your hi-fi tweeter rated a Best Buy in *Consumer Reports?* You get a warning from CR, and it gets stronger with each intentional repeat of the alleged misdeed, until you have a meeting with their lawyers. Try it! Once when I did I found their law firm had an office with a very deep pile rug. I've been told that the deeper the pile of the rug in the office of an adversary law office, the dearer the cost of losing their case. (That theory is one I haven't tested.)

Advantages of the In-house Advertising Manager

Shortly after becoming Radio Shack's lone ad ranger, I began to accumulate reasons why it was better to work for a company than for an ad agency, but, for the record, at that time the notion of an in-house agency hadn't entered my mind:

1. As a company employee, I could learn about the business and the business could learn about me. Any agency would have to learn about the business if it wanted to become our agency; and they seemed to trade their craftsmen at will, whereas I aspired to become a fixture.

2. As a company employee I could gradually acquire a knowledge of all parts of the promotion business—media, layouts, graphic arts, statistics, demographics, the business side (bidding, buying, budgeting), and the approach of our business competitors to our problems and solutions.

3. As a company employee I could build loyalty along with my trade, and conceive of rising higher in the management pyramid. (Or circle, or square, or cloud.)

4. I could quickly insure my worth to the company by saving them money and, hopefully, by doing better and/or more quickly and easily whatever had been done before, if I had anything like the drive and talent I promised Radio Shack when it welcomed me aboard. And it wasn't long before opportunities to do these things presented themselves.

Splitting the Commission

Almost the moment I looked into the matter of November's ads—it was September 1948 when I started work—I found I could eliminate one of the two outside agencies Radio Shack was using, an art studio in Boston to which the company was paying out $400 a month for magazine drawing and pasteup services. I did that $400-worth myself: I was costing $433.33 a month and I'd already whittled it down to $33.33 by playing Lewis the Boy Artist! Big excitement, but

. . . no raise; in those days you were supposed to do well by doing good.

I'd saved time as well as money—no more conferences at the art studio or our office. And no more pen and ink drawings, either. I preferred photographs. Out of the savings I bought a Speed Graphic camera, commercial lens, tripod, and various accessories. Lewis the Boy Photographer thus got rid of the *Boston Globe* lensman who had been doing odd shots for the lazy guys at Radio Shack; he'd had to be told how to position each and every electronic component so as not to get things like capacitors and transformers upside down. No raise. No raise, either, for my other assumed art duties such as astutely clipping borders and other trifles from the rich folks' ads—especially those many nice ways of printing the words "Sale" and "New" and "Now," the finest monosyllables in the entire vocabulary of advertising.

While single-handedly putting out Radio Shack's annual catalog and media ads, it occurred to me that everything was being billed through our ad agency even though I was doing most of the work in-house. "Why don't we split the commission?" I asked my boss, our founding president. His look was that of hiding from his slave the fact he'd just been handed a loose diamond—the greed-is-good look.

First we divided the immutable 15% commission (which works out to be more like 17.5%) and eliminated entirely any billing for costs incurred by my own production. Later, we went to 10% for us and 5% for them. (No raise, naturally. I was hired to manage advertising, not to mismanage it!)

(Finally I learned that if I got a raise it would only be gotten by demand.)

My staff grew from one to two and the work from 100% to 400% and I got to be a vice-president which, as noted earlier, was in lieu of a raise. Eventually I began to understand that Radio Shack was a company which probably had *too much advertising* for a conventional agency to handle profitably. There was *too much work!* Too many layouts, pictures, pages; too much copy; and too little time for the characteristically slow wedding march of client and agency.

If your enterprise has too much work, you, too, will have

to face the paradox that your agency—if you have one—won't be able to afford the luxury of doing it, or that its price will be so high you'll want to think of a better way. Very likely, the better way will be doing it yourself.

Insofar as an actual in-house ad agency is concerned, that's a matter of desire and arithmetic. I can't tell you how to differentiate between desire and logic, but the numbers of advertising can be very easily sorted out. Get all the costs of your last agency year of advertising from your agency; insist on a complete breakdown. You'll know it's complete when it adds up to 100% of everything you paid for . . . except your own time. ADD THAT IN TOO.

Objective: To get it done as well but cheaper.

Compromise: Decide if cheaper is enough cheaper to make acceptable the fact that it might not get done as well. Or decide what might happen if it weren't done as well—something or nothing. Who knows? Who might care?

Research: Check with other companies in your field, in other fields. Radio Shack has no ad agency. Many department stores have no ad agency. Check out the cost of doing what ad people do to get ads conceived, executed, placed. You'll find your peers like to talk. Check with friendly media people. Read my later chapters on the media. Seek out sources who don't think agencies are absolutely the last word; those who do will have already forgotten how great it is to be independent, and they're a dime a dozen.

Flashback: One time I heard Senator Long (D.—La.) talk to a crowd of businessmen on how to make their opinions and desires really felt in the Congress. "Don't go down to Washington to meet with the people who already believe the way you do;" he said, "you already have them in your pocket. And don't go down hoping to convince those who already hold strong contrary opinions. The people in Congress you want to get to with your needs and your argument," Sen. Long advised, "are the *Undecideds;* they're always in the majority and always willing to listen."

See what the Senator is saying? He's saying that if you

want to find out about getting things done without ad agencies and consultants, *don't ask the man who wouldn't want it any other way.*

Man's Second Basic Defect

Man has four basic defects, according to His Divine Grace A. C. Bhaktivedanta Swami Prabhupāda, of which the second—his susceptibility of being illusioned—precisely fits the thrust of this book. "Illusion means to accept something which is not," is the way it translates from the original Sanskrit.

It is illusion to believe that advertising agencies are Aladdin's lamps which, when rubbed, will produce undreamed-of success and cleverness; or that all companies need and use ad agencies and other consultants; or that you need to place your ad via an outside agency to get it into a major medium such as a national magazine; or that the standard 15% ad agency commission may be "collected" only by an independent ad agency so "you might as well use an agency because there's just no way to save that part of your cost." Illusions!

The consumer is also illusioned in the instance of his buying a product that is not "as advertised." He has been, in the colloquial, "ripped off" not only by the manufacturer, but also by the wholesaler, the retailer, and the ad agency which accepted the product and made enhanced claims for it which are in some way illusion.

Speaking to the latter, contemplate a newspaper story which reveals that "only three out of the ten complaints resolved in February (1982) of the National Advertising division of the Council of Better Business Bureaus ended with the dropping of either ad claim or advertising. All seven of the other advertisers were able to support their claims."

What do you think of 70% fulfillment? Of 30% defective? In Radio Shack's business, a 30% rejection rate at any stage of production or distribution would be viewed as abysmal failure. Nor is 70% fulfillment of claims anything to brag about. To me, it's more like an explanation of Japan's recent

100% product acceptance. Note: of the three spanked agencies, two were outsiders, one an insider. Who needs this kind of illusion? Who asked for it? I have thoughts about such things strewn at random through my pages; please handle them with care.

Back to the subject of agencies: the fall of 1981 was a crash of sorts for them as noted in a *Wall Street Journal* story headlined "Rash of Advertisers Switch Agencies, Testing Strength of Long-Term Ties." McDonald's, Eastern Air Lines, and Hallmark Cards all changed partners in mid-dance. And within the prior six months, the same fickleness had been noted at American Airlines, Campbell Soup, Gallo Winery, Nestle and others, some leaving part of their person with old lovers and transferring remainders to newer ones.

What causes these apparently newsworthy divorces and remarriages? Don't ask the partners; ask an outsider like me with a gift for perceptive oversimplification. My three main perceptions are (1) bad times within an industry, (2) bad times within a company, (3) the perennial search for greener grass, meaning rumored or hoped-for newer ideas, smarter people, relief of boredom. Sometimes, of course, it's a matter of personalities and promises (my dream agency is called Sesimorp . . . Promises spelled backwards; but the one I've used throughout this book is called High Yeller, Inc., because it's more descriptive).

Bosses don't fire themselves (usually) when their great new product becomes an Edsel, a Laker Airways, or cans of veggies that carry lethal botulism. Sometimes they do get wiped out by events, but more often they come back to fight and win again. So why fire the ad agency? Because the agency, like the manager of the Yankees and the coach at Notre Dame, is easy to fire, but the *team* isn't! They also fire the National Sales Manager at the company when things are not exactly going great. Why? Because—as I've developed in my chapter "The Boss As Salesman"—the national SM is a lad they've hired to do what the boss is supposed to be doing (and is best at) instead of chairing the alumni association and sitting on the President's council for abandoning Taiwan.

Outside agencies are also easier to blame and dispose of than in-house agencies. You know damn well your in-house people follow your lead; you know in your heart you're a bigger part of the problem than they are.

Even your own ad manager will be spared if you, O Whiz-kid, get trashed by your board of directors in its pursuit of "due diligence." He is a blameless lad who is likely to learn your business as well or better than your smartest lawyer or moola-mover. Unless he gets both of the titles I had from 1958–1970 at Radio Shack, he is not to blame for switching your gunk from insert glass to plastic bottles that leach.

Every time I compare outside and in-house advertising people I come away with more good vibes for insiders, more bad ones for the outsiders. Speaking of "more," my 64th Rule of Marketing says quite clearly: *More is always more than less. And more is usually better than less.*

Thus it is time I meandered into an unusual tale: why and how I hired an outside ad agency because it had more experience than I had in producing TV commercials. More was indeed more than less. Alas, it wasn't better than less!

"Make or Buy" Decisions

Whenever a company "does its own thing" in manufacturing or advertising or electric sign building or display case design and construction—all of which Radio Shack has been doing for many years—there's a covert battle among your own people on almost every new job. Is it smarter or cheaper or timelier to do it yourself or to get it done outside?

Merchandise buyers generally prefer (given the choice) to buy outside where they can cherry-pick the world's offerings and say "no" as often and as churlishly as they like. I've been there!

Bosses and other promotion-minded execs often find it hard to believe that the dummies who work for them in advertising or related professions can actually compete with outside agencies on quality, ingenuity, media insight, understanding of demographics, etc. I've been there, too.

These "make or buy" decisions become less and less amusing in direct proportion to the growth of your outlay for in-house capital equipment and parts inventories and assorted personnel such as artists and copywriters. Having fathered both Radio Shack's advertising *and* manufacturing profit centers, I can show you my related gray hairs and recount for you the following paradox:

> ***ADvisory.*** While manufacturing products and designing ads are my favorite indoor sports, buying them on the outside is a great way to keep your team and its output sharp and competitive!

What's so unusual about doing things yourself? Did you have "parentage lessons" before you started a family, or "love lessons" to set the whole process in motion? Who taught you to have opinions, anyway? And once you had opinions, how often did you have to get hit on the head in order to get one changed?

Radio Shack went essentially all private label in the middle 1960s. It had had private label items since the middle 1950s. Most viewers think that's extraordinary, courageous, or even foolhardy. But Charles Tandy used to say he'd consider changing his mind about private branding the day anyone showed him an Exxon pump in a Texaco station. And when I introduced our first private merchandise in 1954, I thought I was doing something interesting and exciting but—having grown up around S. S. Pierce and A&P—far from unusual. Doing my own advertising seemed, from the very beginning, both enjoyable and worthwhile; that it would also turn out to be cheaper as well was just another happy circumstance.

Deciding between building and making, given that you have that option, is not always without anguish. I recall that in 1971 when I went to Indianapolis to look at the possible acquisition of RCA's blank tape factory, its neighbor, RCA's pre-recorded 8-track tape factory, had refused to buy from them on the basis of the quality of its tape or cartridge.

That was one in-house versus another in-house. "Hell no," I said when asked if I'd stand for that sort of heresy. But just between us girls, it's each case on its own merit, and that one was "make or buy" at its bleakest, simply another problem that should have been resolved before I got there.

Nevertheless, there's nothing more rewarding (to me) than making our own ads for *Fortune* magazine, building our own telephone sets, creating our own annual and quarterly reports. And there's nothing easier or less rewarding (to me) than buying on the outside, be it merchandise, advice, PR, or advertising.

Radio Shack's Maladroit Meander into TV Commercials

So . . . would I elect to buy instead of make when Radio Shack finally developed an irresistible urge to advertise on television?

"Yes I would," I decided. "We don't know a hoot about making commercials for boobtube viewers. And it shouldn't be hard to get us an agency that knows quite a few hoots, now that we're a nationwide company on the rise."

Is that Mister Make talking? Yes, but without that silly decision, what follows in this chapter might be duller than a social-minded Mobil ad. And what's duller? A Gulf ad, or one by almost any insurance company or bank or broker in town!

The best of intentions were exercised in locating an ad agency with proven experience in TV—experience we could see and hear just by switching our TVs to any channel. No portfolios, please! We were inordinately humble: despite our in-house agency and obvious do-it-yourself bias, we were in their hands and would not part from them for selfish reasons.

New York City's Ed Koch once punned that he was "Mayor Culpa." Now it's my turn. I found that agency. I hired that agency. I waived its offer of the usual head-butting contest between it and other agencies. And I explained what we wanted.

You'll soon see it was Mea Culpa all right. But not Major Culpa, because in the end, both agency and Shack are still expanding like sunbelts after our long-ago final divorce.

Before we went out for a tour of our chosen agency's

premises and a bash to emulsify our relationship—and beware: this is a very serious point of no return—our newly elected partners insisted on several surveys. There's nothing wrong with surveys per se, but also there's everything wrong; it's a paradox I hope to illustrate by our example.

Surveys That Don't (sic) Surve

The first survey was to measure our awareness—the number and sort of people who were aware that Radio Shack existed. Up to that point all I'd known of the vulgar masses was that enough were customers to let us pay our bills and grow. But I've always known that a buyer and a booster are like love and money. You can never get enough or have too much!

The second survey involved tabulating our customers' feelings about Radio Shack and its products. *Satisfied? Dissatisfied? Don't know?* And: *Would buy again? Wouldn't buy again? Don't know?* And our prices: *High? Medium? Average? Don't know?*

This inspired our 5th Rule of Marketing:

---

5 Surveys undertaken to reinforce the safety of fairly imminent business decisions tend to arrive at the obvious in a time frame that is too late, and in an amount that is too little.

While I realized these first two surveys wouldn't alter my decision to advertise on TV, the pace was already painfully slow for us. We were used to getting out of bed running!

The surveys also revealed unexpected problems in communicating with our new external agents:

1. The agency needed much too much intelligence about our business before they could settle down to productive work.
2. They didn't seem to appreciate we were already in a business we understood thoroughly and for which we

had onrushing growth plans we didn't want delayed by either surveys or our substantial first test of TV advertising—the latter was a side show to the main event.

3. They apparently needed a road map to drive the next inch, but I'd already described the next inch as TV ads and "soonest," as they say in our headquarters in the U.K.

Then there was an unexpectedly big problem with the agency that reminded me of my regular big problem—namely, dealing civilly with hardheaded employees who don't want to dance to your anthem. My 6th Rule of Marketing defines this nicely:

---

6 A direct order is an instruction that is made clear and workable only when your people have revised it so it becomes their best judgment on what to do next.

Our agency's "best judgment" surfaced when it became de facto that its personnel were to be regarded as highly trained, untouchable specialists, never as our employees.

ADvisory. This applies even if they adopt your theories, take your money, and accept credit for your hoped-for upcoming successes in marketing—ultimately your bonafide prior ones as well. And why not?

Flashback. Charles Tandy was believed by the folks on Wall Street to have been the perpetrator of anything done brilliantly at Tandy Corp. and Radio Shack, and to have had a hand in every important decision. He desired—at his first wife's request—to be known throughout the company and the investment community as CHARLES, not Charlie or Chuck. My favorite gag came out of hiding whenever someone from The Street gave me the well-known *Concerned Analyst Look* and inquired: "Do you get a lot of help and guidance from Charles?"

I'd return that long, thoughtful look, pause, and ask: "Charles who?" (It never failed NOT to get a laugh.)

Resisting Hard-Sell Ads

It was roundup time. "In short," I said, "what we've decided to do is to run ads on television. What we've come to you for is expertise in creating and placing these ads. Our budget," I went on, "is x-dollars for media, art, the works."

"Well, that's pretty straightforward," said I. B. Honcho who, after the first few meetings, retired from front-line duty. "Anything else before we go to work?" (Bright smile.)

"Well, there's one other thing," I replied. "We do *hard-sell* advertising in our newspaper ads and mailers, and we want also to do our TV ads that way."

(Note: none of these quotes is exact, nor exactly inexact. They are history recreated for the purpose of enlivening these pages with material you are certain to find relevant at some point in your career.)

"What's your understanding of 'hard sell'?"

I gave him my 7th Rule of Marketing without even thinking:

---

7 When your advertising asks for the order right out front, with a price and a place to buy and with "NOW" included in the copy, that's hard-sell advertising, and it should invariably be tried before any other kind.

"Oh," said I. B. a trifle darkly.

"And I really mean it," I said. "What I'm saying is Radio Shack is a company that tells its readers, look, here's our little sweetie, here's our regular price, here's our sale price, and don't leave our store without it."

"Don't you say why the 'little sweetie' as you call it is better than others?"

"Not usually," I said. "All our products are good, reliable quality, priced to sell, and available nearby. *That's* what's better. *That's* the benefit."

"Oh, so you'll only be advertising sale-priced items?"

"No. Not only. Sometimes new ones."

Mr. Honcho breathed heavily. "Okay, then the new products will be comparable to other similar things on the market, and we'll want to know why they're better. Can you tell us that?"

I made my very-patient-teacher face. "Look . . . you're not reading me. We aren't interested in claims of superiority and comparison charts. We're interested in MAKING SALES and in determining what causes these sales to be made other than by our guys' salesmanship. Our idea is simply to use TV as a new added way to help make sales we might otherwise not make."

Seeing his expression, I had one of those sick feelings you get when you know (a) you're not making your point after all that yakking, and (b) you're not making your point because your audience doesn't like your point. I could see we were going to be offered stylish—not hard-sell—ads.

Our 8th Law of Marketing looks at the problems with a jaundiced nay:

---

8 When ad agencies or in-house ad employees seem inclined to copy trendy ad themes, rely on comparisons, resort to story-telling, or aim toward winning an award for creative excellence rather than toward satisfying the greater need of their client, these inclinations will NOT be deceiving, and the client must fight them with every available weapon.

When they tell you of the wild merits of the project, how it must be entered into x- and y- contests for PR value . . . PUNT! If you want some free winner's cups, medallions or plaques for your office walls, phone 817/390-3273 and ask for Dave Beckerman.

Could a reason why many professionals dislike preparing hard-sell advertising be that it tends to be instantly measurable? Out, unworthy thought! Let's hope it's because creative types simply find it inartistic, inelegant, boring, and a waste of time and talent. Forget the obvious: that hard sell moves the merchandise and pays the salaries, rents and taxes!

This book's 9th Rule of Marketing continues to address the paradox of hard- vs. soft-sell in advertising. See how quietly it makes its sensitive point:

---

9 Advertising is usually most beautiful when it's least measurable and least productive.

This is not to deny youth and beauty the right to succeed in attracting customers. But measurable, resultful advertising (i.e., hard sell) rarely scores over a 5 on pulchritude's scale of 10. You can ask the man who has paid for both kinds—the ravishing and the homely. Me.

The Road to Hollywood Bowl

My Hollywood Bowl story is a fascinating scenario for studious Monday morning marketing quarterbacks. But why wait until Monday morning to read about a loss that possibly might be prevented by better understanding of the forces at work on your problems and opportunities?

Invariably we were shown pretty ads by our newly hired TV-commercials agency; also situation ads, witty ads, personality ads; any kind of ads but beautifully ugly hard-sell ads. Often, we'd see them too late to make changes.

There was the time they conned me into okaying the cost of bringing a pair of our walkie talkies to the Grand Canyon to show that, wow, yes, they'd sure talk clean across it!

There was the time they requested my okay to take our sale-priced loudspeaker to Red Rocks Park. Get the beauty of it . . . two Realistic speakers alone on that vast stage? They'd sound so great you wouldn't need a live orchestra!

"Do you mean you'd send the same or a different crew—cameras, lights, directors, and actors—from Arizona (the canyon) all the way to Colorado (the park)? Do you *know* how far apart they are . . . how *expensive* your scheme is?" It was a time for executive outrage.

Sure they knew. But calm down, Mr. K., and realize the mind-expanding nature of these visuals . . . what they'll do for Radio Shack in awareness of product and reputation for being a sharp advertiser. You know you can't do these things in your catalogs, flyers, and other media. That is why you came to us and instinctively turned to TV.

I kept half my cool. "Absolutely no on Red Rocks, but go ahead with the Grand Canyon. For the speaker commercial, since most of your photography is shot in L.A.—where your picture crew lives—let's use Hollywood Bowl. It's big, beautiful, and has a stage. Even though your script again isn't really hard sell, time is tight and I'll accept it."

"Ummm, well," said their Creative Type, "we get your point all right, but it's like—it's like Hollywood Bowl has been *reeely* overused on television, and. . . ."

Flashback. We used Hollywood Bowl. And as you must have guessed by now, our walkie talkie and speaker sales went their trendy way without the slightest trace of effect from either our pictured products or our picturesque locations.

Here are a few more of the problems we encountered and which—despite many corrective ideas and suggestions from me—caused me to fire my chosen advertising agency:

1. Back to awareness: insofar as it was concerned, the awareness survey naturally revealed we had less than 100% (as a guess, we had 47% in 1972 and 94% in 1982). So our agency's aim, by gosh, was to go out and get some more! Of course "more" had been our active urge since Day One (Radio Shack was founded in 1921, not, as some believe, when hi-fi or CB or small computers came onto the market).

2. Do you actually need consultants to tell you awareness is grown by consistently giving and improving your services; by locating your business as conveniently as possible

for your customers, not to please you or your employees; by increasing and improving your marketing—especially your advertising?

3. Do you really like meetings which, due to geography or scheduling problems, cause you to spend days doing what can and should be done in hours? If so, consultants will do you just fine.

4. Do you need outsiders to get you to remember to put your name, address, and hours or conditions of business on everything you publish to attract customers? No? Then try on this little anecdote for size. . . .

Flashback. At the very first preview of our agency's very first series of TV commercials, I suddenly realized they had forgotten to say anything that might tell our 53% unaware audience WHERE or even WHAT a Radio Shack was!

"Hey, don't we get better awareness if we tell our TV viewers *a Radio Shack is a store in their town?* And by telling them our products are *not available in other stores?* Isn't exclusivity a terrific benefit?" I asked.

Unabashed, they allowed these were, yes, very fine points, quickly inserting such advisories as "the Nationwide Supermarket of Sound" and "Near you wherever you live or work." What's a major omission between doctor and patient?

> ***ADvisory.*** Don't run an ad that overlooks such elementary awareness builders as Who, What, When, and Where! Even where Radio Shack has too many shops in any one location to be able to print locations in ads, flyers, and catalogs, it tries to squeeze in some identifiable place—even a phone number—to let the public reach it and to reassure the public that it is available on call, at least in the phone book.

Campaigns Are for the Military

"Campaign" is a venerable buzzword used by agencies and businessmen alike to describe a proposed plan of attack. Me, I think campaigns are for the military. I have never ever initiated or talked about advertising campaigns. Advertising should be an ongoing process just like buying and selling.

I had a chance to prove this when I faced the challenge of marketing Radio Shack's biggest breakthrough—its TRS-80 personal computer (for which I get fathership credit because when the buck stopped on my desk in 1976 I said "BUILD").

Believe me, Dr. Gallup, there was no survey, no test, no call-in of technical ad men, no search for a red hot PR firm, and *no campaign.* On my primitive skull the scrimshawed graffiti reads: A Campaign Is Forever, or Until the Product Poops Out, Whichever Comes First. (See Chapter 11.)

Some of you think, and with commendable accuracy, that merchandise and ideas and tickets sell better during the Christmas season. You know it's an "in" season with specific chronological parameters. You invoke the Goddess of the Ad Campaign. And you proceed to demonstrate the time-dishonored practice of opening your promotional purse—a vessel that has been closed for so long that you've succeeded once again in having an "off" season.

The 365-Day Selling Season

Some of you brag about your luck in having not one but several "in" seasons, each about 30 days long. For example, the wristwatch and candy seasons, with their sudden glorious agency-inspired campaigns to attract buyers who remember such recipients as dads, grads, moms, and brides. You spend (on ads) like a drunk; then you lay low until the next "in" season—Christmas, Easter, or St. Patrick's Day. I've got news for you in the form of my 10th Rule of Marketing:

---

10 No one should allow his selling season to be shorter than 365 days in any calendar year, or allow ad funds to run dry before they have somehow touched each of its 52 weeks.

I had intended to close this chapter by saying some nice things about ad agencies, even showing some sample agency ads that win my accolade (five pitchforks), but space ran out. In the mite left, I pause to acknowledge that part of the chapter's title came from that of Robert Townsend's best-seller *Up the Organization.* He says right there under the letter "A" (the book's contents are in alphabetical order) to "fire the whole advertising department and your old agency [and] get the best new agency you can."

I say not to do either, offering the following gentler suggestions:

ADvisory. If you have an old ad department or an old agency, start today to make them do what you need to get done. If they know what it is better than the boss does, fire the boss.

ADvisory. If you decide to retain an outside ad agency, give it one small task to test the water. A trial marriage in today's unisex world won't offend anyone. Ditto for any other kind of consultant.

ADvisory. Be certain your understanding of one (1) small task is mutually understood and agreeable. Otherwise, don't blame your outsider group if they try to grab whatever's loose . . . the annual report, the company table of organization, the merger initiative, the warehouse system, the EDP program, the makeup of your board, or—oh nasty mind—a key employee or two who might better serve an even better client.

ADvisory. If Radio Shack can start and run its own in-house agency, why can't you? It wasn't until 1970 that it became clear we could do this successfully and, at the same time, build executive strength and save important time and money. First you need an inside Ad Manager whom you can trust and let grow. Then a department. Finally enough sales to warrant your beginning to harbor the thought of setting up a complete shop on your own. Cost it out every year. GO when the light turns green!

THREE

The Boss As Salesman

Fear of 400,000 Ball Point Pens

It's true about you, isn't it? I mean that you'd raise hell if your top five people went out and ordered new gear for their offices at $25,000 per office? I remember going into a Radio Shack store in Minneapolis and finding 96 ball point pens (in boxes of a dozen) in the manager's back room, and raising hell about it at our regional meeting attended by that manager and 399 others. As if the specter of 400 × 96 = 38,400 pens wasn't bad enough, we also had enough other regions to make it a theoretical 400,000 pens in back rooms. Another point to remember is that Radio Shack doesn't sell pens, just as you don't sell Louis XV furniture or Jasper Johns prints and the other stuff your top five people bought to cushion the shock of being overpaid for another straight year.

What it's about, and not for the first time, is how tough you/I were about furniture/pens when all during the fiscal year there was a *really big leak* at Ye Olde Outfitters, Ltd., and you acted as if nothing new was going on. The leak was 3 or 5 or 7 or some other % of sales going down the SG&A-drain called your Sales Promotion or Advertising Budget.

Why down the drain? Because it was inadequately planned and insufficiently accounted for.

I'm not talking 400,000 ball point pens at 16¢ = $56,000 wasted, or 5 × $25,000 = $125,000 blown on executive environmental protection, because I'm talking BUCKS, not peanuts.

The $2,000,000 Handout

Flashback. [Disclaimer: The following essentially true story actually happened, but any similarity of its *dramatis personae* to persons living—or embarrassed to be—is strictly coincidental.] Once upon a recent time I was privileged to visit the comfy home offices of a large NYSE company where I and one of its major domos (actually higher than a major) began to compare marketing notes (our merchandise lines were completely unlike).

"You operate on an ad budget . . . I'm sure of that," he said.

"Of that you can be sure."

"How closely do you adhere to it?"

I looked at my nails without counting them. "That depends on conditions. My experience is that one never subtracts from an ad budget. One adds to it if the pace is too slow, or stays with it if things are either okay or better than okay."

"What would you think," he asked, warming to his point, "if your people came to you and asked for 20% more dollars than budgeted at the start of the year?"

"That they were out of their minds."

"Because?"

"Because I would have known two things—first, that business conditions didn't warrant the change, and second, that they weren't smart enough to buy us an additional X% sales increase."

His look twinkled with the radiant good will of two members of an elite golf club meeting at a Friendly Ice Cream counter. "That's what I thought you'd say."

I smiled. "And you sent 'em away, huh?"

"Oh no, I couldn't do that after all the work they'd put into the plan. I gave them an additional $2,000,000," he confided, "because after all what's another 'two' on top of a budget that's so many times bigger?"

This time he didn't read my smile, I hope, because what I was thinking was: why don't I go downstairs under your office window and you try to throw $300,000 into my outstretched hat? (It was a lot less than $2 million. In fact he could thank me for saving him $1,700,000!)

If I were sure your scales of commercial justice weren't likewise tipped toward under-consideration of marketing expenses and over-consideration of toilet paper expenses, I would have spared you that grisly example of TGMWOTWP—The Great Mind Working on the Wrong Problem; but alas, as Rodney Dangerfield says, you "can't get no respect" from anyone who was never poor and pensive. Why? Because, Mr. Honcho, I watch your TV commercials, read your ads and mailing pieces, squeeze your cartons, visit your retailers, and occasionally do with a little dab of your product.

My market research, Mr. Honcho, even if 66% huncho, tells me that you, too, need a few "sadness lessons." Your customers are not as happy (with anything) as High Yeller, Inc., your ad agency, has let its ads for your product pretend. In fact, I shudder to think what my purchase of a Piaget watch tells me about myself, as I quaff your American-made German beer and choose a broker who believes in "old-fashioned things like money" (which, to be practical, sure does beat the idea of a bull running happily around the country in a bear market).

Man's First Basic Defect

Of the four basic defects of man, sourced from His Divine Grace A. C. Bhaktivedanta Swami Prabhupāda, #1 seems to me to be the most obvious and least excusable: "that he must commit mistakes . . . to err [is a] defect of the conditioned soul." The other defects?—propensity for being illusioned, propensity for cheating, fact of possessing imperfect senses.

Okay okay, Swami, but why should humble *product*

marketing be burdened with so much defective humanity? Perhaps it's because *selling* is an unnatural act? Would it be more natural simply to have a Packard car in stock and wait for the man who doesn't own one to come and get it? No, we tried that.

Anyway, look what doing what comes naturally can do! David Attenborough pinpoints "the real threat to human life [as being] the failure to plan our use of the environment. At the moment," he goes on, almost matter-of-factly, "we are engaged in destroying our own planet." But not, surely, by forcing sales to be larger than necessity dictates, or smaller, as they are behind the Iron Curtain. Those are indicative of plans in operation, and if a better (counter-) plan is indicated, the Captains of Industry will be called upon to help forge it.

For now, I'm interested in planning to avoid waste motion and money in marketing, and not to avoid terracide —which is a little beyond my reach. (Surely you remember that the Mouse said, "Because I've been sick," when asked, "Why aren't you big and strong and king of the forest like me?" by the Lion.)

One of the biggest wastes is manpower, conspicuously the lack of making good use of—you guessed it!—the boss as salesman. He was a salesman; he was THE BEST SALESMAN at Ye Olde Outfitters, Ltd., if you'll recall, before getting sidetracked by geography (the corner office) and philosophy (you just take care of the government and the shareholders and leave such mundane matters as product and peddling to your loyal troops, O Shananshah). Philosophy is dangerous to life, as I just demonstrated two paragraphs back when I suddenly began brooding over the browning of our planet.

In my case, the farther removed I got from the product-planning and promotional arenas by dint of moving to "better" offices, the farther I had to run to catch up with them. Here is a small pro and con of it:

Flashback #1. The day Kornfeld arrived on Radio Shack's doorstep in 1948, its president gave him the sales promotion job (at which The Man was a natural) and never looked back. In 1958 I also got the merchandising job because, I suppose, some talent was perceived, but even more obviously (to me) because of a lack of defining such a task as worthy of VIP attention. The attitude then was something like: you just keep on buying, selling and promoting, and leave the money-grubbing to us—things like borrowing, credit, G&A, and other B-School stuff.

Sending the Boss to Japan

Flashback #2. In another part of this opus I make anecdotal note of a chap named Murao who had a lofty export position at Toshiba's central offices in Tokyo . . . how he invited me to explain to his merchandisers the matter of Radio Shack's inexplicable success. Once at a product-planning session between Toshiba and us in our own import-export divisional office in Shinjuku, Murao made one of his deep, samurai-type sounds:

"Ummmmrahh," Murao reflected meditatively but aloud, "maybe Radio Shack is success because president and vice president, ummmrahh, come to Tokyo, Osaka, Tapei, all places, and not just send somebody to do the work? Umr—yes, I think that the reason. . . ."

He'd suddenly remembered that it wasn't every day the foreigner buyers who came to Japan were top management. In fact, it was downright unusual—in fact, very few Japanese execs from the upper echelons came to such meetings. Of course some came but left after the felicitations were over, and most came to dinner (as host) with us at least once every few years.

Was it perceptive of Mr. Murao? You bet! And do I make an ADvisory out of it? No. It depends upon company size and nature, and upon management talents and priorities. But it's a wonder to me that so many C.E.O.s put product and marketing on automatic pilot and get away with it as long as they do.

A missing ingredient, surely, is *the boss as salesman* somehow communicating his own touch of class or persuasion instead of the offerings of High Yeller, Inc., as worked out between HYI and somebody within the corporation whose purpose in life is getting things done on time—which can be as far removed from selling as good news is from journalism.

One of my oldest ideas on how bosses can maintain their perfect pitch returned to mind in 1974 and subsequently showed up in public as the "Flyer-Side Chat." As I wrote in Chat #1: "From time to time I'm going to have a chat with our readers so you can know it's *people* who run Radio Shack—not machines. My first essay coincides with our 51st birthday. The Shack was born when I was seven. I've been with it 25½ years. Those are my credentials."

How My "Flyer-Side Chat" Turned Junk Mail into Class Mail

When I sat down to write my column "Flyer-Side Chat" for our monthly 10-million customer circulation, it was as salesman, not as surrogate Ernie Pyle or Art Buchwald. Its success is neatly summed up in this fan letter from a gentleman in Webster, New York, who said: "I must admit I have always read the 'Chat' before I checked the flyer for bargains. *See how, with a little class, junk mail can become interesting communications and good business.*" (Italics mine for emphasis.)

With just "a little class" you can clean up the "junk" side of your mail, the man says.

Surely not with overweight corporate ads which have almost zero effect on anything—not even common stock prices, the one thing they're supposed to achieve. One expert comes right out with it: "Investors don't look to advertising for information about the performance of a company." To be blunt about it, "Messages about the American economic system's glories, excessive government regulation and world hunger are losers on Wall Street," says its very own *Journal,* meaning corporate ads on these subjects. Clear enough, Mobil?

PRESIDENT'S MESSAGE

Flyer-Side Chat # 1

By Radio Shack's President

From time to time I'm going to have a flyer-side chat with our readers so you can know it's *people* who run Radio Shack—not machines. My first essay coincides with our 51st birthday. The Shack was born when I was seven. I've been with it 25½ years. Those are my credentials.

Sometimes when we run out of a "sale" item we get accused of (1) bait-and-switch tactics, (2) never had it in the first place, (3) only had a few to sell. The plain truth is (1) we rarely sell out of an item although it's *always* our intention, and (2) there are over 2500 places that had to be stocked so you know we had at least several thousand to begin with, (3) we've never used bait/switch tactics in our lives and—like the Miami Dolphins — just win by plugging away at the line.

I apologize to any and all our customers who have missed out on a "sale" bargain because of our stock position. Can you *please believe* we love to sell what we advertise? Will you give me a chance to find it for you if we let you down?

Now I don't promise to search overseas for that sold-out special. Too much red tape! By year's end we had 8 stores in Belgium, 1 in Holland, 9 in England, 4 in Australia, 163 in Canada, promises in Germany but no action . . . *ach du liebe* our Chairman is mad!

As a last word on "specials" I can promise you they're real and—what with shortages, currency changes and inflation—usually irreplaceable at the price. But, our industry, loosely known as "consumer electronics," has a great way of coming up with price-saving technology that keeps our merchandise in the bargain category no matter what. And I think you'll perceive that our particular candy bar doesn't get shorter and shorter. When newspapers were 2¢ apiece and hamburger 33¢ a pound, radios were more expensive and less reliable than they are today in 1974.

L. F. Kornfeld,

Lewis Kornfeld

President

In a five-paragraph column, I was able to make these additional selling points in that first Chat:

■ In reference to accusations of bait-and-switch tactics: "We rarely sell out of an item although it's *always* our intention . . . and over 2500 stores had to be stocked so you know we had at least several thousand (of the item) to begin with."

■ In reference to disappointed customers who miss out on a sale bargain because of our being sold out: "Can you please *believe* we love to sell what we advertise? Will you give me a chance to find it for you if we let you down?"

■ In reference to our prices being low when compared to familiar items: "Consumer electronics have a great way of coming up with price-saving technology that keeps our merchandise in the bargain category no matter what. And I think you'll perceive that our particular candy bar doesn't get shorter and shorter. When newspapers were 2¢ apiece and hamburger 33¢ a pound, radios were more expensive and less reliable than they are today."

Get the idea . . . that such things are difficult to say in almost any marketing approach unless it's personal? Soon I was to write: "Last month I promised our readers I'd invade their privacy in these pages by occasionally inserting a personal message. The purpose is not gratification of my ego. The way I see it: you pay my salary and are entitled to know what I'm doing to earn it."

In that column I went for a few more "brownie points" with our customers:

■ In reference to our sale of things not made in one of our factories: "Most of our non-companymade equipment is actually *custom made* for us alone using our designs, features, tooling, and engineers. . . . Radio Shack *does not* sell "private label" goods where our name is merely stuck on in place of somebody else's!"

■ In reference to our preference (which is genuine) for quality even before low cost: "We won't buy unless we're certain *all doubts* as to reliability and performance have been removed as per our specifications. . . . *Price,* old friend, is only a *part* of how you keep customers coming back!"

Selling your institution or enterprise as a place to do business with and ENJOY it, is right up the boss' alley. How to do it with utmost credibility is the problem I'm positive I solved by chatting instead of b-s-ing, although I naturally couldn't convince some readers that (a) I really did the writing, or (b) that I wasn't just grandstanding.

"The First Thing They Look For"

You can see how it takes one to know one, when the highly regarded newspaper columnist Milton Moskowitz sent me a letter which said in part: "I have always enjoyed your column. You have a pithy style. All newsmen should write as clearly as you do. I was pleased to see my name mentioned in your column." The one-time under-secretary of commerce (under Carter) wrote me: "I read with interest your commentary in Tandy Corporation's Annual Report. Your obvious responsiveness to market trends insures your corporation's continued success."

(Both Sec'y Harman's and Mr. Moskowitz' letters adorn my office wall in more than mere paper testimony to the good uses to which management can put its frequent opportunity to sell something more potent than the divine right to clone itself.)

As I got more and more into the spirit of flyer-side chatting, and our managers around the country repeatedly told us "customers say it's the first thing they look for when the flyer hits their mail box," I was able to broaden my selling base into current events and national policy. Here's how I handled the latest of many increases in postage.

"Your increases in postage play right into our hands, Sam, because the costlier it gets to put envelopes into boxes and retrieve 'em from other boxes, the sooner electronic mail (cf. TRS-80 Videotex) gets affordable in comparison. Aside from being faster, it eliminates stamp-licking and mailman-biting. And you cranky ones who think flyers like this are 'junk mail,' think twice when you say that about a 4¢-item that now costs about 16¢ for fewer pages."

In the same chat—it seems I mentioned Moskowitz more than even he knew about—I noted that "syndicated columnist Milton Moskowitz recently found we've passed 7-Eleven and McDonald's in numbers of stores, observing, 'Today there are some pretty big companies trying to figure out what Radio Shack did and how they did it.'"

I immediately followed that with this pitch for our 60th Anniversary Sale: "Well, one thing, fellas," I wrote, explaining what we did and how we did it, "is we have a blessed event about every four weeks. If you drop by to see this one, our Snazzy Sixty Sale, please leave your hamburger wrappers outside. And BUY something. Okay?"

Selling Made Pleasant

Selling "made pleasant" was essayed in almost every essay. This example shows how you can try to pitch and please at the same time: "Hey—want an honest USA-made bargain? Right here on this page . . . realistic C60 and C90 cassette tapes at half our low regular price. Visit our tape factory if your summerfest takes you to Fort Worth. Tell 'em LK said to treat you like a customer.' (Real nice.)"

Right there in *less than 50 words* I was able to make six clean shots on goal: (1) We had an American-made bargain for a change. (2) The bargain was detailed alongside, on the same page as my column. (3) The deal was half-off on the two most popular lengths of cassette tape. (4) The tape was our own Realistic brand. (5) The tape was made in our own factory. (6) Our factory was in Fort Worth and LK personally invites you to visit it; the welcome mat was out in a believable manner, as I made clear every time I could remember the importance of that little marketing point.

Go ahead!—challenge your ad'xecs to make a valid, positive point about your business SIX TIMES IN 50 WORDS OR LESS. I did it in 48 words—that's making one point every 8.333 words, friend. And it's almost this easy:

ADvisory. On personally making a noise like a cheese: First, you need friendly feelings and the urge to make them relevant to your enterprise. Next, you need at least the semblance of enough authorship to get them on paper in telegraphic form (a welcome change from your everyday memos!). Finally, you need a suitable forum for presenting your friendly, relevant feelings so that they seem *warm and fresh* . . . not *cool and canned!*

On selling Christmas for the umpteenth time: "Christmas is, yes, coming. Could be that TRS-80 is the unique, perfect gift that will have a payoff beyond your wildest dreams. Joseph," speaking of a kid owner who had written us, "aged 13, also sent us some of his tapes, three games and a math test, all executed without his Dad's assistance. Verily, a child shall lead us!"

On making an opportunity out of a failure: "A lovely complaint letter from a Lindenhurst, N.Y., customer had buried in it this diamond-studded accolade: 'Enough brickbats. Every piece of equipment we have bought from Radio Shack, even going back thirty years, is not only working, but working perfectly.'"

On revealing, by quoting a magazine article, valued praise from the co-inventor of the world's first electronic digital computer: "The late Dr. John W. Mauchly . . . enjoyed pointing out that 'that little TRS-80 has more power than the ENIAC did.' Ten words from Dr. John are worth a thousand pictures!"

On revealing we have competition, but . . .: "Two dazzling quotations from *Business Week* magazine. One, in respect of their opening of a retail store—'Xerox is obviously going to have a hell of a lot to learn, declares Tandy's Kornfeld.'"

On being chastised for my views: "Some of my correspondents think I'm a right-winger because I talk about such things (as Uncle Sam deserting Taiwan) and occasionally wave our flag in print. In truth I'm not even entirely conservative. What I want to be is your electronics salesman. And free, at the same time, to speak my piece. At age 61, it really doesn't take much guts. At 21, I didn't have either the courage or the forum!"

And on politics in general: "I wish the heirs of the founding fathers would please get us a new foreign policy, a new oil policy, a better economics policy, a solution to busing problems, and lean quite a bit less heavily upon us who provide the jobs which in turn provide the taxes which in turn let the government govern." Since that was offered in 1975—but could have been 1935 or 1995—"present company" is very likely not excepted.

A Problem of Awareness

The legendary boss of Neiman-Marcus, the by-then retired chairman Stanley Marcus, once received a "Hey, what the hell's going on?" letter from me which he answered promptly, with a carbon copy to (son) Richard Marcus, his successor.

"I am most appreciative of your interest," Stanley wrote, "in writing to me about the food service in our restaurant in Fort Worth. You may be sure that this matter will receive top priority and that we will undertake a radical change in the quality of our food operation. Sincerely, (signed) Stanley Marcus."

Most impressive! An elegant example of the boss as salesman, and if you care to see it, it's hanging on my office wall along with other prized mementos of leaders out in front of their troops showing how to go sic 'em. As visitors to N-M, a.k.a. Neiman Markup (all the way to the bank), may be aware, Mr. Stanley has written several books about his life in merchandising, one of which, *Minding the Store,* seems not only never to be out of stock but also never to be laid out on less than several sales counters. So you see . . . even if you had to rent the lecture hall, the audience will pay to hear you if you're entertaining as well as frank, and manage to sound democrat—pardon my grammar—instead of autocrat.

Positioning the Carter Cabinet

My loftiest platform ever was the White House, Washington, D.C., to which I'd been a very surprised invitee by means of a telegram signed "Jimmy Carter." About 30 other businessmen were invited, all promised lunch and a multi-hour meeting with the Carter cabinet and the Carter himself.

What's this if not another instance of the boss selling, this time Business on the perception his government was pro it, not anti? You went to be sold because it's such an honor to be asked, such a rare compliment to your company.

At that November 1977 meeting in the historic cabinet room, the various secretaries talked about their concerns and solicited points of view. My first big moment came when Secretary of Energy James Schlessinger spoke of the "seven or eight years of grace" left before a real disaster if energy problems weren't attended to promptly, but, alas, "nobody . . . wants change." It was then I had a fabulous idea, raising my hand to signal a request for response time. He saw it.

"Mr. Secretary," I said, introducing myself, "in my business of marketing, we have a word for the condition you have just described. It's *awareness,* or, in your situation, lack of awareness. What I mean is that while the public knows we have a genuine energy problem, it's not aware of the problem in the classic sense of having a symbol or metaphor to catalyze that awareness into action. As we know, awareness without a following action is useless.

"And so," I went on resolutely, "I have an idea to help achieve two of the goals you so earnestly desire . . . first, that the public be made aware of the seriousness of the situation, and secondly that it take an appropriate action—specifically energy conservation, especially gasoline.

"Where better to attack the problem than right here in the nation's capital?

"Why? Because the focus of all eyes around the country is Washington, and the people in it whom the beholders have chosen to represent them are here.

"How? *By having all persons in government, from President Carter on down, drive small cars.* Rabbit-sized cars, though I certainly am not selling Volkwagens."

I wrapped up my sales pitch with this thought: "The country is waiting for Washington to lead it, and I am suggesting that it will 'buy' leadership BY DEED quicker than by word. Putting all the government's leaders into small cars will give you both awareness and emulation!"

While this is a cleaned-up version of my "Rhapsody in Sub-Compact," it's the genuine essence. I would like to think somebody heard (instead of listened to), but if you're an owner of, say, Ford or Chrysler or GM common stock, you'll note I didn't even lay a glove on the entire then-present cabinet of the President of the United States, judging from their noncompliance with my rather simple automobile fuel-use reduction program. (It's enough to give me gas when I think of it!)

I also wrote monthly editorials for our company magazine, one of which mentioned my White House visit although not the above story. I told our employees of how I raised my hand in response to a question from the President and was promptly recognized. More than merely recognized. . . .

"Mr. President," I said, "my name is Kornfeld."

"Yes," said Jimmy Carter, with a glitter of blue eyes, "you're from Radio Shack, aren't you?"

Is that "the boss as salesman"? It is, indeed! Never mind how he knew me—perhaps by the small feat of consulting a map of the collected execs. Who cares? He was out there selling. Hell, we were both selling! Yep: everyone in the room was selling, because when we were put in the pilothouse it wasn't to become architects, altruists, art collectors, or aviators.

Remember it the next time you see the hint of an opening to do something personal in front of your customers. And "personal" doesn't mean okaying a State of the Company editorial on Page 3 of your annual report, written by someone at High Yeller, Inc., or even by one of your own best and brightest. (Junior's time will come, Dad, but not today.)

Radio Shack's entire top team has for years been seen, heard, and visited with by every manager in the entire country, every August, and in person—not on a video tape or in a PR movie. You can call these tiring trips and get-togethers *noblesse oblige* or even 50% waste, but I call them selling sessions. We get to sell the company, the product line, the promotional plan for the year, the track record, and ourselves (on both sides of the podium) as people who all put their pants on the same way.

Year after year, new employees stop by during the cocktail hour or at a coffee break to tell me: "I worked for Zerodefects Corporation for seven years, and you know what—we rarely ever saw anyone from the home office, and never the bosses." Had #1 at Z-D stopped selling by dumping marketing at the Sales Manager's office door? Probably. A long time ago.

Don't be too surprised. Just ask yourself why of 112 students who enrolled in the MBA program at Columbia in a recent year, only 16 said marketing was their major interest. But 23 preferred international trade. And 25 picked finance. Is marketing too menial . . . too primitive . . . too embarrassing . . . or perhaps too difficult and/or insecure a calling? Somewhere among those questions is the root of problems you encounter when you wonder how England lost its commercial zing, and Spain before it. If it were merely a matter of losing colonies, Japan wouldn't be selling anything today!

Radio Shack's 9% Blockbuster

A lot of companies, including those whose leaders have stopped selling personally or who rose to the top from non-selling positions and so never had the honor to ask for an order, view marketing—advertising and sales promotion in particular—as something to be done minimally. Why not?—they've probably never been exposed to maximization.

They tend to identify four things worth spending such dollars for:

1. *More sales.* If the product or service is not a new one and gross margin isn't shot to hell, "more is always more than less," to quote one of my rules and rarely a bad goal.
2. *New sales.* If the product or service is just now being brought to market, or if some new audience has been located, these are "more sales" of a different kind.
3. *Positioning.* If you need a shot at changing the competitive pecking order, positioning is always a place for spending promotional dollars without getting too much flack from your internal Scrooges.
4. *Institutional awareness.* A frequent excuse for telling the world how Zerodefects Corporation has raised its

> dividend (or lowered its boom) again is—Hey, it's time to get that P/E multiple back up! The abundant evidence that such machismo is rampant in the media suggests (to me, at least) that gray hair is no assurance of adjacent gray matter. I do agree, however, that there are "ways and *ways*" such money can be spent, not all of it in a predictably wasteful manner; we'll have to look at each proposition as it comes across the Louis Quinze desk . . . and be prepared to say no.

It's not true, obviously, that more sales, new sales, positioning, and institutional awareness are the whole ball of wax when it comes to promotional dollars; those imply mostly overt media expenses. So let's add another four categories just to be neat:

1. *Premiums.* For example: extra discounts to dealers, rebates to customers, contests, free catalogs and samples.
2. *Displays.* For example: booths for conventions, banners, stickers, pins, posters, billboards, signs, special fixtures for selling goods and services A-V tapes and films.
3. *Awards.* For example: trips to internal contest winners, prizes as internal and/or external awards, charitable contributions—especially if synergistic (business related).
4. *Internal items.* For example: spiffs, ad department costs not charged off against specific productions, PR costs, entertainment, employee magazine, annual report, and so on.

What say? It's incomplete? Forgot all about distribution and mailings? Remember . . . I never promised you a textbook!

Or perhaps you've noticed that your company doesn't call advertising what Kornfeld calls advertising. But don't be too sure you know what he does call advertising; he's not always sure himself, he just likes to think and talk about it, mainly to *be sure you've thought of everything it takes to make a sale, and have an account number for every expense category*.

If you do that, you'll be even more surprised to learn that Radio Shack's "ad" budget for the last many years has been budgeted at 9% of sales. N-I-N-E percent.

How it got to be 9% is what happened before and after 1963 at Radio Shack. Before, it was about 3%, but the three was stretched to 4% by the inclusion of co-op ad money. I was a reasonably adept fund raiser from our suppliers, because I knew that many of them—in their turn—knew we would spend it more effectively; after all, we had an internal ad department and an annual catalog and were hot to trot!

If there was anything unassigned in those "key city" co-op funds, I went for all of it. One of my favorite projects was getting newspaper ads fully paid for. Yes, there are some ad'xecs who could, and probably still do, get back over 100% of cost. I felt 100% was reasonable and right, and anyway, as it turned out, I came to understand that the natural limitations on what you can and can't say in co-op ads made them an unpleasant, ineffective way of soliciting sales.

Charles Tandy's arrival in 1963 led to the following agreement between him and me in respect of Shack's ad budget.

Tandy: Lew, how much do you think our ad budget ought to be?

Kornfeld: Six percent is what I think.

Tandy: I can live with that number.

Perhaps it was typical of the two of us, but we never did get into all the nits and lice of what was advertising and what was some other department's expense, not even of whether the 6% included ad department costs. Of course it did. We always agreed that such costs—labor, repro proofs, pictures, etc.—would run around 10% of budgeted dollars.

A nice thing about working with C. D. Tandy was that he never let debates over expense allocations disturb either his equilibrium or his thinking. His greatest of all virtues quite possibly was that he never forgot to remember to line up ALL THE COSTS where they could be seen and counted. His hackles were more easily raised by unaccounted-for expense items (which later returned as surprises) than by going over budget by any amount so long as it had been done for reasonable cause.

As the years went by, the 6% went by the boards. Over the six-year period 1976–1981 its progress (USA retail only) was 7.7%, 9.3%, 9.4%, 10%, 9.5%, 8.6%. The 7.7% year was aided by CB radio's boom, and the 8.6% says something about selling a good ratio of TRS-80 computers and accessories.

When you consider that those are percents of an ever-increasing sales number, you get a better insight into Radio Shack's blazing desire to keep on expanding. During the same six years, sales (USA retail only) went from about $553 million to about $1.23 billion—an increase of 123%, with roughly corresponding increases in advertising outlays.

> ***ADvisory.*** Those "roughly corresponding increases" in promotional expenses were mostly *planned* before the start of every new year, not improvised to meet emergency situations, although the latter were not exactly rare. It is, however, very rare for sales gains to precede corresponding ad outlays. In my entire business life since 1948 I can recall only one situation—the CB radio boom—when we had growth without a need to beef up selling costs. Actually, we had to cut back Citizens Band promotions due to a lack of merchandise to meet the demand. (In Chapter 11 I give you my reasons for predicting that the personal computer boom will not follow CB's so typically human, tragic, and American rags-to-riches-to-rags scenario.)

Eventually the figure of 9% of sales became the figure generally budgeted for advertising in Radio Shack's retail operations in North America. Overseas, in Australia, England and the EEC, it settled out at about 10%, but during our first few years abroad the price of admission was about TWICE that amount!

According to a reliable source—and by way of giving

you something to compare against that 9%—in 1979 these were among the 50 top advertisers who had advertising costs at a percent of sales of *3% or less:* Sears, K mart, Penney, RCA, GE, AT&T. These were included in the range of *3.1% to 6%:* Proctor & Gamble, Pepsico, Coca-Cola, Philip Morris, Anheuser-Busch, CBS, Time Inc. Only four of the top 50 had outlays of *8.8% to 11.4%:* Richardson-Merrell, Sterling Drug Co., Chesebrough-Pond's, and Heublein Inc.

Drugs, cosmetics, booze, cold drinks, cigarettes, soap—all enterprises with one thing in common provided they hadn't dramatically changed their mix via acquisitions. Need I say what that is? Yes, as a reminder to those who may be unfamiliar with it by choice or ignorance: *adequate gross margin.* Adequate to what? To paying the piper. No less, no more. There are indeed many other trade routes to take in the wide world of commerce, but the one paved with affordably excessive (by the conventional wisdom) advertising expenses offers the best scenery and smoothest passage.

How to Pay More and Like It

A prime objective of the Boss is to find and trim excessive fat. Long ago, I suggested that an obvious way was by solving Wanamaker's Conundrum. Remember?—he knew half of his ad cost was wasted but he didn't know which half. And all through my pages I've targeted solutions such as these:

1. *Stay close to the product and promotional picture,* by participating in marketing plans and decisions.
2. *Examine closely the conventional wisdom* that insists that you need outside agents—advertising, PR, consultants; that you can't do all or most of it in house; that you should follow trendiness—in media selection, art, copy, themes, campaigns, use of models or famous personalities; that 3% or less is the way to go in budgeting ad costs because Great Soporific Incorporated gets along okay with 2.9%.
3. *Don't buy what can't be counted,* meaning simply that

your results attributable to marketing costs—and particularly ad costs—are as suspect as any asset swap until you've accounted for what you received in exchange. Even staying under Great Sopo's 3% isn't reason for throwing away $10,000 bills "because we're still under budget."

4. *Don't spend less because it's cheaper.*

The last of those four saving graces is the most difficult for businessmen to swallow, particularly those who have been denied a whiff of Entrepreneurial Elixxer (trademark pending) because they were hired *to manage and control,* not to blow dream bubbles with Zerodefects Corporation's money.

ADvisory. If you can't aspire to Radio Shack's 9% because the gross margins aren't there, try to get them "there" by changing something—cost, sell, package, distribution, SG&A, or your whole damn business. Try, even if you don't plan to spend it to get and grow your business!

ADvisory. If you can't see the benefits of 9% versus 4.5% or 2.25%, try remembering that almost any sort of promotion has corollary "givens" of more awareness and solid positioning, and that when the promotions are both affordable and productive, the "givens" are given free!

Radio Shack advertising is believed to be everywhere and in most media, according to even the most observant people I meet. Actually, it is tightly controlled to something like 33.3% for direct contacts with recent customers, 66.6% for "cold" contact with recent non-customers, and 0.1% for cigars. The simple fact that you think you see a K mart ad whenever you look up doesn't gainsay the probability that its ad expense in 1979, expressed as a percent of sales, was no more than 2.3% (or anything less than $287 million).

But not to worry if that 287-megabuck figure attributed to K mart is five times bigger than Zerodefects Corporation's turnover from 1980–1984 inclusive. Fundamentals still apply. If you want to grow you've got to invest. Charles Tandy's pet figure was that for every additional $1 in sales, an additional 50¢ had to be invested in the business. That means to get that extra buck, another half had to be anted up; part of it, of course, would pay for the extra advertising required.

But in advertising there's another consideration. What if your average sales ticket (retail) was $15 before the new $1 in sales was bought for 50¢, but afterwards it went to $30 or even to $45? You might be able to produce more sales from the same size (cost) advertising—right? Not necessarily!

By increasing your average sales ticket it's probable you'll run into a new group of competitors or the cost of plowing new ground, and that the encounter will reduce margins until you have re-sighted your gun. Some time ago I concluded this: simultaneous expansion of selling and advertising is on the leading edge of marketing technology for reasons which—if not made altogether clear in the foregoing paragraphs—most assuredly merit your best thinking seven days a week.

A Shopping List of Problems and Solutions for Bosses

An inveterate reader, I am always tearing articles out of magazines and newspapers, particularly out of the *Wall Street Journal.* The WSJ periodically runs a marketing column that's worth wading through a lot of bad and questionable advertising to reach. Today I culled my file for items relevant to bosses (owners, managers, movers and shakers) who are still sufficiently interested in moving their product to give a hoot how it's done and measured. For example. . . .

Reaching the boss was said to have been on Data General's mind when its computers seemed not to rank high enough in bosses' awareness, and there was also the problem of some nine other computer makers with either "data" or "general" in their name.

SOLUTION: Television commercials in tennis, golf and news slots, to attract top management's attention—not to make sales directly but rather to get on corporate shopping lists and, as a Data General man was quoted, "If there's three bids, we want to be one of them."

COMMENTARY: I'm skeptical of TV's ability to deliver in terms of cost effectiveness. Just for a random better idea, suppose the company had a book on computers with a value of $25 per copy, and mailed one to each of the Fortune 1000 companies—directly to the boss—with a personal letter from its own boss. Estimated cost 1000 × $15 (book cost) plus other expense items such as postage = $20,000. The finished film of their first commercial probably cost several times that figure, never mind airing it. But given that they had other ideas, too, TV would have been close to the bottom of my shopping list for sorting out the datas and the generals (Goodrich, with just one other nominal competitor, has spent quite a few bucks trying not to be Goodyear which, if I were Goodyear, I'd appreciate).

Management training and sales training are ever on the executive mind, possibly because THEY never had any themselves—"they" meaning people like myself.

SOLUTION: During the recent (or current, depending upon view) recession, department and specialty stores were found to be 57% holding the line on training expenses, 43% cutting back in various ways.

COMMENTARY: I know little about management training since all I've ever approved was done on the job by doing the job. On the matter of sales training—aside from considerations of having to learn computer science or the operation of new equipment—I'm a genuine iconoclast, especially in the matter of elaborate teaching materials and time away from the sales arena. I'd rather teach togetherness, loyalty, job security, company history and direction, and so on, at the proper places and times for doing so. (Most Radio Shack management people got "educated" on someone's sales floor.)

"No agency got results like we got ourselves," said a gentleman in the industrial cleaning equipment manufacturing business, after trying for six years. "We got tired of wait-

ing for agencies to live up to their assurances that they could 'position' us properly and solve our complicated marketing problems."

SOLUTION: As reported in *Inc.* magazine, a really nice source for small business news, the exec found they'd "been looking for someone to do our work for us," and so, after years of frustration, "we decided to set up an in-house agency . . . and go outside for our specific artistic requirements." Their own in-house research gave them three yardsticks for applying promotional solutions: (1) Watch and learn from your competitors' growth, including size and make-up of product line. (2) Watch the sales of major component vendors to see how you stack up in who's getting what. (3) Watch your warrantee cards for signals and useful data.

COMMENTARY: You would have thought I'd written that article for *Inc.* But I can write you this: in an adjacent article, there was an agency guy's story about good things agencies do, and I've omitted them all out of considerations of bias, space, and lack of novelty.

What makes a good ad once (at least) was the subject of a thoughtful article in *Consumers Electronics Monthly,* one of my regular sources for non-advertising data. It suggests you ask yourself five questions about your customers—YOU, not Joe Blow down the hall: (1) Who are your customers? (2) What do they need to know? (3) How should they be informed? (4) Where should they find out about you? (5) How often?

SOLUTION (and equally plural): (1) Occasionally buy some outside research. (2) Choose between direct-selling and awareness ads. (3) Avoid too much info in your ads, but don't forget that attention-getting copy can make or break your ad. (4) Design ads around the locale where the product will most likely be used. (5) Measure media ads by using coupons, premiums, offer of a pamphlet or catalog, traffic count.

COMMENTARY: All the solutions point toward the ad and away from the product, whereas my own solution always remembers that the boss (as salesman) cannot hope for healthy advertising or salesmanship to make a sick product well. This may be where the famous Japanese consensus system comes in handy . . . referring to some sort of consensus on whether it's the right product in the first place. Most salesmen, however, get a product to peddle on the basis that a product is a product, a peddler a peddler. Why the agency or in-house bunch may be perceived by management as having failed to sell again may, in fact, be because Merchandising slipped them a lemon, an Edsel, a Pringles, or even an RCA mainframe computer.

"The richest 40% of households account for 60% of all U.S. retail sales," says a Shearson Loeb economist. That's 40% of roughly 80 million = 32 million households. Those 32 million households give us advertisers a population to sell, of, say, about 90% the size of Japan's entire population, and double that of England, Germany, and France, taken separately! Need more?

SOLUTION: Consider electing a president who's a Democrat or at least not an older Republican. The article spoke of how much worse the statistics would have been if budget-cutting got serious: "Spending by the bottom tier could decline sharply, dampening the strength coming from the upper tier."

COMMENTARY: I included this ADvisory from a tale told in *Business Week* magazine to show you how easy it is to locate your customer. Most of us sell to the 100% of households including the "bottom tier," and we also depend upon the latter for a lot of the elbow grease. It's nice to play with the private sector as being composed of two basic tiers—top as contributor, bottom as consumer—except that too much play may end with the bottom tier consuming the top! (Tell them you got this notion out of a book on marketing and advertising, and they'll say, "You're kidding.")

"Who's minding the store at Sears?" asks a columnist writing for *Retailing Home Furnishings,* a trade paper. "Did the management of that once paragon of performers in retailing become so infatuated with its non-retailing operations that it took its eye off its retailing ball?"

SOLUTION: Recent management changes—more accurately, the latest round of same—might have augured better for Sears, in my opinion, had they not just bought one of Wall Street's bigger brokerage houses. However, the fact that this giant also planned 45 office equipment stores for 1982 instead of a rumored five, is a plus on the retail side of the ledger.

COMMENTARY: A market test of five special stores (see above) seemed inadequate to one (myself) who planned 50—the Radio Shack Computer Center—with a smaller product base than that envisioned by Sears. When we think of Sears losing its way in the merchandise marketing jungle, it's a bit like the world's richest retailer getting lost in a bank vault, and not at all like Montgomery Ward (#5) getting squirreled up on the one hand with competition and on the other with advice and a big allowance from its foster parent, Mobil. When Sears decides it can't be all things to all of the people, as it once apparently envisioned, it will disappear from marketing critiques and go back to being a cash cow. (Memo to Sears: I know you didn't ask for my advice, but any PR is better than no PR as I point out in this book. Any advice, however, is not always better than no advice, as I now point out.)

Why big companies fail when they try to start new businesses was the subject of a fine *New York Times* article by an NYU professor who also entrepreneurs. Among nine reasons for failure, one is a favorite of mine—the observation that many failures are caused by the timing and amount of investment.

SOLUTION: Keep the cost of the failure low by not thinking "too big too soon."

COMMENTARY: While the above solution is only a fraction of the thinking expressed, my own thoughts—assuming the investor(s) to be rational and logical people—tend to run the other way, no doubt because I'm such a critical critic. What I've seen too much of, in the way of generating failure from possible success, is timidity. When you couple innate timidity with adversary accounting, you can hardly win for losing. After Tandy's 1963 acquisition of Radio Shack, the latter was taken aboard "service free" in respect of costs in its behalf paid for by the parent and not charged to the acquisition (which was then in the red). When Radio Shack could pay its own way, it was charged by the parent for everything provided. By doing that, the division was able to continue rewarding its good people for jobs well done; without that kind of thinking, they might have jumped ship. The moral: keep the load light until the ship can float on the open sea. Or, to paraphrase Shakespeare, "Load oft sinks itself and ship."

"Pricing of products is still an art, often having little link to costs," headlines the *Wall Street Journal's* first of a series on how prices get set.

SOLUTION: This is another item I've slipped in for your delectation, because we so often think our genius lies in writing price tags instead of many-splendored memoranda. And if we think we're scientific in doing it, one quotee offers up the opinion that "often, the process is incredibly arbitrary." (My solution, actually, is to write the price properly the first time, because rewrites generally cost you a bundle.)

COMMENTARY: The foregoing is meant to arouse all readers to the importance of dealing with price as a basic component of marketing. When pricing becomes a formula, i.e., cost plus 52 or 92 or 112 percent of itself, throw out everyone and hire yourself a robot whose handwriting is legible. When pricing is not reviewed by the Host of Hosts, you have only him to blame, and you'll note I used a lower case "h." In a later chapter (on Marketing the TRS-80) I reveal my strategy in using $599.95 as our introductory Model I system price despite rumors that $888 or $1199 might have worked as well.

"Advertisers and their agencies have too much faith in advertising," says a veteran adman named Gus Priemer in one of the *Journal's* best-ever marketing columns, because "they use the wrong definitions of productivity and offer little incentive to budget less—rather than more—for advertising." He even goes so far as to say—as I have said throughout my text—that management needs to "act more responsibly toward the investment of their advertising (funds)."

SOLUTION: Included suggestions are close the circuit between sales and advertising; don't assume advertising is doing something without knowing what; don't assume good sales = good advertising; don't assume that distribution, packaging, product appearance and pricing aren't crucial ingredients to affordable advertising that pays its way; and don't ever assume that circulation—actual or potential viewers or readers—is bought properly on a "more the merrier" basis.

COMMENTARY: The time for being merrier about "more" is when you've closed your cash register for the day and . . . the cash is there!

FOUR

The Media (External)

Media is the plural of "medium," and what a neat, multi-purposed word medium turns out to be! My dictionary sees it as *that through or by which anything is accomplished; as, an advertising medium.* But just one definition away, medium becomes spiritualistic: just one prior, it is a substance through which forces act or effects are transmitted . . . for instance (my examples): air, water, space, time, the ripple effects in matter from micro- to macro-cosmic.

Most media are places of privilege, clubs to which an admission charge is levied each time you enter, the price of membership varying with the amount of privilege desired and the number of people (circulation) predicted to show up at the club as spectators.

In Bhagavad-gita it says that the Lord—although probably not the Press Lord!—"reserves the right NOT to expose Himself to anyone and everyone but [only] to those souls . . . surrendered unto Him." Most media lords who sell advertising space wouldn't know what to do with a soul if one were presented; what they want surrendered unto them are your promotional dollars in exchange for their exposure of *your representation* of your business or other enterprise.

Lords of the news media, however, have a constitutionally protected, primary holy calling: dissemination of all the news that's fit to print and presumed accurate. Thus the surrendered soul may appear in the news columns as well as the advertising columns, often for a feasance instead of a fee. If the lords of the news media additionally deem it their secondary holy calling to entertain, that one is entirely self-imposed. In my more ornery moments I define the press, which was one of my former employers, as a disseminator of bad times, mediocre entertainment, and excellent sporting news; I have plenty of such moments whenever the *New York Times,* the *Wall Street Journal* and the *International Herald Tribune* are not available.

The diminution of competition among newspapers in the big American cities—a trend since the 1929 depression, an avalanche since 1959—now gives the press de facto power that is as immense as it is immediate, and neither TV nor other "electronic" news seriously threatens the hard-copy press during at least the 1980s, no matter what they tell you or what other publishers (like AT&T and Dow Jones) do.

What the latter are contemplating is touched upon in Chapter 14, "Future Schlock." While "schlock" refers to advertising and other marketing techniques, the press will add its fair share by packaging "fabricated" news and rewritten PR handouts to look like the real stuff.

Newspapers as Today's Mail Today

Advertisers in the retail business usually find results from newspaper ads to be more immediate, affordable, and measurable than they are from other conventional methods: radio, television, mail order, billboards, stuffers, word of mouth, PR, brouhaha of whatever description. Advocates of one or the other media—particularly mail order and radio—will question this assessment. At times they will be correct, but my 33 years in merchandising and advertising allow me the luxury of not waiting up for exceptions.

Newspapers are today's mail today; you can change your message as often as they have days and you have dollars. Your "mail" can have a number of shapes, sizes, and privileged positions—the latter usually at extra cost. I'll run a few of them by you just as a reminder:

Classified advertising: Every paper has a classified ad section in which, for modest cost and often without the requirement of special art work, a vendor can sell anything from an entire company or business service to the smallest item imaginable. Because this section is typically indexed by type of goods offered, it's an extremely quick way to reach someone looking for something specific, say a CB radio, motorbike, flute, typewriter, tennis racquet, Rolex watch, sports car—all things I've looked for at one time or another.

ROP section. The acronym stands for Run of the Press, meaning roughly that your ad will run anywhere the paper puts it (except not in the classified section or in an extra-cost position).

Extra cost sections or positions. When an advertiser requests that his ad be located in the Amusement, Entertainment, or Financial section of a newspaper, the line or size rate is usually higher. It may cost a premium over ROP rates to guarantee a position such as sports, first news (or back of any) section, etc.

Special sections. The Sunday TV pullout magazine, the comics pullout section, the magazine section, whether local, regional or national, are special regularly scheduled domains usually carrying ads. In addition, a newspaper may publish limited-time inserts dedicated to activities such as sportsmen's or motor car shows. Circulation considerations aside, these sections are run to produce advertising revenue beyond what the "regular" paper can raise; their news value is wishful thinking.

Private newspaper inserts. Many large advertisers, Radio Shack being a good example (along with Sears, K mart, Montgomery Ward, Target, White Auto, catalog houses such as Best Products, and local or regional department store or home improvement store chains) create their own "newspapers" for insertion into local newspapers on specific days. These publications are called "inserts" and they are frequently *not* printed by the inserting newspaper or even locally, because of such criteria as print technique, economies of printing and distribution cost, labeling technology, size of print run.

Let's take a look at these basic newspaper elements with ideas and opinions on which might be the right one for you to use and at which times, heavily loaded with the experience and bias that caused me, in part, to write this book.

Classified advertising is a rifle among the many advertising shotguns. If you have a Powell flute to sell and I want a Powell flute, classified may be the best approach for you, assuming you've considered music school bulletin boards, flute teachers, etc.

Flashback. When Tandy bought Allied Radio, we found that Allied had a special store in Chicago where only discontinued and blemished or out-of-repair goods were sold, and that the basic advertising method it used to attract buyers was a lengthy, multi-item classified ad. Want to bet the "selling cost" of these ads was lower than anything else they did in the way of advertising?

Note: "selling cost" or "cost of sales" is a term used to state *the promotional cost of getting something sold.* Very simplistically, a $1 cost to get something sold for $10 is a 10% cost of sales when we talk about c/s in advertising. Classified's c/s is likely to be both the lowest AND the easiest to measure.

So why not do all your advertising in the classified section as most car dealers do? Darn good question. Don't be afraid to ask it each time someone asks you to okay an ad. Simply say: "Have you considered running that in the classified section?" (They won't have. And you'll be more respected for your inquiry than for your okay to run it ROP, because they'll know Big Brother knows something about advertising . . . and it'll be your secret how much!)

The ROP Section, meaning Run of Press (or Paper), is supposed to be up for grabs, i.e., not controlled by an advertiser, so never fear to request (a) a right-hand page, and (b) top billing.

I think right-hand pages are better ad sites than lefts, but the margin of choice is small. I think ads are read from top of page to bottom, so I prefer top billing and remind you it's possible to shape and size your ad to get it without much hassle. The back page of any section is also desirable.

The notion that ROP space isn't good enough is usually bunk. *But* . . . if you're selling a movie, and movies are lumped into an entertainment section along with such benefits as movie reviews and timetables, stick with the herd. *But* . . . even so, don't even do that without thinking about some other (or additional) spot such as—yes!—two-line classifieds on the front page, or wherever they put the weather map.

Extra-cost positions can be justified by assumptions such as these: Men read the sports page and men buy the tires, so run your tire ad in sports. . . . Businessmen read the financial section and cause or influence the purchase of office equipment, so run your copier or word-processor ad in the financial section and smile when you pay the extra cost. . . . People who go to the movies often eat out before or after the show, so run your pizza shop ad in the entertainment section. . . . Most of your competitors for women's wear sales run their ads in x-section, so specify x-section and run with the herd.

Every second thought I've had during my professional life has been *not* to run with the herd. Nevertheless, when we started making and selling personal computers in 1977—the first year of any significant sales push of this sort of product to the public at large—we immediately started to run ads in as broad an assortment of computer, office and business media as we could identify and afford. Even if we were #1 in the herd, it was herd instinct at its most obvious and least ingenious. (See also Chapter 11.)

Special sections such as comics, TV magazine, etc., all have their own ad/herents or you may be sure the paper would package this info in some other way. The general thinking is they theoretically cast the strongest, narrowest beam on the segment of the circulation you perceive, by fact or fancy, as your primary target or customer.

Approach these sections with extreme care. Remember: aside from extra cost, they may offer the added negative of having *zero reading interest* for a quite large chunk of circulation. To my mind it makes a lot of sense to pass up these dear little country inns for places where the most cars and trucks are stopped at noon: the ROP Hog Wallow. That's where you'll find the new news, kids!

Inserts: the Private Sector

Just to show you he wasn't always in step with his times, let me state that our late Chairman, Charles Tandy, once said to me, "And we won't run any newspaper inserts . . . right?" "Wrong," I replied, "I'm already running them and I intend to continue to do so."

On another occasion, after I'd put us into the wire and cable manufacturing business, Tandy advised: "And one thing we don't want to do is to extrude wire." I laughed, saying, "I don't know where you got that idea, but if you want to see *four* extruders in action I'll drive you over to the plant."

Inserts are also called "supplements" or "preprint sections." Some of you know them as what drops out of the Sunday paper when you pick it up carelessly. Though most are run on Sunday (bigger circulation, longer reading time, easier stuffing for the newspapers), some are run on a weekday such as Thursday. (Maybe Tuesday will be your good news day?) (Ask K mart why it inserts in Dallas-Ft. Worth on Thursday.)

If the big guys use newspaper inserts, why might it be smart *not* to do so, since we're always interested in at least two of the four sides of every question? A chap at Target told a magazine one of the reasons: *Final item selection is done 12-16 weeks PRIOR to publication, and pricing must be set about 8-10 weeks PRIOR to publication.* That's two to four months of lead time, and when you compare it to the week or less you need for the regular part of the paper, you quickly perceive the risk. Styles go sour. Items get sold out prematurely. QC problems suddenly prevent shipment. Strikes occur. Management changes its players and its philosophies.

Let me itemize a few of the advantages I found when I got Radio Shack into the insert game on a regular basis:

1. *No competition.* Your supplement carries only your

own advertising messages, always without interference from the news, makeup or ad department of the paper.

2. *Better paper.* Newsprint is generally of a lower quality than any paper you'd choose to print your ads on, unless they were scheduled for a well-printed, well-dried supplement printed by the newspaper itself. When you use your own printer, your choice of stock is quite wide, although the better grades (whiteness, smoothness) always cost more.

3. *More and cheaper color.* As you've seen from the various efforts by the local newspapers to mess around with four-color printing, it's more mess than miracle. Newsprint can't satisfactorily reproduce the fine screens needed for realistic color; but rotogravure and offset can. (Think of "screen" as the size of the smallest acceptable bit of printed space . . . the finer the screen the finer the printing quality, the coarser the screen the coarser the printing quality. Two common screens: 133 fine, 65 coarse.) When color's cost becomes incremental, the more you use the cheaper it costs; once you've passed the low six-figures of circulation, color's just about a freebie.

4. *Enhanced image.* Here's an example of utilizing a medium that—when proved cost-effective—gives you both short- and long-range status among advertisers in your community *as perceived by your readers.* The insert is a class publication delivered within a mass publication, always assuming you've done a decent job of preparation. And, in a way, it does the job of a mini catalog (whatever you think of catalogs, the public always respects them as efforts beyond the ordinary ad effort).

Target on Target

In the early 1980s, my choice among inserts is Target's; this division of Dayton Hudson regularly produces inserts which lift Target's discount store image far above its competitors'—at least to whatever heights a quality publication is able to levitate a business.

According to a trade publication, Target's preprinted

supplements run between 8 and 16 pages and "account for about half of Target's yearly ad budget. They are also an integral part of the chain's unquestioned success." Target's Charles Miller, in discussing the image projection mentioned earlier, said he "didn't accept the concept discount needs to be schlock [either] in the stores or the advertising."

My admiration of the Target insert still lets me wonder if paper of the quality they use is actually required. Where does practicality end and gilding the lily begin?

ADvisory. Never forget to ask.

5. *Measurable results.* If you have ever paid the price of an insert—for convenience use six cents each for total unit cost and multiply six cents times the paper's circulation—you know that the cost is so steep as to demand prompt justification for using this particular medium during any but the highest of the "high season" weeks or months. Obviously there are some of us who have measured results and found them acceptable. Equally obviously there are others who haven't. And less obviously, there are some who use inserts whimsically, with no intent (or need?) to track response.

6. *Miscellaneous pluses.* Among the pluses are wide option regarding the number of items (SKUs) advertised versus traditional ad sizes (but be careful—space makes waste) . . . *the pullout insert may have longer life than the body of the paper—can be hopefully regarded as a "keeper"* . . . avoidance of adjacent price competition—it's YOUR paper within the paper . . . *benefits of best positions—front page, rear page, center spread of two adjoining pages are all yours* . . . benefit of overrun use—the insert can *in addition* be mailed to customer, occupant or prospect lists, and used as a high-class in-store or in-trade-show promotion piece, with or without changes . . . *an insert helps you "shape up" your buying and advertising and distribution people by making them plan ahead for a really serious, immovable deadline* . . . insert size, usually eight pages because that's usually the most economical, allows you to mix some institutional advertising in with your sales pitches—stuff like extra-long new product in-

tros, PR about your company, job openings, changes of location or hours.

TV and Radio as Ad Media

On a recent trip to our nation's capital, I was riding with my cousin to play tennis indoors when I suddenly decided to involve him in my current project—this book—at least to the extent of finding out what his outfit, Hechinger Company, thought about advertising on radio and television. Since my cousin is Richard England, Hechinger chairman, he seemed to be the right person to ask. Hechinger, being the largest retailer in the D.C. area of things for home improvement, including lumber, and a profitable nine-figure company and large advertiser, is a witness whose testimony is worthy of our attention.

About television advertising, Dick England was quite candid and laconic, in the manner of many of us who come from the northeastern corner of the country: "We just don't seem to see any positive results."

About radio advertising: "Well, what little we've done didn't seem to show us any positive results." As with Radio Shack, so with Hechinger: a POSITIVE RESULT is a SALE to a customer. Ask your preacher or teacher if this isn't gospel!

Shortly thereafter I visited a nearby True Value Hardware store in West Fort Worth. After introducing myself, I asked the managers—there seemed to be two of them—about their advertising and what worked best. They ranked the media as follows: *1—newspaper 2—television, 3—radio.* Newspapers were #1 by a long way. Cost of sales was unknown to these men, as was their percent of advertising vs. sales, possibly because the store was only seven months old.

My own experience with TV advertising has led me to the positive but unspectacular opinion that for most of us it's affordable only if (a) the cost doesn't frighten you, and (b) you don't anticipate or need a response that's 5X to 10X WORSE—yes, that's five to ten times worse—than you usually get from your best measured advertising medium.

Radio Shack did get a not unanticipated benefit when it went into TV advertising in the early 1970s. At that time we had decided that the best way to sell our wares in the "grass roots" areas of the USA and Canada was to open small-town dealerships in markets too small to support a company store. "Too small" in 1965 was 20,000 population; by 1977 it had shrunk to 8000 because it turned out that, after all, a company Shack could survive in lonelier places than our number crunchers had prophesied.

This led to my 11th Rule of Marketing (one Tandy would have loved):

---

11 Don't let your bookkeepers make book on your marketing decisions.

(Better they should tabulate your losses when you follow my rule. And better they should keep their jobs when you lose yours; as they say in Texas: "It's only right. . . .")

The small-town dealer would be a profitable retailer who was *already* in business. He would keep his name over the door and simply add ours, in contrast to the typical "franchise" where the franchise uses our name only and *goes into business* as a result of joining our team.

From a standing start, and with no guiding precedence, we opened our first dealer in January 1972 in the town of Eastland, Texas, a place so small it failed (along with its neighbor towns of Cisco and Ranger) to make the World Almanac's 1981 list of Texas towns of 5000 and over. By 1982 there were over 2000 such outlets carrying Radio Shack's merchandise to the hinterest lands, meaning they'd been added at an average of 175.72 per year net of closures. But the real point here is that I have excellent reason to credit our TV ads with having increased awareness of us so we were more credible when we knocked on our prospects' doors. Yes!—they told our knockers they'd seen our TV commercials.

Lest I deceive you into thinking just any old sheaf of TV commercials will do the trick, I remind you—better still, tell you for the first time—that Radio Shack used and uses what is known as *network* TV, or, loosely speaking, all of it. Very few advertisers have outlets in all 50 states, but Radio Shack does; and not only in all the states, but virtually all of the cities and towns; and now, virtually all the hamlets (except the one soliloquizing "There are more things in heaven and earth than a Radio Shack"). That's the kind of reach that allows The Shack the assurance of *no waste circulation* when it attempts to govern by videocracy.

Most advertisers buy x-amount of waste circulation in any ad effort, and the amount of waste is rather easily determinable. In fact our 12th Rule of Marketing goes to the heart of the matter:

---

12 Always investigate the amount of waste circulation you have to buy when you buy space or time in a medium; always evaluate the value of waste vs. non-waste and see if there's a better way to spend your promotional bucks.

All publications make their circulation figures available, including their figures on circulation per area (distribution).

But after Awareness, What?

Radio Shack still had to SELL its dealer-prospects who had been made (more) aware of us; needless to say, there's many a slip between notoriety and a purchase order. It came right down to the product itself—the Realistic, Archer, TRS-80, Micronta, and other lines we offer. When push comes to shove, Podner, your product must satisfy, even if it's wood for wooden nickels.

Those who can't indulge in renting time on the entire network can indulge in local or area "spot" commercials. Sometimes, as happens in great moments in pro football, the local advertiser's spot is shown at a much more favorable time than your network ad, causing bile to rise and faith to fall.

TV advertising may be bought in a wide variety of time slots and costs: as with meat, prime is Grade A and priced accordingly. You may also buy viewers by the age group and/or by the sex. (There are more age groups than there are sexes, but the latter—with uni, ambi and homo—are gaining.)

All this can be taken too seriously. The reason there are so many lures in fishing goods shops is that there are a lot of opinionated people in the sucker population, as I have so often demonstrated by personal example.

In an article on marketing, the *Wall Street Journal* headlines: "Retailers Buy More Ads on TV, But Many Still Question Results." Yes, they do, despite newspaper space being infinite in quantity for all practical purposes, and TV time being finite and layered with virtually viewerless segments. The article supports my newspaper love affair by crediting that medium with carrying "about 75% of all U.S. retail ads." And somewhere deeper into analysis we learn: "While most retailers who do use television are sticking to conventional messages that convey store image, some are experimenting with ads about specific products and prices. Many, however (my italics) *still harbor doubts about how suitable and effective the tube is.*"

The "many" referred to are, I must add, among the most active retailers in the country, folks who understand quite a bit about awareness and cost of sales (c/s). Since TV advertising has been around since the late 1940s, that's quite a put-down. So why not a knockout as well?

Perhaps Marshall McLuhan gave us a clue when he ventured the opinion—in respect to TV—that "the medium is the message." Therefore nothing on TV is nearly as significant as the TV set (with program) itself. But he visualized the impact of TV commercials as greater than that of actual programs . . . not so much as a force for the delivery of buyers as for the delivery of reshaped lifestyles and attitudes. In short: it exists, therefore it is: *hic et ubique.*

But more likely the lure of TV as a medium for advertising is the certainty of large numbers of viewers in a captive position (seated, eyes on the fat of the tube, mouths in the fly-trap position) at precise, well-known times. Barnum's memory does not need to be evoked when so many vendors are aware of so much positive exposure at times of day or night which are so limited in number and so obvious in viewer popularity. There's a new vendor born every minute who thinks this is his little secret. But the truth is, lads, all is not gold that flickers.

Earlier I warned you to expect five to ten times worse results when you use TV instead of an equivalent medium at an equivalent cost. "If a newspaper ad costs me $1 to get $10 in sales, do you mean, Brother Lewis, that I might pay $5 to $10 to make that $10 sale on television?"

"Aye, that I do, Your Clientship, and it could cost you $20 to make that $10 sale, except that if I'd said that first, Sire, you'd have put me away."

So it could be that TV commercials have the same luster as fine art in the executive suite, the company jet fleet, or—as canny Matsushita reckoned when it came to the USA to try to put Panasonic on the map—a slew of offices in the Pan Am Building in New York City. (I used "canny" because they've since moved to New Jersey.)

So it could be a convertible status symbol: held one way it delivers a few instant sales, held another it delivers a short ton of prestige, held upside down, as it were, it rains awareness so that sales conversions may be harvested at some later date; furthermore, if abstained from, it can be read as a sign of poverty, weakness or ignorance. If I may speak for Radio Shack, those are all valid reasons . . . but not quite ALL the reasons.

Occasionally there's an item that starts selling the minute it goes on the v-tube, more than likely one that's priced under $30 and on sale at a price representing a genuine saving. Occasionally there's the event, say a store or computer center grand opening, that responds well to a modest saturation of local TV spots within a tight time frame. Occasionally there's a new item or service that needs a heavenward launching aspect (and damn the expense).

These are use-excuses for which I don't have to apologize. And when you discover that not all networks are profitable all the time, you realize that Channel Manna is as far from being divinely supplied as other wonders of our time—cf. nuclear power, supply side economics, bubble memory, and advertising guaranteed by its creators to succeed (or they pay for it).

"Radio Ads Ride a Comeback"

No less a harbinger than the *New York Times* finds "the advertising medium many gave up for dead in the 1950s and 1960s . . . is making a comeback." Frankly, I'm less concerned with comeback than with payoff, and less concerned with payoff to the medium than to the advertiser. (If I'd inherited the *Times* or *Washington Post* I'd be concerned about biting my tongue; but as it happened, fate laid out for me a career in turnover instead of hearsay.)

The bad news, however, is that the *Times* story seems to be based on observations and findings derived from the president of the Radio Advertising Bureau (the graph, too), leading to our frosty 13th Rule of Marketing:

---

13 Never base a business decision or philosophy on information supplied by an industry bureau or association unless your main requirements are bias and optimism.

The president of the RAB, Miles David, while bragging that radio's price increase of 65% since 1968 is the lowest of all the media, says the value "wouldn't be worth much unless the medium worked." Right-on to that, but why hasn't it worked for Radio Shack (with minor exceptions) and Hechinger (with no notable exceptions)? My answer to that is to suggest that we didn't use it properly or long enough. And my answer to that is why mess around with Mr. In-Between when both companies know perfectly well how to attract lookers and buyers?

Flashback. That reminds me of a story about my friend, Jimmy Schaye, when he was chief cook and bottle washer for the once-great Boston department store chain called Raymonds. As a stunt he had Sugar Ray Robinson—could be before S/R/Leonard was born!—spar with another boxer in a ring set up in Raymonds' ground floor. Traffic? Excitement? "You never saw so many people in the store at the same time, not even at Christmas," Schaye said glowingly.

Ever interested in sales-generating stunts, I asked him how big an improvement in sales had occurred as a result. "Improvement in sales?" he replied. "The only thing that improved was shoplifting."

Other revelations of the Radio Advertising Bureau follow. Over the same 1968–1980 period that saw radio advertising costs rise 65%, magazine costs rose 71%, television 121%, and newspapers 132%. (The period being 13 years, none of those increases is too depressing, especially when I think of gasoline and first-class postage.) An average of 30 million people listen to radio during an average 15-minute period, and 95% of us listen to it at least 15 minutes a week. Well, weller, wellest!

There are a lot more statistics where those came from, and it's not necessary to pay an advertising agency to dig them out for you. What is necessary is worth repeating for the nth time: To get your product sold, consider all the media . . .ask other *advertisers* in your area what they think about each one and why . . . and GO! . . . I'm trying to give you the big picture without the big price.

Co-op advertising aside, radio is probably a medium that will work better locally than nationally for you, and probably will do better with an event ad than a product ad.

You don't know what co-op advertising is? It's advertising paid partly or wholly by your supplier, but eventually wholly by you in the form of higher prices or other legerdemain. (You don't know what legerdemain is?—it's when you neither put down this book . . . nor pay for it!)

Magazines: Top Banana?

"It was around two decades ago, in the city room of the Boston *Evening Transcript,* that I first became aware of the elongated-yellow-fruit school of writing," said Charles W.

Morton (1899–1967), recalling a story about fugitive monkeys and policemen trying to recapture them by using bananas as bait.

Time and again when I read the seductive promises made in picture and headline on magazine covers, and their pathetic realization within, I think about the elongated-yellow-fruit school of writing. To enter this school you must use three words which 88% inadequately describe a subject and/or appease hunger. After 10 or 20 years of trying to ignore this deception, which is, of course, the magazine's bright way of advertising itself, I begin to admit to myself:

—the article on which zoom lens is best for you will be a letdown instead of a pullout;
—the guarantee of a better sex life will be a solecism:
—the how-I-did-it-and-you-too-can-become-a-millionaire (by various routes) will be GIGO (garbage-in, garbage-out);
—the ee-zee-duz-it article on building something will probably include an unavailable component, leave a part out of the parts list, and certainly won't make it ee-zee for you to construct anything.

Given this mind set, you can still get a reasoned look at the magazine as a medium from me, perhaps because it takes me about 10 or 20 years to develop all-out skepticism . . . you'll note I still want to have a better sex life, to be assured that one zoom lens will replace all my other photo glassware, to make millions in clever, novel ways. And I'm quite sure most of my readers have fully evolved illusions they've clung to long after they had carbon-dated proof the earth is 4,500,000,000 years old—not the 45,000 they'd prefer.

Magazines have become increasingly specialized since WWII, certainly since the Great Depression that preceded it. Specialization makes it easier for you to target your audience in all important respects: distribution (mentioned earlier), age and sex (mentioned earlier), income and interests (mentioned now). Every magazine has available propaganda which explains why it is your BEST BUY among apparent peers and obvious betters. They also have printed rate cards (but you should haggle just in case). And rules about such things as bleeds, colors, deadlines, screens, locations; sometimes they are fussy about what they will accept as advertising.

Flashback. Radio Shack once had its hi-fi ads rejected by a very famous magazine and never could find out the reason. The magazine went so far as to tell us we "wouldn't like the results." And I even went so far as to reply, "The only result I want is to appear in your advertising section and pay you for the privilege." This experience taught me a lot about turning the other cheek (and remembering I'd only one left).

Among the leading kinds of magazines are seven major categories of such magnitude as to be written about in still other magazines—as for example *Magazine Age,* where this data is gleaned: News, Business, General Interest, Women's, Fashion, Shelter, and Sunday magazines (the latter in newspapers). "Leading advertisers" gave them over $2 billion in 1980, according to Leading National Advertisers, a source.

But that's not what interested me when I stumbled across their data. I was more interested in seeing *what products* these "leading advertisers" were advertising *in which categories of magazine.* For example, in shelter magazines:

—18% was spent on business products!
—1% on apparel.
—17% on food.
—8% on liquor.
—4% on automotives.
—4% on toiletries.
—14% on cigarettes.
—30% on home products and services.

As that adds up to about 96%, it certainly doesn't leave much for schools, books, and travel advertising! What it shows is where sellers go to find buyers. And where they don't.

Business magazines, for another example, lured practically NO advertisers of apparel, food, or toiletries; and less than 1% of their ad revenues came from cigarettes. In a last example of selectivity, automotive ads accounted for less than 1/4 of 1% of major category advertising in women's magazines (and you can bet none of that was for trucks).

How Magazines Multiply

Give any publisher a hint that there's a new industry brewing and he'll rush to be first in line with a new magazine for it. Why? Because the publisher knows the new industry probably doesn't know where to advertise.

When CB was hot—ca.1972–1978—a legion of new magazines entered the field. And EVERY ONE of us CB manufacturers meekly joined the fold, grasping for cover positions and more product reviews. When the personal computer entered the scene, an unprecedented number of magazines got born—and I can tell you, it didn't take 'em nine months.

One magazine, *80 Micro,* got born simply because our TRS-80 became such a standout product; it was aimed at owners of our computers, even though not sponsored or circulated by us. Its publisher couldn't understand why Radio Shack didn't want to distribute a magazine containing (a) advertising by competitors and knockers-off, or (b) articles which are occasionally adversary in nature . . . or (c) why we don't peddle ANY magazines of ANY kind—logistics is the reason, but he failed to perceive it as a genuine problem.

I'm the kind of guy who likes rough figures, neatly rounded. Here's one: there are about 2100 magazine titles in the *consumer magazine* list section of the most important source of such data, the Standard Rate & Data Service—hereinafter known as SRDS. Its "Consumer Magazine and Farm Publication (Rates & Data)" also lists 500 farm magazines!

Right there you have 2600 magazines from which to select, and we haven't gotten into the zillions of other luscious possibilities. Fortunately, there's a relatively cheap way to get data about magazines that is even more complete than the Bible . . . because the data is changed on a weekly, monthly, bimonthly, quarterly, or semi-annual basis.

It's All Yours for $1081

Lucky you! For $1081 you can get each and every SRDA publication FOR ONE YEAR, INCLUDING POSTAGE AND HANDLING. You get 17 different publications containing current info in incredible detail, covering rate and data of such media as (1) business publications, (2) consumer magazine and farm publications, (3) direct mail lists, (4) networks, (5) newspapers, (6) spot radio, and (7) spot television. The seven categories listed would cost you only $667, but the remaining ten for $414 would be like money in the bank if you got only two paying ideas out of them over the entire year.

The consumer/farm magazine SRDS is a monthly, typically 700 pages BIG, packed with definitions, classifications, new listings, deletions, even ads by magazines wanting to stand out in the crowd. At $106/yr. (of the $1081) how can you miss?

To order or inquire about these gems, contact the publishing and executive offices of Standard Rate & Data Service, Inc., at 5201 Old Orchard Road, Skokie, Ill. 60077. Skokie: 312-470-3100. Chicago: 312-583-1333. New York City: 212-935-7593. Los Angeles: 213-651-2311. These numbers should get you at least the next number to call. Tell 'em you read about them in this book. Prices are recent, not necessarily current. No, I don't get anything (except satisfaction) for introducing you to SRDS. My satisfaction is in knowing you don't need a consultant to find out about the media.

After you find out about the media for $1081 or $667 or $414 or $106—and remember that's per annum, not per month!—then a great way to find out about successes and failures is to telephone the boss and/or ad manager of a variety of advertisers. You'll be pleasantly surprised at your reception. It will be casual, comfortable, candid. Smart businessmen like to talk to their peers; dumb ones don't.

The Troubles Multiply, Too

To an extent, a basic trouble with advertising in magazines is one of timing. Take a magazine like *The Atlantic,* better known as *The Atlantic Monthly*. It goes on sale at newsstands on the last Tuesday of the month *preceding* the publication (cover) date. Ergo, your January ad will go public in late December, a minor problem that can be worse, depending on the particular magazine.

More of a problem is that the "closing date" for your ad is *the 15th of the second month preceding the date of issue*. This means your January 1984 ad had to be at *The Atlantic* no later than November 15. And when they say "no extensions granted, no cancellations accepted after closing date," they mean it. Many businesspeople simply can't cope with time lags of more than a few days or weeks, and, essentially, the ad that ran in January and hit the stands in December and closed on November 15 quite likely had to be planned on October 15 for timely subsequent layout, copy, pasteup, and mailing to the magazine; all in all a two-and-a-half-month project.

Then there's the probem of space. The typical magazine ad is (the ad itself) a mere 7 × 10 inches, and even if it "bleeds" (runs off the edges) the text of your message will be 7 × 10 inches or close to obliteration. So the format itself is troublesome to many advertisers, particularly retailers accustomed to vast playgrounds of newsprint. For that reason, only a few of the latter go national with sale-priced ads—conspicuously Sears, K mart, Radio Shack.

The net result is reducible to a few observations: that magazine ads tend to be institutional or introductory, that magazine ads tend to be looked on by advertisers much as one looks at the sign-in log outside a wedding or funeral parlor—proof of your attendance, or in this analogy, proof that yes, you, too, are very much in business. Many vendors advertise in magazines in direct support of their retailers; even if it isn't called co-op advertising, you can bet it's somewhere in the cost of goods sold.

Then, alas, there's the problem of where the circulation resides, otherwise known as distribution; and this problem is serious. Take *The New Yorker* magazine, with a recent territorial distribution of 512,000 copies. Take yourself, in business in the part of the USA called the Pacific states, meaning West Coast. Only 80,400 readers of *The New Yorker* live on the west coast, meaning if your business address is located there, and you're not soliciting mail orders, you may reach less than 16% of the circulation. Some magazines circumvent this by breaking their circulation down into regional pieces—you can buy any or all. All is cheaper. But what's the price/value of waste circulation? Some advertisers hope to defy waste with mail-order ads, but those only acerbate the time-of-year (deadline) problems just enumerated.

The first part of our 12th Rule of Marketing read: *Always investigate the amount of waste circulation you have to buy when you buy space or time in a medium. . . .* I now offer a 14th Rule of Marketing to help make things clearer:

---

14 You can anticipate that the order-number results of national advertising will be roughly in proportion to the population of the affected states or localities, except that the results in your "home" area—100-mile radius from address in ad—will be well above this proportion.

(Sorry, exceptions to this are too variable to allow for a corollary rule or deeper insight.)

Billboads' 53-Century Hype

An imaginative writer for *The Dallas Morning News* tells how Egyptian merchants "etched their trade messages in stone along the roadways that led to the town markets," all this in the year 3200 B.C., when scenic pollution presumably was not a problem unless the Pharaoh said so.

Then we're told revenues in the billboard industry "have grown at a faster rate than any other form of advertising, outstripping television, radio, newspapers and magazines." It was when I read that that I knew the info came from a source like the Institute of Outdoor Advertising, a source which had cleverly helped to make its business worthy of a news story.

Imagine!—they got a freebie of a third of a page on the first page of the business section, replete with a four-color picture and a nice graph, by claiming a renaissance of the billboard. (When you try this one on your PR department, remind them of the value of a touch of antiquity, such as the way it was when roadside ads were only a twinkle in a camel's eye.)

The first slice of good news from this enhanced PR tale is that billboard advertising's cost per reader "statistically beats any other advertising medium in its ability to reach the general public." I like the second slice better, the one that tells me the billboard population shrank from 400,000 signs in 1965 to 250,000 in 1981 and is still shrinking.

Flashback. When I moved my headquarters from Boston to Fort Worth in 1963, one of the first surprises I encountered was that my friend, mentor, and employer, Charles Tandy, not only admired billboards but indeed drove me out to see one he'd rented that actually *moved*. For the next 15 years I would resist this urge of Tandy's, finally succeeding in turning it into a love for store signs that were either *very large* or *very large and rotating*. There's simply no comparison!

Is there a billboard in your future? Are you a circus? If you are a circus, okay. Is your hotel or restaurant off the road and easy to find? Are you a gas station in a really special spot that's likely to be really important to onrushing drivers? Okay okay. Are you running for office? Why?

Mail Order Memories

Most readers of solicitations for orders by mail fully believe that most solicitors are paradigms of success. And conversely, most solicitors for orders by mail fully believe that enough solicitees will *eventually* become customers to make the whole dream come true. To put it more simply: if you hope to live by the mails you can expect to die by the mails unless you have other fish to fry at the same time . . . if, for example:

—mail orders are only "plus business" for your regular business but you want them for certain reasons;

—your product or service is so expensive and/or your

gross margin so high that you clear your costs quickly and the rest is gravy; a high average mail order—say over $29.95—can cover up a lot of gambling losses;

—the cost of soliciting mail orders may not be recouped on the first round of sales, but your product or service is such that re-orders are almost automatically generated and before long you're taking it all to the bank.

When I came to Radio Shack in 1948 the conventional wisdom was that the mail order business was a natural for us. Look at our successful competitors, I was told; look at Allied Radio, Lafayette Radio, Hudson, Burstein-Applebee, Olson, etc., all busy opening envelopes and packing and shipping orders like no tomorrow.

Flashback. By the early 1980s it really WAS no tomorrow for most of those old boys. Only Olson Electronics, a small Akron-based consumer electronics division of (by acquisition) Teledyne, was waiting for the postman to ring twice. But—and PLEASE pay attention—in the period between 1960 to 1980, its mail order volume had declined from over 90% of total sales to under 10% of sales!

Four factors make Olson's incredible transition from mail-order to store-floor dominance understandable:

1. The company went from a few to over 40 stores, replacing mail sales with store sales.
2. Surviving competitors—such as Radio Shack—did the same thing.
3. Every effort to stem the loss of mail order sales was made and proven futile.
4. As the nature of consumer electronics merchandise changed over those two decades, its distribution changed, bringing more competitors into the fray—discount houses, music shops, audio/video "warehouses," department stores, and "catalog showrooms," just to name five!

As the nature of the merchandise changed, more electronic components went in out of the heat—into cool, opaque integrated circuits and other solid state devices—reducing or altering the hobbyist population and hence the fundamental nature of our kind of consumer electronics business. Why is this important to you? Because a similar transition is probable in *any* business you happen to be involved in today. The coming of age of so many electronic systems and devices that change the way you cook, communicate, file, type, read, write, learn, fix, and get your kicks should be telling you to be prepared, old scout, for the Quartz and Beep Generation, or you can color yourself distressed oak!

Tandy's first words to his newly acquired Radio Shack team in 1963 included this macho pronouncement: "We're going to put stores everywhere the mail orders used to come from."

For the next 18 years the rate of new store and dealer openings would scare hell out of 333.33 a year in the United States and 111.11 a year in Canada and abroad! But back to our subject—mail orders: we stopped soliciting them in 1972 when their contribution to sales had shrunk to 0.4% of a $183 million business, down from nearly 50% in 1962! We stopped; we didn't sit around debating the point or making surveys.

Many a starry-eyed character has called me up over the years saying: "Kornfeld, how would you like to increase the business by 25 or 50%? I've got a fabulous idea for you."

"I know exactly what it is," I reply quietly.

"How could you . . . I haven't even told you my idea," says starry-eyes irritably.

"It's mail order," I rejoin, "and we don't want any today."

"I'm talking hundreds of millions of added sales and *he doesn't want any today!* God, there's nothing worse than a closed mind."

"It's simplicity, not stubbornness," I explain, "I don't want to *open envelopes,* I want to *open store doors,* and that's the way my managers like it, too." There are other reasons I don't get into. But here's one I do: most electronic merchandise doesn't travel well in the mail. Okay?

Nearest and Dearest Friends

Just because Radio Shack fell out of love with the U. S. mail service's inability to deliver us from evil with bags of order envelopes* and white mail** averaging over $15 a pop, it didn't follow that we would abandon mailing propositions to our nearest and dearest friends*** asking for their business. But a pause for those asterisked notations:

**Order envelopes* are usually self-addressed (prepaid postage) envelopes included with packages and invoices and designed to make it easy for recipients to mail you orders. Nice as they are, they are costly and, in my opinion, wasteful. I discontinued their use years ago, first scrapping the prepaid postage feature, finally the envelope itself. Their best use may be for collecting accounts receivable and bank-by-mail deposits. Yes. When I get one, I use it.

***White mail* is mail—in this instance a mail order—whose origin by the order-taker cannot be traced to any coded coupon or other media-measuring device. Forget this definition and get all you can.

****Nearest and dearest friends* are your MOST RECENT customers. Forget this definition and get all you can.

P. S. With respect to ***, above, don't pay too much attention to those who advise qualifying *most recents* by overt concern about *how much they spent* or *what they bought*. You can stay up nights programming down to where your computer can tell you the size and location of the customer's smallest mole. Forget this kerrapp about knowing all the minutiae about customers and *get all the customers you can.*

There was one thing we former mail order experts—meaning Charles Tandy and his acquired Radio Shack team from Boston—knew and agreed upon: There's no customer like—well, it really merits my 15th Rule of Marketing to immortalize it:

---

15 Your customer most likely to become a repeat customer is your most recent customer.

This is a really fabulous rule that's worth at least $10,000 (which you may mail directly to me c/o Prentice-Hall if you are abnormally grateful). But it requires care and feeding, not lip service and coronation.

We decided to continue two of Radio Shack's famous publications—the catalog and the monthly flyer—but to discontinue (a) mailing them to purchased lists of names, and (b) soliciting mail orders. When you stop soliciting mail orders you STOP asking for them with coupons, mail order blanks, phone numbers, postpaid envelopes. If necessary, you start using such lines of copy as NO MAIL ORDERS ACCEPTED, or NONE SENT BY MAIL.

The reason I describe this process in such detail is that it's extremely difficult (a) to break old habits, or (b) to tell people how *not* to do business with you in a particular manner. If this is your present situation, as it was ours in the 1970s, you must instantly activate our 16th Rule of Marketing:

---

16 Never tell a customer or prospect what NOT TO DO unless you immediately tell him WHAT TO DO in the same or next sentence of your message. A negative command is a no-no.

Last In, First Back In

You've heard of FIFO (first in, first out), and LIFO (last in, first out), and you probably know these acronyms pertain to merchandise in respect of accounting. You also probably realize merchandise is valuable . . . worth storing securely, counting regularly, and turning over several times a year. But your customer list? As merchandise?

Meet LIFA, and get this through your head and, if necessary, through the rear ends of your donkeys. LIFA means *Last In, First Asked Again* and it refers to customers. It may even be applicable to inquirers, people who have asked specifically about your merchandise or service but who have not yet converted to actual ownership.

Who says LIFA is the truth, that your last buyer is the most likely to be your next buyer? The *record* is who! Of course if you don't have a record of the comings and spendings of your customers you're one of two things:

—*Lucky* to have such a "demand" business that you don't need to track who buys; or

—*Dumb*. Ignorance is not an acceptable defense when your commercial life is on the line.

In most cases, tracking your customers is both feasible and desirable because of LIFA. You record three details:

1. *Recency*. Date of last purchase.
2. *Frequency*. Number of purchases made in a given time.
3. *Monetary*. Amount spent on last purchase (or all).

A fourth often-watched factor is *item-category of purchase*. As an article of faith, take my word for it that the first three factors are much more important.

Sure, there are many other clever little trackable details, *most of which will simply increase the cost of your tracking and the bulk of your reports*. In the end, they will prove not worth the paper or punch card or disk they're recorded on.

It's not a rule but a postulate: *Too much knowledge is often a dangerous thing*. And this is just about a postulate: the customer's address being a "given," *recency and frequency are the only two customer-knowledge factors that are absolutely essential* unless you are tracking accounts receivable at the same time as you're going for those repeat, add-on, or new sales.

Most of the businesses with which I trade really don't believe in LIFA, the primacy of the most recent customer. But I'm not terribly surprised: their salesmanship is virtually non-existent . . . why should they believe in repeat sales?

Here's a living tribute to lack of salesmanship. Over recent time I've bought four (4) Volkswagen automobiles for members of my family. On no occasion was I offered—at the moment of sale—an add-on! Not a radio. Not a right-side rear view mirror. Not a locking gas tank cap. Never a bumper protector, a roof carrier, a special wheel or tire, or any other option. (Dumkopf: you're not alone . . . Radio Shack has its own share of salesmen who only take orders.)

A customer is to be made love to . . . loved, not raped. How is this done if she's gone home and you don't know her name or address and she doesn't have a personal computer you can access?

Of Time and the Seller

It's like this about time, when you're talking mailing list: *Time waits for no customer beyond 12 months.*

To put it more succinctly: a mailing list that's over a year old is on balance too old to make love to. A customer who hasn't bought after a year should almost always be taken off (purged from) your mailing list . . . after or without prior notice. Prior notices cost money. Prior notices without super inducements usually fail. Better to forget that lost sweetie and hope to catch her on another safari into lioness country.

One of C. D. Tandy's great unwashed theories was that multiple-time customers should be treated more kindly than one-time customers because they had shown unusual devotion to your cause. Good thinking. Try it. It's a hell of a lot smarter than dropping dollars into dollar slot machines.

Some time back, before my mailing list chit-chat began, I promised myself I'd tell you about a neat little paradox . . . namely, how Radio Shack increased its mailings at the same time it stopped doing business by mail. Come to think of it, it's a promise I may have made in the Table of Contents.

First and by far the most important factor, we opened the stores and brought in the people. Then we captured their vital statistics on our sales slips. And then, at long last, we had access to customers who might, who could, and who absolutely trackably DID become repeaters.

If you don't have stores, you have something equivalent to which this activity applies. The main principle, obviously, is to bring 'em back alive—the car buyer, the parishioner, the registered party member and voter, the mail or phone buyer, the season ticket holder, the customer. And how you know they're alive is this: you or someone else sold them something *recently!*

When Radio Shack made its store personnel keenly aware of the importance of the customer's *curriculum vitae* the names of recent customers really started pouring into our computer center. And the merchandising/advertising people really started pouring out the mail.

What's so new about sending out mail to bring buyers in? Hell, it's as old as the carrier pigeon. Scratch that! It's older than the handwriting on the wall. What's new is the extent of Radio Shack's devotion to this duty: monthly mailings of 24 pages of four-color advertising to recent customers.

What's even newer is adherence to such a program when your "recent customers" become 1,000,000, then 5,000,000, and finally over 10,000,000 names to be mailed monthly. Note: at roughly 9¢ per piece for mailing out 10 million pieces, the P.O. bill is $900,000 *every 30 days!*

Is that $10,800,000 per annum, Mr. Ripley? Well, well, how cunningly the price of love escalates when inflation rages. My point is, however obscurely I've approached it, that it takes courage to follow one's destiny when the end-zeros multiply. At any rate, it explains how Radio Shack's mailings increased even more quickly than its mail buyers disappeared.

On the matter of 12 flyers a year, please get this straight: first you have one, then four, then eight flyers per year. You have what you can afford, not what I tell you you can afford. You have:

1. *Recent customers* whom you care for just as if they were valuable merchandise, or, more precisely, inventory.
2. *Frequent customer contacts* which you make as often as possible with the ultimate aim of at least one a month.
3 *Measured results* kept in writing and not kept secret from your employees.

4. *A clean customer list* with a one-year cutoff for old one-time customers, and an 18-month cutoff for old multi-time customers.
5. *A well-conceived program for getting new customers,* which is more or less touched on throughout the book.

It will pay you, in regard to #5 above, to order this 17th Rule of Marketing as an hors d'oeuvre before going for an entree:

---

17 It takes at least twice as much money to attract a new customer via newspaper or other form of advertising as to re-attract a recent customer by direct personal contact; budget to spend 33.3% on recent customers, 66.6% on very old or non-customers, and 0.1% on cigars).

Does my recounting of Radio Shack's exit from the mail order business mean that the latter is a dead issue for other companies? Definitely NOT. There are many mitigating factors for it, not to forget that it might be cheaper and more effective to solicit by phone than by mail:

1. You may be able to work on a smaller (or no) inventory.
2. Mail orders may be incremental to your regular business.
3. You may have an item priced high enough to get by costwise on as few orders as one.
4. You may be able to use mail orders to test a product or service which you ultimately intend to sell another way: the result of the test could be amazingly accurate.
5. Electronic techniques for ordering may someday preempt shopping in stores; your earlier experience could pay off.
6. Another oil shock or two may make traveling about so costly that mail will be a better (or more equal) option.

7. Emphasis by traditional stores is on reducing stock-keeping units to best sellers only; what they eliminate could keep a lot of smart mail order folks in clover.
8. Present success: if you've got it, keep it (but past failures are better heeded than fought against).

On Premiums and Rebates

Let's throw contests into a group of klutzes, along with premiums and rebates. I don't like contests but listen, gals, it's certainly one of the ways to become Miss America. And premiums . . . well, the Radio Shack Free Battery card was one of my finest improvisations, according to the late Charles Tandy, of whom it may be said greater love for the common zinc carbon radio and flashlight battery hath no man. (The card is given out free to shoppers in participating Radio Shack stores; it entitles them to a year's supply of certain Radio Shack brand batteries at the rate of one free battery a month.)

Flashback. In November, 1977, I was invited by President Carter to attend a three-hour White House session attended by most of his cabinet members and about 30 businessmen from around the country. The idea was sort of a Project Interface between big government and big business. Realizing I would have a chance to speak personally to President Carter, I had our people create a LIFETIME Free Battery card for him as a gift from the company.

At the opportune moment, I handed him the card and described its intent. A few months later the card was mailed back to me with a note from Carter's chief assistant, Jack Watson, which said something like this: "Regretfully, the President returns your card because he is unable to accept gifts of significant value."

This unique premium had at the time a "significant value" of $7.08 *a year* (at the rate of 59 cents a month) which perhaps is indicative of the high moral component of that particular administration! My flashback has, however, a happy ending. Four years later I mailed the same Lifetime

Free Battery card to Citizen Jimmie Carter in Plains, Georgia, and received the following greatly prized letter:

"To Lewis Kornfeld: Thank you for the lifetime free battery card. I appreciate this expression of friendship and thoughtfulness on the part of the 25,000 people at Radio Shack. With best wishes. Sincerely, (signed) Jimmie Carter."

My definition of a premium is "something given away." A dictionary definition, in one part, reads, "A gift provided with a purchase." Tandy's theory was that a premium should be something not ordinarily sold by the company, i.e., a radio as premium would deny the sale of a radio to the premium's recipient. In sum, everyone's right and everyone's wrong. A good product or a good deal should be self-supporting. What that means, Mr. Kellog, is that perhaps most products and most deals aren't quite good enough?

My definition of a proper contest is an event in which all the prizes are won by the entrants, and which, in the instance of businesses that are not in the gaming business, is characteristically something to fall back on when the wells of ingenuity have run totally dry. With unaccustomed generosity, I admit that contests as charitable fund raisers or scholarship providers are okay, even in my philosophy, but you will do well to think of another way of making a noise like a cheese.

That brings us to the pernicious rebate, generally a "refund" made directly to the buyer by the manufacturer. If anything in advertising's bag of tricks has epitomized the problem of making sales in the early 1980s, it's the Factory Rebate.

"Trying to Get Something Going"

My subheadline is attributable to a Ford official during one of Ford's forays into the rebate jungle. *"We're all just trying to get something going here. We can't afford to stand still."* Whether you offer lower than "market" interest rates à la GM, or $2 back on a $5 purchase of Gillette Atra blades, or larger mini-refunds on GE appliances or Zenith TV sets, the name of the game is the same. And rebates are mean little drains on gross margin and dangerous little substitutes for classic advertising.

What is "classic advertising"? It's advertising at its least shrill moments, when it tends to offer:

—something new in the way of goods or services;
—something desirable at a reduced price;
—something in overstock which must be closed out;
—something for which its owner, in order to stimulate and/or maintain momentum, needs more awareness by the public without delay;
—something, in summary, newsworthy.

I wonder, is it a coincidence that the rebate bellies up to ALL FIVE of my (certainly incomplete) criteria? Why, then, is it so often a device of last resort? Because, if you'll pardon the oversimplification, the rebate is too powerful a medicine for use without an expert's prescription.

Take this quote from the *Wall Street Journal* on the Ford program in question. "As it has in earlier rebate programs . . . Ford . . . is requiring its dealers to put up an average of 36% of the advertised rebates. Car dealers don't like this . . . and critics maintain that it lessens customers' actual savings by narrowing dealers' leeway for bargaining." Some of the defects of rebate advertising surface quickly!

If the era of the giant rebate was stimulated by problems endemic to the American auto industry, what about the increase in the use of rebates by smaller businesses? Some just plain copy the latest ad fad. Some say, hey, that's something we haven't tried since the Spanish-American war!

Some see it as a way to confront the perennial problem of maker/vendor relations: Who IS supposed to do the job of selling to the public? The answer, inasmuch as really splendid salesmanship is a fiction, is . . . both!

Rebates are within the province of most manufacturers, yet they're a technique that the average retailer—with his pinched gross margin, his instant price-cut weaponry and his ability to tell it to the world in tomorrow's newspaper—is reluctant to employ. At best, rebates seem to me to be merely an implied threat of the manufacturer in his never-ending war against (what I perceive as their perception of) the sloth and infidelity of their typical retailer.

POEM

I've never made a rebate, I hope I never make one;
It's a fishy kind of bait that's liable to break one.

FIVE

The Media (Internal)

The First Thing They See Is Your Advertising

My paternal grandmother had a theory about men in the hard world of commerce which coincided with the theory about advertising that boils down to this: when people see you or your business, what they notice first is your advertising. Her advice was stern and appropriate to the (1930s) times: "Be sure you go out with your shoes shined, because that's the first thing they see."

Unfilled, guilt-ridden, lobe-deep in angst at the age of 14, my mind nevertheless had a sensitized bit of film on which her warning registered, apparently for all time—otherwise how could I deliver such a sharp print of it to you over a half century later? It took me many years to understand that without exception the first thing shoppers and lookers see really *is* your advertising. Not necessarily your published advertising, but more likely the internal kind: shop windows, carton art, caliber of salespeople, and, yes, maybe the color, style or gloss of your shoes.

Once a Radio Shack district manager sent me a book dealing with the psychology of clothing oneself, recommending that I buy 5000 copies for distribution to our store salesmen along with one of my cage-rattling "shape up or ship out" memos. He was positive the members of our floor personnel were our worst advertising and were the only thing preventing achievement of the 25% sales gain I'd requested. Bad appearance = bad internal advertising? Granny would have liked him better than me!

Ignoring proper sales training for the moment, I open these proceedings with a plea for shipshape interiors. The notion is that if you provide the latter, the occupants will shape up to the ship . . . clean courtly Neiman-Marcus contains clean clever Neiman-Marcus people. To a large degree it works, but alas, not without constant persuasion, retraining, and the occasional pilloried victim. Such analogies as "You'd never use the floor of your own home as an ashtray," or "At home you'd never leave the lights on and the water running," etc., operate, figuratively, only at gunpoint.

Flashback. The second Mrs. Charles Tandy desired that her husband look more like a millionaire industrialist and less like a millionaire Texan, starting with his shoes. "You know these damned Gucci loafers," he once said, looking at mine, "just aren't built to hold a man of my weight. Yesterday Anne made me buy six pairs . . . and whoo-ee, do you know the price tag?"

Shoes as internal media are supremely important in my native Boston as well, it being an imprimatur of caste that gentlemen's brogues be worn only when—seemingly—three creases from a final parting of the leathers; also, the only proper style is plain-toed, rubber-soled and flat as a flounder, always in no-nonsense brown. On State and Federal Streets if shoes aren't seen first, they're seen eventually. What is this if not vintage bottom-line elitist advertising?

But since the pre-flashback subject was shop interiors, and since you've probably never visited a Radio Shack which in any way resembled a Neiman-Marcus in full bloom, you must do as I say—not as I've done. Public interiors aren't the only exemplars of internal advertising; the look of your parking lot, your behind-counter areas, your WCs, the way you flaunt your printed disclaimers and other legal notices—these are all advertising and should be treated as assets at work. Meaning? Meaning change housekeepers ASAP if the old ones don't know your assets from a hole in the wall.

There's nothing sorrier than a store sign or front that needs paint, relighting, patching, cleaning, or its i's dotted. Well, maybe there is . . . seasonal decorations left in place after the season's come and gone, sale-event signs that aren't in place when the starting gun goes off, new price tags askew over old price tags (always the higher prices on top), smoking salespersons, random cups and cans, litter blown into your architect's wind socks. They're all ads, and I've said again and again: *good ads must combine news and benefits,* so do not ask for whom the mess tolls, it tolls for thee.

Packaging: Boxes, Bags, Stationery, Name Cards

When Rupert Brooke saw the Cantabrigians as people who "never smile" but are "packed with guile" his ad metaphors got mixed. In fact: advertising *is* a smile. But, in fact: advertising *is* packaging. And, in fact: advertising with a tad of guile *is* the real stuff, otherwise why bother with such make believe as tight jeans, scent, a string of pearls, lucent eye shadow, lip rouge, body jewelry?

The Japanese have taught those of us merchandisers who like to think of ourselves as observant a new thing or two about packaging and packing . . . mainly to *do it better than the customer has a right or need to expect.* After all, a purchase is a precious thing. Who ordained that the wonder and pleasure cease when I trade my gold for your gazebo?

Those scrutable rising sons and daughters give you that double inner protective wrapping, that extra glossy instruction manual, that special mounting hardware, those costly box stiffeners and snow boxes, those many multicolored touches which could easily have been economy-black. Why the handsomely knotted elasticized gold string instead of tape? Is it good . . . advertising AFTER the sale? Absolutely, but if you do it:

> ***ADvisory.*** Get it back in gross margin if you want to live long enough to enjoy the best of both worlds (being in—and staying in—business profitably).

While your letterheads and other statements don't have to be *nouveau* to be *riche,* give them your best effort insofar as mirroring "the real you" is concerned. If you frankly don't give a damn, well, that's "the real you" and it will eventually take more talent than you have to get away with it.

That evokes this 18th Rule of Marketing:

---

18 Guard against small details which can needlessly downgrade your image: printed materials, use and size of logos, the area around the cash register, doors that bang when they shouldn't, things whose cost would be the same for a rose as for a bramble.

Maybe Confucius would have said: "Is trouble when enterprise has slob manager and fancy art director." I guarantee you my paternal grandmother would have had a maxim to cover the situation. ("Nichts for der Kinder" was one I heard fairly often, meaning for adults only.)

Name cards, like manly handshakes, can be executed in the extreme. Adequacy is next to godliness! Keep your card size standard for easy filing and retrieval; standardize your company card and avoid the hideous ingenuity of associates who lack your, ahem, classic taste. On author Isaac Asimov's name card he modestly lists himself as Isaac Asimov, Natural Resource. Many of my friends, on retiring with financial distinction to play gin rummy for acres of ranchland, list their business as Investments, others as Unemployed. (Yes, there are times when I wish the Greenhouse Effect were more effective than it is.)

Don't use transparent or translucent cards—people will see right through you and find someone nearly Neanderthal. Don't use brass or sterling cards, i.e., be off your mettle. Pause to refresh your image by removing and ditching the sign on your desk that has your name on it, even if your wife or secretary thus gifted you. Blame me. Say I said redundant advertising gimmicks are worse than lonely long-distance joggers, and that I'm ready to trade in my Rolex Presidential watch and British attaché case. The moral is something like this: If you don't believe you're a big cheese, you can't make a noise like one by wearing a label that says Brie.

On Matchless Advertising

There are two things most new and many small businessmen feel they must have to be pros: a large cash register replete with beeps and gushing tapes; a bottomless supply of book matches replete with company data, often with interior contest or bonus. I'll give you one brief squeeze of each lemon.

> ***ADvisory.*** You don't need to give away matches unless you're running a bar or restaurant, and even then they don't need to be customized. If you enjoy trashing money, light up a dollar bill every day of the year; the savings will be $157.88 or some variant of that number.

> ***ADvisory.*** You don't need to rent or buy a cash register until you've investigated the *cash drawer,* a push-pull device that works the same way your desk drawer works; it's ideal for those who do their sales slips manually. Cash drawers have the added virtue of being quiet and circumspect. Which reminds me to add that you probably don't need a cashier either, except possibly for Saturdays and high seasons. Why prove you're only as smart as the other shopkeepers in your zip code? Cashiers who don't sell, who mostly read and yawn, would tell you how lazy *you* are (for hiring them) if they weren't too lazy to.

One of internal advertising's ritual acts is the placement in every customer bag or envelope of a stuffer, usually provided by the co-op vendor free under the tacit understanding that it really isn't. Well, a stuffer is, after all, for stuffing, and even I would eventually have to admit stuffers are bonafide advertising. So cuss 'em out when they forget to insert one along with every invoice and parcel. But keep tabs on results. In the long run it's smarter to stuff *your own ad material* on the basis that you'll try harder to sell something. Maybe then you can get a co-op vendor to pay for the effort and have a real freebie? . . . Tell them Kornfeld said to let you do your own merchandising, which will have the added virtue of testing the freedom of free trade.

The paper bag (now often plastic) is an adequate advertising medium simply because your logo comes with the territory at essentially no cost. Your designated bag can also do double-duty as a competitor-irritant, and how I know this is that once upon a time . . .

Flashback. When I became VP Merchandising at Radio Shack in 1958, I also had a sudden brief reign as king of the LP record business in Boston. Naturally I did a lot of record advertising, so much so that one of my competitors paid us a visit to complain.

"Your discount prices are too low," said my soon-to-be former friend, a friend since our high school days.

"And so?"

"And so if you don't ease off," he said, "you'll have a record war on your hands, and it'll be TOTAL WAR."

My president remained silent; I did not. "Coming from you that's amusing," I ventured. "After all, you're the one who started LP record discounting in Boston."

"A discount is one thing," he replied, "but senseless, profitless price slashing is another. What's your choice?"

"If there's a war, you'll have to wage it alone," I said, "and in case you're interested I make a profit in my record department. But what gives you the idea my prices are too low; what makes you say that?"

"I see too many Radio Shack record bags in my stores," was the answer. And it was good enough for me. From that day forward I've had a high regard for the logo'd bag. My only advisory is contained in this 19th Rule of Marketing:

---

19 Don't put any words on your shop's bags except your company name. Put your name on BIG.

Catalogs by the Millions

Charles Tandy was the most dedicated proponent of the annual full-line catalog I've ever known. And in fact this major internal advertising medium is the best unifier and teacher of your personnel you will ever put to work for you. What it will do in the way of producing direct sales is often difficult to measure precisely unless you're an active mail order house, as opposed to one that accepts random mailed-in orders as "plus" or incremental business. I'll give you just four typical benefits of issuing your own catalog:

1. *Whimsy's end.* Publication of a catalog tells both your customers and your employees that you are in x-business with y-items for z-time. No drop-ins, drop-outs, switcheroos, sudden novelties.

2. *The compleat spec sheet.* How large, which colors, what weight? On and on go the intimate practical product details you know damn well only a few of your executioners can recall on demand, even for an unhurried customer, prospect or phone inquiry. Funny, isn't it, and sad: you know exactly how much and what kind of money you paid for the goods, but you don't really know exactly what you bought (and your financial officers and lenders believe in you)! I can't make a Marketing Rule about this paradox; it's a permanent paradox, the way a zebra isn't a horse.

> ***ADvisory.*** If you don't produce a catalog, at least give your people a pocket line-compiler with stock numbers, colors, and prices in ascending order (so they can sell up logically instead of prayerfully). Otherwise it's off to search for the suppliers' spec sheets—no two alike, all usually lost or missing. A third option is *actual knowledge,* but even that is no guarantee of actual salesmanship. So . . . might as well play the Rhapsody in FFF: 60% Fact, 30% Finesse, 10% Fib.

3. *The fearless pricer.* You may be too chicken to say this is my *firm price* out loud, but your catalog isn't. It says, "This is my price and I'm proud to be caught in bed with it."

It also verifies your price; someday when the IRS or the Old Price Freezer comes around, you'll be glad I reminded you of the joys of verisimilitude.

4. *The upscale image.* Back when we were gabbing about positioning, I had upscaling yourself in mind. None of the four dictionaries I use knows about "upscale," not even the one that contains 6000 words "that have become firmly established in the language largely during the past 15 years." I think it means—however unfirmly—improvement as perceived in you by others. A catalog gives you that special look of better quality, greater substance, and appealing maturity. The more it's your own private catalog, the more upscale you appear; vice versa if it's a catalog composed mostly of pages created by suppliers. Your enhanced image also rubs off onto your associates, so never downscale (underestimate) the power of a catalog until you've first made a proper estimate!

Flashback. Eons ago I was interviewed for the job of merchandising boss of a Radio Shack competitor, meeting the head hunter for this purpose in the bar of Chicago's Executive House hotel. It was after my second Tanqueray on the rocks (with two large olives) that the guy suddenly said: "How do you feel about the annual catalog? We think it's a total waste of money."

Having just finished publishing our 14th consecutive edition, I was able to be honest without being frank: "Well," I said, "you sure as hell can do business without one." (Why do head hunters seem to ask the wrong question in the right way at the right time and end up selecting the wrong head?)

Of course the cost of a catalog like the one issued by the American section of Radio Shack—something like $4,000,000 at a recent look—is one of those armpits every treasurer suggests deodorizing on a regular basis. And it never hurts to take a spray at a target of that magnitude, as I now confirm.

Back in the early 1970s, having always mailed our annual catalog to our best recent customers and our hoard of unfilled inquiries, I got the urge to test NOT mailing it to customers anymore but simply to advertise its availability—"New! Still free!"—in our monthly flyer and newspaper ads at the appropriate time; we'd just tell the people to "come and get it." Maybe we could distribute more quickly and to better qualified customers—better because of being more recent? The idea not only worked, it also gave us three super benefits:

1. *Savings in cost* because the postage would have amounted to more than we spent for media advertising.
2. *Increased traffic* because our great American freebie suddenly became something *wanted* instead of something given.
3. *Quicker feedback* because our salespeople had their copies before the customers, they had time to learn the line; and our customers didn't have to wonder when we'd mail because we told them their copy was waiting for them in the store.

Like many another test at Radio Shack, this one was conducted under what I call the "BF Method." The latter is a market study combined with an action, where B = Brute and F = Force. You just put your head down and charge! Failure of the BF Method is immediately followed by a switch to the "NAD Method" (where N = Never, A = Again, D = Dummy).

> ***ADvisory.*** To be valid and successful, the BF Method is employed only when the entire company is behind the program and fear of reprisal removed. Would this method have saved the Edsel and kept RCA in the computer business?

In an early Rule of Marketing I told you how most market testing tends "to arrive at the obvious in a time frame that is too late and an amount that is too little." The decision to refrain from mailing (by rote, of course) the Radio Shack catalog saved us $500,000 in the cost of postage and wrappers alone; a less than national test would have postponed those savings for another year, and the slightest screw-up in a small test might have caused the whole idea to be scrapped.

Of course a test based on judgment of experience past and conditions present is a more sensible application of the BF Method than, say, putting an H & R Block into every Radio Shack store (which was one of Tandy's notions) only to discover that we'd just screwed up two valid enterprises!

When you fund and circulate a catalog in any quantity, much less the ten-million circulation of a Radio Shack book, and when you don't ask for mail orders, obviously you can't expect your catalog to produce sales as measurable as those that drop through the mail slot. What you expect and get is better-informed salespeople, customers and prospects. I'll belly up to this cost much more confidently than to the price for television commercials—prime time, Olympics time, any time!

Aren't there other ways of showing the world your entire product line in total clarity of detail and intent? And cheaper and easier ways as well? Sure! As the man says, "Only you and I are irreplaceable, and I'm not sure about you." My point is: I haven't found a better way to inform the troops.

I have to laugh when people say Radio Shack doesn't spend enough money on sales training. Some of our otherwise most perceptive employees forget how their $4 million catalog tells every man on the sales floor exactly what our business is all about; they'd rather train salespeople with one of those fancy new electronic ways of telling it ("it" being the lesson that disappears when you turn off the switch).

The Xemplary Xmas Xtra

Speaking of internal advertising, I give you the typical merchant who wakes up just in time for Christmas and who worries the rest of the year about the one that's coming next. But I don't give him to you quickly, because first there's an interesting reason why the December quarter is less of a problem at Radio Shack than at most other retailers.

Example. Radio Shack's consolidated sales for the 4th calendar quarter amount to about 32% of a typical year. This leaves 68% of sales to be divided among the remaining three quarters—an average of 22.7% per quarter. Comparing the two numbers you get a picture of Radio Shack's holiday quarter sales running about 41% above the normal average quarter.

Example. For comparison, I've picked another large company which, unlike the giant retailers, uses the 4th calendar quarter as a scoreboard quarter, i.e., Oct/Nov/Dec. Best Products is a new-styled retailer which sells general merchandise via more than 50 catalog showrooms. My look at five recent years of Best's sales tells me that Best's 4th quarter sales amount to about 46% of its total year. This leaves 54% of sales to be divided among the remaining three quarters—an average of 18% per quarter. Comparing the two numbers you get a picture of Best Products' holiday quarter sales running about 155% above the normal average quarter.

If Best's Christmas quarter sales run something like 15% above a normal average quarter vs. 41% for Radio Shack, to me it means Best's results during that period are infinitely more crucial to its fortunes. Note: This is not meant as a detraction, merely as a comparison of different enterprises.

Naturally, for all of us retailers Santa's our patron saint, and we dassn't say "Xmas" in our external media ads for fear of upsetting the little old lady in tennis shoes. Your quality consumerist consumer, on the other hand, is against all commercialism no matter how it's spelled.

So what do we make of all this? We make our Christmas catalogs, asking you please to buy early. We examine our Christmas quarter to other-quarter ratio, and try to get it into better balance with the other three but without taking anything out of it to make those nine non-Christmas months more bearable.

ADvisory. Spend more time worrying about building sales from January through September. Make your first target *no losing months*. If you think that's impossible, change jobs with the guy who knows damn well it isn't.

When your calendar says August, Kornfeld says you're already too late to mount a coherent Christmas sales plan.

For example, your Christmas catalog (for mail orders) must be mailed out by early September; if it's merely for building an in-season boom, it must go into the mail on or before November 15. Buying for a big Christmas catalog begins in March at the latest.

Who gets your Christmas catalog? *Customers,* unless you like to shoot craps with rented mailing lists, occupants in selected zip codes, and mail boxes and slots in random locations. Which customers? *All the customers on your mailing list* including those scheduled for elimination.

Christmas is the one time of year you don't give super special treatment to your (most precious of all) most recent customers; you mail them ALL.

> ***ADvisory.*** Don't purge (i.e., cull) your mailing list until some time after Christmas; I suggest mid-February, the only month with two Rs in it.

> ***ADvisory.*** If the Christmas season is the only time you use the mails to generate business, you need, if you'll forgive the expression, a keeper. No mailing list that's used only once a year is of real value, and the same goes for horses and whatever else needs activity to maintain bio-feedback status.

Recently I went into the GHQ store of a small chain and was waited on by the boss. We talked "catalog" while he wrote up my sales slip—one copy for him, one for me. His catalog mailing list was a fairly stable 100,000 names, he said, and "didn't grow much." I found out why. He didn't ask for my name and address to get me on his mailing list! I'd just spent an above-average $100.75 and I was his most recent customer!

How I Became Superman's Best Editor

Among the real masterworks of internal advertising is the lowly comic book, a not necessarily funny—albeit funny-paper styled—publication used by some of us merchants to generate interest in our business. The proprietary comic book is a freebie and may be aimed at any desired age group.

The first such Radio Shack effort, "The Science Fair Story of Electronics . . . Man's Greatest Discovery," was born in 1971. Of course electronics is not actually man's greatest discovery; that was said to please Tandy and me. (Love is.)

At a recent count, "The Science Fair Story" had gone into its 4th edition and the company had given out a total of 18,000,000 copies over a 10-year period. Edited in the in-house ad agency, the booklet is 24 pages long and measures about 7×10 inches; the printing method is "comic book color" rotary offset. Its per-piece cost rose from 3¢ to 6¢ from 1971 to 1981 but—unlike the ex-nickel Hershey bar—it has neither shrunk in size nor gone up in cost to the consumer. It's still free to him, as is the annual catalog whose piece cost rose 50% in that time frame (controlled down by artful dodges such as cheaper paper).

You well may ask, "Why not charge for these publications? The public is inured to paying token amounts for things that used to be giveaways." The reason is simple, at least to me. *Videlicet:* a few pennies saved to attempt to recover costs will be a few pounds that never get into the cash register.

"The Science Fair Story," and incidentally Science Fair is one of my oldest and favorite registered Radio Shack trademarks, is a young person's guide to electronics history and inventors. Given the keen interest kids have in Radio Shack products, the booklet's aim is twofold: to entertain while it educates, and to develop future customers. If you're in my age group, you recall the old free sample days when Hinds Honey & Almond lotion, Mentholatum, Grapenuts, and Ipana could be sampled by mailing in coupons. Why do I remember them after 60 years? Because I sent for them and they came. Because young people's minds are like 400 ASA film: fresh, fast, forever.

Please don't mention the fact that some free-sampling 1920s products are now off the market. That's not the fault of their advertising, or lack of it. *Lack of management* is what puts good companies and viable products into ancient history! And the free-sample technique is still with us, proving it's good enough to consider trying before you ignore it and complicate everyone's life with factory rebates and contests.

Teachers are invited to write or phone for additional free copies of "The Science Fair Story." Does it interest teachers? Only to the tune of 75% of 18,000,000 copies!

ADvisory. Press gently on the overt advertising button if you want distribution like that. Restrain yourself to a coupon solicitation in a back corner. Coupons, as mentioned a moment ago, are as old as Kelsey's keester, and coupons can be *counted.* Posilutely, Mr. Skaggs? Absotively, Mr. Albertson!

All that being as true as almost anything you'll read almost anywhere, and Radio Shack having (in 1977) introduced the world's first mass-produced small computer with a whole new audience from graybeards to pre-teenyboppers, I directed our advertising department to produce an entirely new comic book on computers to complement our old one on electronics. By another glorious coincidence, my phone rang at the very moment I was wondering why I hadn't been seeing any progress.

"Hello, Lewis. Remember me, Jimmy Berger, your neighbor when we both went to Brookline High School?"

The 1930 memory banks glowed faintly. "Yup, um, yeah; what are you doing now, and where are you?" This is a fail-safe method for saying everything and nothing.

It turned out Jimmy had a position with Warner's DC Comics division in special and premium sales. Comics!

"I'm working on a comic book right now," I said, "one about personal computers because we have a leadership position in that business to defend. I want to bring the understanding of computers down to at least the 5th grade level, what they call expanding 'computer literacy'—God knows where they get such terms—and 'computer architecture,' for God's sake!"

"What would you think about using Superman in the book?" Jimmy inquired. "As you may know, he's our hottest property."

"Gee, I don't know how fantasy would be appropriate

when we're dealing with something as real as computers. But, no question . . . Superman's great . . . tremendous awareness . . . and if I could direct the story line—"

"You can do it! I've read your 'Flyer-Side Chat' and I know what you can do," Jimmy shot back enthusiastically. "What kind of circulation are we talking about?"

"Millions," I said, "but there's also the question of price and speed. I need this comic like yesterday."

Jimmy was like yesterday and competitive; thus was born Radio Shack's second booklet, "The Computers That Saved Metropolis," starring "The TRS-80 Computer Whiz Kids," all under Superman's supreme command. On my office wall is a poster of Superman saying "Lew Kornfeld, you're the best editor I ever had," a token of my determined effort to keep a maximum of fact in the fancy. Within the first few months of publication, 1,500,000 copies were distributed, a second version being drawn, and a third being planned.

The next time you're dreaming about offbeat internal advertising, remember the comic book. You don't need to print millions; just don't let your order quantity gather dust on a dark shelf. Would you let money do that? Ask your associates that question whenever your assets get Ripvanwinkled-off!

Up the Company Magazine?

Some brain-trusters think the in-house magazine is a waste of time, money, and whatever talent is turned loose on it. I disagree. But I had to get a few things changed before Radio Shack's monthly *Intercom* really pleased me:

—all sections of the company must receive editorial space in each issue;

—the editorial people had to quit using "fillers" from non-approved sources such as the U. S. government and Ma Bell because we could write our own or pay for desired material from such periodicals as the *Wall Street Journal* ($50 charge for some material) or *Harvard Business Review* (no charge);

LEW KORNFELD... YOU'RE THE BEST EDITOR I'VE EVER HAD!

—our divisional managers had to quit publishing their own monthly newsletters (we'd drifted into 20 different rags!) and settle for one page each;
—our merchandising manager had to quit mailing his monthly newsletter separately and settle for a bind-in centerfold position in *Intercom;*
—our advertising manager had to quit reprinting and mailing—separately, of course!—full-scale repros of each media ad to each store and settle for reduced-size batch reprints in our monthly unified attempt to centralize our armies of internal news releases.

In the end a lot of money was saved, but, more importantly, our 4000-plus store managers and other folks now had to open only one envelope a month to keep tabs on their corporate world: news of internal sales contests, messages from management, kudos for achievement, a calendar of social events, and 12 shots at improving interpersonal relations. Got a better idea at the price?

Up the Annual Report?

There's an old saw about annual reports, namely that their quality and size are in inverse proportion to the kind of business success the company had over the prior fiscal year. I've done no research on that allegation, but there's no doubt the annual report is a great American pastime like Chevvy's "baseball and apple pie" (but we'd best forget about U.S. cars for the moment since their advertising has outrun their management and there are too many Toyotas in America's present).

The most important readers of the report, aside from employees, Wall Street, the financial community and the competition, are present and future stockholders.

Aside from keeping old owners owning, the publication is often used to induce new people to become owners. It becomes an internal medium that gets advertised externally, which explains its tendency to present the business in the best possible light: if last year was poor and this year is more promising, the former gets the numbers and the latter gets the glitter.

Headlining what it called "E. F. Hutton's Regal Report," the *New York Times* saw its $400,000-cost 1980 version as a venture "that immortalizes in museum-quality black and white E. F. Hutton's executive elite and their photogenic clientele." Contrary to the fail/spend theory, it commemorates Hutton's best year, not its worst. Nor was it a matter of letting them eat cake; their dividend was increased and the stock split in the same time frame. Nevertheless, I was an EFH customer at the time and viewed the report with a groan. At a time when food stamps and subsidies were being talked about more actively than usual, it did seem like rubbing it in—even though management reports to owners are scarcely the place for discussing society's balance sheet.

Once at Tandy Corporation the new blood decided to make a run at one or more of the various prizes awarded by the financial medium for the best edited annual reports. I was invited to write a by-lined piece called an "Industry Perspective," aimed at showing our readers that we were alert to trends in electronics, even such electronics as were not made or sold by Tandy's Radio Shack division.

This resulted in some great fan mail, presented here just to show you what you can do with your report if you decide to be different (i.e., entertaining instead of boring). One reader wrote: "It's the first time I have read ANY annual report that didn't use all kinds of jargon to puff itself up, and also the only one that had a sense of humor. What a pleasure! And what a relief from all the others! And who would ever think of footnoting an annual report!"

I hope you'll get a point beyond noting that my prose and research had been singled out for praise. The point is: you can do a lot in your annual report if, as I said earlier about your common stock, you'll treat it as merchandise. Fancy angle shots, "silver paper imported from Germany," dull-as-dust paragraphs ghost-written for the CEO by High Yeller, Inc., reproductions of the company's art collection and new office complex, and the happy faces of minimum-wage gals on the assembly line . . . these are NOT merchantable anywhere but in the smoke-sweet security of the boardroom.

Should the annual report almost always promise you a rose garden? Aside from satisfying SEC and NYSE (for listed companies) requirements, you're pretty much on your own in what's committed and omitted. The requirements are *last year's* material, and whether it came up roses and buttercups is a matter for sober analysis of numbers (which most readers aren't sober enough to do intelligently). So the report is a document that, in its other areas and by its appearance, "merchandises" your enterprise to those who have a need to be sold or remain sold. Why promise them a rose garden when you can give them a compass rose? Let them take their own course and substantially create their own illusion of the direction of your realtime and sometime!

After all, when they get your just-published annual report you will be into "next year" by anywhere from weeks to a quarter. Your report should try to do these things:

1. *Be the first to tell it,* whatever "it" is; if you fail to do this, you will be preempted by some other medium in which your chance of looking "the way you'd like to be seen" is less than outstanding.
2. *Be the last to promise it,* whatever "it" is; because an outright promise is a debt of a sort that's almost impossible to repay with alibis and further promises.
3. *Be the most reliable place to show it,* "it" being your company and its people and directions, using the time-honored logic of good advertising—namely that when your ad (meaning the annual report in this case) takes up the full page, you don't have to fight off adjacent advertisers; you merely have to do the best advertising job you can on selling whatever you're trying to sell, usually . . . yourself!

When you own all the space in the medium, as you do in your own annual report, whom are you fooling with acres of blank white (glossy enamel) space, beauty shots of your directors and officers, and most-favored perspective shots of your products and real estate? Certainly not your directors and officers; both of those groups are informed shareholders. Certainly not your lenders; they typically mistrust people who waste money on fluff. So why not try to "tell it like it is" with a nice blend of candor, humor, modesty, and blue sky; and an absence of boredom and bleep? P.S.—show some other smart faces beside your own; you may die on the next plane to Reno.

Flashback. One of our retired top executives once told me: "This company, here, the Oak Electro/Netics company, ought to be a great one to invest in." Asking him how he figured it, I got the following answer: "See this picture of officers and directors in their annual report? Well, now, did you ever see a finer looking bunch of men? I mean these are faces you can bet on!"

Can an annual report win friends and influence readers? May I modify my remarks on beauty shots of directors and officers?

The Annual Report as Negotiating Tool

Flashback. Once, at a business meeting, I was asked to give our gross margin expectation by the top brass of a multibillionaire Japanese company that was considering selling us a product. "See," I said, shoving a copy of Tandy Corporation's 1978 annual report across their enormous polished table, "in that graph on page 24 you can see that our current gross margin as a percent of sales is 53.6%, the same—within 2%—as it has been for the past five years. Now while I know there may not be 54% in the video cassette recorder you're thinking about making for us. . . ."

It's Q.E.D. that printed facts are 100% more disarming and credible than spoken ones, particularly if your facts are above the industry norm. How uncomfortable it would have been for this manufacturer to offer me a limp 30% or even a strong 40% when IT SAID RIGHT THERE that again and again we rack up a number that scares hell out of 56 percent!

Your annual report can be designed as a very sharp or

special negotiating tool, or even as a Buy-Our-Tax-Loss sign, but only if treated as an important piece of advertising. Sell, don't brag. Talk, don't mumble. Spend your 50¢ to $2 (each) wisely; why make it look like just another chore you've dumped on your VP finance and your outside auditors?

To summarize, yes, your annual report IS valuable for internal advertising, institutional PR, and conceptual selling. Let an agency prepare it?—why? Let an art studio give your did-it-yourself job a facial?—sure. And yes, send copies to your suppliers and giveaways to your store managers (unless last year was a stinker). It's your best business card!

PR and Insider Information

The most obvious sources for communications about your enterprise are the boss, the rest of the management team, your inside or outside PR people, your inside ad manager, and perhaps your personnel manager. Frequently, however, some of the less obvious sources within your company family are tapped, particularly those who like to talk and those who like to be quoted in the media. The usual method by which these worthies are contacted is the telephone.

We had this not particularly dazzling or nice saying in the Marine Corps, which was, "Keep your bowels open, your mouth shut, and don't volunteer for anything." Anyway, I could fill ten pages with flashbacks and advisories on this form of internal advertising, but it would boil down to the basic advice contained in our 20th Rule of Marketing:

---

20 News, plans, moves, changes, guesstimates and rumors about the company must be responded to by DESIGNATED PERSONNEL ONLY, and all other persons contacted must refer their contact to the designated personnel.

Too darn bad if all the designated folks are in Antigua today. Too darn bad, as well, that outside board members

AREN'T designated; most of the company brass is in the same category (and if you don't know whether you're designated or not—you're not).

The above wouldn't be necessary if you had better luck with the often tricky desire of the press, and sometimes the government, to interview accessible *talkative* people.

The amount of untimely and mis- and dis-information that gets aired is mischievous, to say the least. Since the advertising value of *correct company-line info dissemination* is high, it doesn't bother my conscience a bit to have "the gospel" purified before release. Saving sinners is a real service to society; salvation in advance of sinning is the noblest act of all in advertiser and advertising matters. *Magna est veritas et praevalet:* great is truth, and mighty above all things. Amen? And the most passionate correction or retraction of an internal advertising error is about as useful as a honeymoon hotel on Mars.

SIX

Ad Copy Made Memorable

A nice way to open this chapter is, I've decided, with an assault on the current American pastime, in advertising and packaging, of emasculating copy with a *disclaimer.* Let's belly up to the real meaning of this irritating noun: it means the repudiation, renouncement, limitation or denial of a claim you have just made or are about to make. There's also a verb in the family, and another noun (disclamation).

In the index to my 1750-page edition of *Bartlett's Familiar Quotations* the word "disclaimer" does not appear even once, although Calvin Coolidge is listed as having made a speech in which he said: "Inflation is repudiation." Made in Chicago on January 11, 1922, if it's a disclaimer it could be the least effective one of the 20th century. Mr. Coolidge's record for ineffectual disclamation (disavowal) is due to be broken soon, however, most likely by someone from California.

American advertising has been drugged to the brink of silliness by its normalization of the use of disclaimers in squinty 6-point (1/12″) type sentences included to ward off class-action lawsuits and satisfy the misanthropy of such organizations as the FTC.

Interestingly, the latter now claims its mandated cigarette ad warnings aren't effective after all; the caption that for over ten years has been telling you smoking is dangerous to your health isn't doing its job, i.e., scaring you off the habit. Why? Because FTC studies reveal you don't know about the diseases smoking can cause and exacerbate. Also, they say, only 3% of us read the copy anyway. They (the FTC) also think funeral homes should be required to provide advance listing of the cost of their goods and services, and have persuaded Congress to make it the law of the land. I can magine the thrust of the disclaimers on those price lists: "Casket length and materials and weight may vary due to. . . ."

You can write all the scintillating ad copy you want to about the wonders of the new Y-car or Z-car, but there's still that matter of their EPA rating. The EPA rating demands quite a lot of expensive ad space to explain that its numbers are probably not accurate. What numbers? The numbers just printed relating to miles per gallon you can expect from the car. What do you mean, "probably not accurate"? Well, what we really mean is *inaccurate,* but the use of probability is within the guidelines. And then there's California, where the inaccuracy is always slightly greater and the probability even more likely.

> ***ADvisory.*** Write your congressman that, since EPA ratings are high in illusion content and low in factual content, we should be allowed to term the numbers given for each car its "variable EPA rating" and to dispense with the rest of the disclaimer. Tell him it was my idea.

The Nay of the Beholder

Perception of beauty has been limited by poetic usage to the eye of the beholder but, even so, TV manufacturers are required to state—by disclaimer, of course—that the picture printed on the face of their advertised TV set is simulated. Not a real picture taken of a turned-on set but a picture taken under ideal conditions and pasted onto the picture tube. My oh my, what nasty deviousness!

Playing under the same rules, Ms. Lauder, all women shown in magazine ads in the process of being cosmetically altered to become something they aren't, so should be disclaimed. My suggestions for such ad copy include these statements:

1. The lady shown is not meant to be posing as anyone's specific wife or companion.
2. The cosmetics used are not guaranteed to make any woman more glamorous or beautiful; they merely suggest a method by which such conversion might be attempted.
3. The colors of the makeup and model will vary according to the paper and ink used by this medium, the speed of its presses, its drying time after printing and before binding.

The TV industry is plagued by a second caveatal disclaimer: the size of the picture tube given in any ad must be stated as its DIAGONAL size. Restrictions of this nature, however crucial to civilization, help inspire the general reduction in ad copy quality that makes this chapter so important to would-be writers and curious readers.

The video set industry might have been told to cite tube size the way we cite room size, i.e., in x-many square inches or feet, thus reducing inaccuracy to zero. As it is, don't be surprised when your body's height goes into Big Bro's computer as a diagonal measurement.

Perhaps the most famous disclaimer in world advertising history is the American Surgeon General's mandatory repudiative warning on cigarette packages, signs, and ads, as mentioned a few paragraphs ago. The paradox is that a similar—or even more specific—warning has never been legislated for poisons, guns, cars, booze, and other items whose kill-time is typically more rapid than even (perhaps) an Allied or Bekins vanload of cigarettes.

How come? As I see it, our great all-pro copywriter Oliver W. Holmes had disclaimers in mind when he observed that "Insanity is often the logic of an accurate mind overtaxed."

Flashback. My column "Flyer-Side Chat' appeared regularly in the Radio Shack monthly flyer for many years before I got around to the barest mention about guns—particularly handguns—being dangerous to your health. By coincidence that column appeared less than two weeks before the handgun assassination attempt on President Reagan. Nevertheless, I was inundated with hate-mail by what you might call "friends of the NRA and/or upholders of the 9th amendment." (With them for friends, who needs an enemy?)

What surprised me the most, in retrospect, was that no one joined my column's savoring of this quote by a financial analyst in the *Wall Street Journal.* In commenting favorably on Olin Corp.'s plan to sell its Winchester Arms division, the man said: "It was the right decision. Despite what's happening in the Middle East, the gun business isn't a growth market."

Kornfeld Adds Four More Disclaimers

So you'd think, wouldn't you, that after all my griping I don't have disclaimers of my own to attach to this chapter. But you'd be wrong. I seldom violate the chicken-hearted 21st Rule of Marketing which reads:

---

21 Color yourself yellow when marketing tactics recommend a retreat and basic principles are not endangered.

(As in wartime, the retreat is to the place we call our Previously Selected Fortified Position.)

The following disclaimers apply to the title and contents of what we call in my part of the country "this here" book:

FIRST DISCLAIMER: All opinions in this book are my own unless otherwise ascribed; they are made to instruct and inform, not to ridicule; and their accuracy is probable within a tolerance of 25%.

SECOND DISCLAIMER: All quotations in this book which may appear to be verbatim may actually be either (a) hypothetical, or (b) to the best of my recollection, or (c) enhanced.

THIRD DISCLAIMER: All data in this book which may later be proven totally or partially inaccurate will be totally or partially corrected in a subsequent edition if issued.

FOURTH DISCLAIMER: All disclaimers in this or any other publication shall not be considered exceptions to my 22nd Rule of Marketing.

My 22nd Rule of Marketing is outstanding for its elegance of declamation in a sentence of 12 words or less:

---

22 Anything in advertising that needs to be disavowed probably should be disallowed.

Why Robert Young Says "Sanka Brand"

Along the same gruesome lines as the disclaimer, today's ad copywriter has to observe recent dismal interpretations of trademark law which seem to be telling us trademark owners: That's a real nice mark you have there, Podner, but if folks start using it like, er, say, a dictionary word your Uncle is going to *take it away from you* and give it to the people to use just like any four- or however-many-letter word.

So Robert Young, simulating a doctor simulating a TV commercial spokesman, says "Sanka Brand" coffee instead of merely "Sanka."

So you'd better not "xerox this page," Lucille, or else Xerox is likely to lose its name. Try making a "Xerox-brand copy copy" or something equally silly.

So you'd better watch it, ReaLemon and Formica, because our government (particularly the part that's *by* the people) will re-open its complaint that your famous trademarks are in fact so popular—hence valuable—that they're to be given to the Webster dictionary @ n/c except for the legal fees. You, too, Masonite and Frigidaire, and all you fellows who thought toxic shock syndrome was frightening, just remember Generic Word Shock Syndrome, and my own special recipe for avoiding it, thereby saving that precious old trademark for the stockholders and posterity. The formulation is given as our 23rd Rule of Marketing:

---

23 When loss of a trademark is threatened due to people's use of it as an ordinary (generic) word, its advertising must always include a REVERSE DISCLAIMER claiming that the product IS WHAT IT IS, as demonstrated by use of the word "brand" after each use of the trademark.

In other words, Sanka is a brand of coffee, actually decaffeinated coffee, so . . . say so! When you say "brand," Uncle says "Uncle," and you'll never have to go to court again to protect the name you own, except when someone other than the government tries to steal it. Had you read *Alice in Wonderland* recently you wouldn't have had to learn this valuable lesson from this particular Lewis.

ADvisory. Should you seek to harm another company—say Panasonic—the course of action is now equally clear. You just go around saying, "That sounds absolutely panasonic," or, "Come on up sometime and let's panasonic," or "One more yip and I'll panasonic you." With a little presence of malice you could make "brand" the most-used word in ad copy in America!

An Obit for Funny Copy

There's scarcely anything that's more fun or easier to do with advertising copy than to make it humorous. And that explains its ubiquity (as Tandy used to put it: "They're always going to do what they like to do best," referring to the eventual behavior on the job of practically anyone you hire). All the more reason, then, for blocking that punt before the kicker gets the ball. Use this argument and follow it up with broad slashes with a blue pencil.

> ***ADvisory.*** Humor in advertising is too easy to create, thus a lot of it gets created; it should be eschewed and regurgitated because (a) either the right person laughs at the wrong place, or (b) the right person doesn't laugh. But that's not all! Real humor in advertising is very difficult to achieve; most attempts fail because they don't try hard enough to be funny *and relevant* at the same time. And *that's* not all! Humor typically detracts from the advertiser's message by *calling attention to itself,* and (Newton's Law about actions having equal and opposite reactions) *away from the product.*

If you will just take the time to follow one example of humorous radio ad copy to its conclusion, you'll find the copy will end with a boffola that'll make you forget everything that was said before . . . a crash of falling furniture, a play on words so the advertised piston ring gets turned into a wedding ring, or a yes-ing Dick Cavett finally saying "no" after being asked if a personal computer will "clean my room."

Probably the worst place for humor in advertising is in a headline. The headline is sure to be only the opener of a set piece that has everyone at the agency—High Yeller, Inc.—rolling in the aisles. Here's a relatively harmless example from a computer magazine that just popped open on my desk.

Combining funny art with funny copy, Epson offers us a blank photographic print over a headline that reads, *This is a picture of all the printers in the world that outsell the MX-80.*

Is that funny? No. Do we see relevant art? No. Is the model number (MX-80) sufficiently newsworthy for a headline? Probably not. Is Kornfeld's 27th Rule of Marketing—the one that says the headline should always be expanded upon in the first line of body copy—observed? No! The first line of body copy says, "The one thing you can't beat in the market-place is value"; that's one of the things NOT mentioned in the headline. And this isn't a really funny ad, George, it's just a sort of smiley ad!

"What would you do," Charles Tandy asked an errant accountant at a Saturday talkathon in his office, "if a horse came into your kitchen and (bleeped) on the floor? Huh? Well, I'll tell you what you'd do—you'd get him the hell out of there and *never let him back in.*" Which is precisely what Kornfeld recommends you do with humor in advertising!

Avoid That Double Windup!

In various chapters I dealt with the phenomenon of copy that goes around and around, like a pitcher's arm, and never delivers the ball. Well, not "never," merely not until you've lost your audience. The double windup may "double" as a crashing bore, exemplified nicely by this quotation from an ad for a Mercedes diesel car: *The 240D driver's seat: not so much a piece of furniture as a biomedical support system.* This guff is accompanied by a small drawing with numerous directional arrows, or—not so much arrows as biomedical effluvia, or—inasmuch as it's double windup time—wild pitches.

Mercedes' would-be rival, BMW, also evidences double windup symptoms. In an ad headlined "AS LUXURY SEDANS BECOME MORE EXPENSIVE, THEIR INHERENT WORTH BECOMES MORE CRITICAL," the following body copy refuses to pitch the ball. First it says: *Due to a variety of economic ills, the day has finally arrived when the price of a luxury automobile can rival that of a small house in the country.* And then: *A disturbing trend that has forced many otherwise casual automobile buyers to scrutinize their potential purchases as never before.* And then: *At BMW we are not overly alarmed by this newly enlightened customer. . . .*" Because, because, and etcetera.

The theory is quite clear. "Dear Copywriter: When you talk to people of substance, sound substantial and don't be afraid to talk big tickets because people of substance aren't fazed by them." The theory is clear but it is also moderately full of prunes; people know when they're being "talked up to"

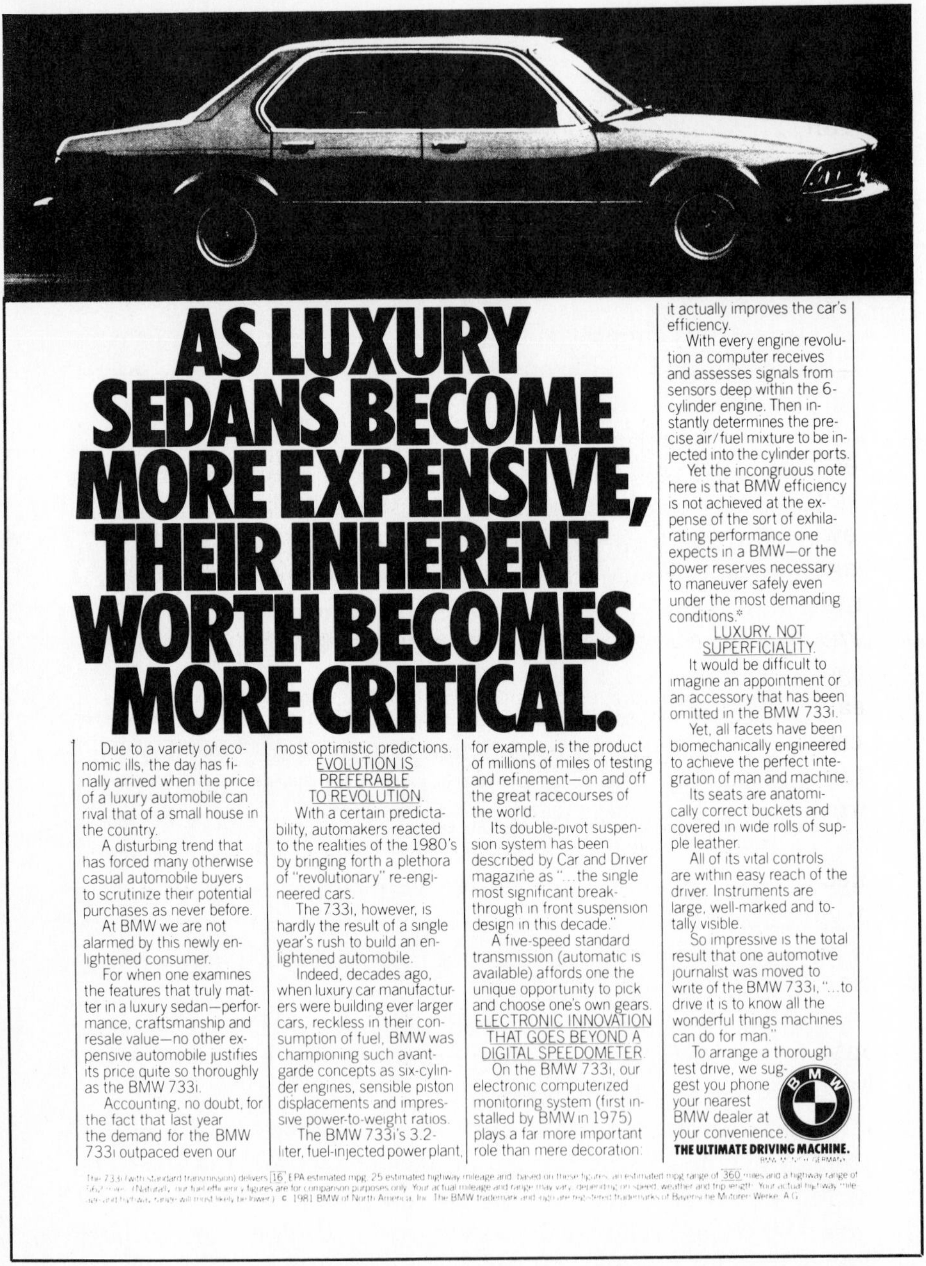
AS LUXURY SEDANS BECOME MORE EXPENSIVE, THEIR INHERENT WORTH BECOMES MORE CRITICAL.
Due to a variety of economic ills, the day has finally arrived when the price of a luxury automobile can rival that of a small house in the country.
A disturbing trend that has forced many otherwise casual automobile buyers to scrutinize their potential purchases as never before.
At BMW we are not alarmed by this newly enlightened consumer.
For when one examines the features that truly matter in a luxury sedan—performance, craftsmanship and resale value—no other expensive automobile justifies its price quite so thoroughly as the BMW 733i.
Accounting, no doubt, for the fact that last year the demand for the BMW 733i outpaced even our most optimistic predictions.
EVOLUTION IS PREFERABLE TO REVOLUTION.
With a certain predictability, automakers reacted to the realities of the 1980's by bringing forth a plethora of "revolutionary" re-engineered cars.
The 733i, however, is hardly the result of a single year's rush to build an enlightened automobile.
Indeed, decades ago, when luxury car manufacturers were building ever larger cars, reckless in their consumption of fuel, BMW was championing such avant-garde concepts as six-cylinder engines, sensible piston displacements and impressive power-to-weight ratios.
The BMW 733i's 3.2-liter, fuel-injected power plant, for example, is the product of millions of miles of testing and refinement—on and off the great racecourses of the world.
Its double-pivot suspension system has been described by Car and Driver magazine as "...the single most significant breakthrough in front suspension design in this decade."
A five-speed standard transmission (automatic is available) affords one the unique opportunity to pick and choose one's own gears.
ELECTRONIC INNOVATION THAT GOES BEYOND A DIGITAL SPEEDOMETER.
On the BMW 733i, our electronic computerized monitoring system (first installed by BMW in 1975) plays a far more important role than mere decoration: it actually improves the car's efficiency.
With every engine revolution a computer receives and assesses signals from sensors deep within the 6-cylinder engine. Then instantly determines the precise air/fuel mixture to be injected into the cylinder ports.
Yet the incongruous note here is that BMW efficiency is not achieved at the expense of the sort of exhilarating performance one expects in a BMW—or the power reserves necessary to maneuver safely even under the most demanding conditions.*
LUXURY. NOT SUPERFICIALITY.
It would be difficult to imagine an appointment or an accessory that has been omitted in the BMW 733i.
Yet, all facets have been biomechanically engineered to achieve the perfect integration of man and machine.
Its seats are anatomically correct buckets and covered in wide rolls of supple leather.
All of its vital controls are within easy reach of the driver. Instruments are large, well-marked and totally visible.
So impressive is the total result that one automotive journalist was moved to write of the BMW 733i, "...to drive it is to know all the wonderful things machines can do for man."
To arrange a thorough test drive, we suggest you phone your nearest BMW dealer at your convenience.
BMW
THE ULTIMATE DRIVING MACHINE.
*The 733i (with standard transmission) delivers 16 EPA estimated mpg, 25 estimated highway mileage and, based on these figures, an estimated mpg range of 360 miles and a highway range of
Naturally, our fuel efficiency figures are for comparison purposes only. Your actual mileage and range may vary, depending on speed, weather and trip length. Your actual highway mile
© 1981 BMW of North America, Inc. The BMW trademark and logo are registered trademarks of Bayerische Motoren Werke, A.G.

and they don't like it. People know things like BMWs are costly in comparison to the norm, so stop mealy-mouthing and start *selling*.

BMW's ad also violates our lofty 24th Rule of Marketing, but that shouldn't faze them because folks like J. C. Penney violate it deliberately and in spades. It simply says:

---

24 Every ad should carry your logo and/or company name in an upper section, preferably at the top, unless your name can be incorporated comfortably within the headline. When the latter is done, use it in headline type, not as a logotype.

I admit to being extremely provincial in the matter of getting readers to *know whose ad it is* as quickly as possible, provincial to the point of insisting that all Radio Shack newspaper inserts carry the name prominently on *every page*. Since "Shack" and "The Shack" are also registered trademarks, they are acceptable substitutes. Every page. Every ad. Prominently. Why settle for a smug little BMW logo at the lower right corner of an ad that could have at least given the swiftly cruising non-reader a subliminal scrimshaw? The day a hotel fails to give you stationery with its name and address on it is the day I'll consider being less provincial about "the quick horn blow," the horn being mine!

If you issue a catalog or other multipage promotional piece, print your name in it prominently, as often as you can. In advertising, talk is never cheap. Your name is probably your #1 product, so don't be embarrassed to mouth it; be mortified if you don't.

General Electric gets *both* its full name and full logo onto its smallest piece of consumer electronics merchandise. From my own travail in seeking room for graphics on products, I'm sure GE designers are forced to position all 17 letters before finding space for feature call-outs and knob labels.

The fact that I haven't succeeded in getting Radio Shack copy people to put the company name into body copy until it hurts, doesn't mean it's wrong. Here's how you say it:

—because you're looking for good music at a good price, you'll appreciate this Radio Shack sale-priced receiver . . .
—and only Radio Shack has it for $88 . . .
—when Radio Shack puts a CB transceiver on sale . . .
—this built-by-Shack computer system is better . . .
—all 580 employees of Radio Shack's cable factory want you to buy their TV twinlead before the price goes up . . .

Most advertising I read fails to do much for the company—any company—except to drop in the name, address, and other vital statistics on a grudging one-time basis. Why? Are you the only advertiser in the medium who's pushing your kind of merch? Do you think everyone knows who you are the minute you get into print? Do they care? NO, times three!

ADvisory. Any damn fool can pay for white space, so why not try to figure out ingenious ways to use it to re-introduce yourself. To get and keep awareness, print your name on every available threshold: then they see it coming and going!

My immortal 25th Rule of Marketing says:

---

25 The copy of every ad should be regarded as "survival copy"—the kind of copy on which many employee lives depend. If all you do is pay for it, learn to recognize "survival copy"; it's copy with a lot of "I" and a lot of "me" in it. If it's only your resumé copy, put your NAME ON TOP of every page; you're not the only one trying to get back in the game!

The Pheromone Factor

Since pheromone is the magic substance animals release to attract other animals, as you learned in Chapter 1, it should permeate your copy like the odor of fresh bread, but not like the aura of a red-light district. The song that advised you "to be sure it's true when you say 'I love you,'" is what I mean. Pheromone is nature's own thing: it stands to reason that if you're not natural you'll get hissed instead of kissed when you make a noise—in ad copy—like a Roquefort.

Along with having a high pheromone factor, copy should be empathetic; the "imaginative projection of one's own consciousness into another being" shouldn't be difficult when you're trying to sell me something, because you want to get your product "into my mind" where it will satisfy what its occupant (or container?) craves. "I understand you . . . you're like me . . . you want and you damn well deserve what I'm proposing . . . a nice cool can of Coors."

It takes at least these two copy ingredients to make successful advertising out of the common clay of words: a high pheromone factor (= animal magnetism), and a cup of the kindness we call empathy (= one-ness with the audience). It follows as the night the day that truth must also go into the pot. Also two other spices I've mentioned often before—news (= news value), and benefits (= what's in it for me?). The acronym BENT-P might help you remember them. But brains, body heat and basic ballyhoo might do even better!

Five Ingredients of Successful Copy

From the foregoing you'll observe that I've called out what I consider to be five really basic elements of effective advertising copy, especially for print ads. To dramatize them, I'm entering a summary of them in this book as its 26th Rule of Marketing:

26

Prior to acceptance by the advertiser, the copy proposed for every media ad must be tested for inclusion of these five essential components:

1. Benefits.
2. Empathy
3. News Value.
4. Truth.
5. Pheromone Factor.

If the presented ad lacks any of these five elements, it probably needs revision.

Note: For most advertisers, the order in which I have given my factors is in ascending difficulty of achievement. Why is Truth so difficult to employ? Because most of the people who work on your ads put Spandex (noted previously) into their copy for two reasons: (1) ignorance of the facts due to lack of reportorial diligence, and (2) assumption that hyperbole is the God-given license of salesmen and other manufacturers of propaganda.

The definition of pheromone needs repeating, especially because of its omission from both the Webster and Random House dictionaries I use. (It was in the *Oxord American Dictionary* which, aside from using a type face about 2⁄12″ larger than Webster, is also valuable because it is directed "at students of the American language all over the world," where we have spread Americanese and where it is least understood—not only our ad messages but also our geopolitical views. We should bomb the capitals of the world with the "OAD" dictionary and keep our military and our money at home, says Kornfeld's insular 1st Rule of Doing Unto Others As They Continually Do Unto You.)

It is said dogs smell fear. It is said certain people exude sensuality. It is said charisma excites the very ozone surrounding whatever has it. It is said in Oxford: pheromone "is a substance secreted and released by an animal for detection and response by another of the same species." Pheromonal ad copy is incredibly difficult to write because it is so purely *natural* in composition, delivery, and recognition.

"Love" is probably its most swiftly evoked word, and a very nice word it is. But can you believe a love affair with, say, Cuticura soap, or the stuff that's supposed to take the brown spots off your hands, or the Chevvy called "Luv"? It won't fly! Such love's as far from pheromone as the scent of Brut from that of Morning in Provincetown. In fact, my experience with pheromone is that it's a glorious, dangerous essence you can sometimes sell . . . but never buy! Even so, when you think "copy," think "pheromone"; the world runs on it!

If you'll pardon a one last return to the matter of truth in advertising, truth is divisible in increments of 1⁄100ths—

Japan, now only $3.75

It's the new low price. $3.75 for a 3-minute call to Japan when you dial the call yourself any time on Sunday.

If you don't have International Dialing in your area, you still get the same low rate as long as it's a simple Station phone call. (Person-to-person, credit card and collect calls, for example, cost more because they require special operator assistance.) Just tell the local Operator the country, city, and telephone number you want.

Here's how to dial Tokyo:

INTERNATIONAL ACCESS CODE / COUNTRY CODE / CITY CODE

011 + 81 + 3 + LOCAL NUMBER

(If you are calling from a Touch-Tone*telephone, press the "#" button after dialing the entire number. This will speed your call along.)

$3.75! What a nice surprise! Or, as they say in Japan, "Wow-ie, How Wonderful!" *Trademark of AT&T Co.

Want to know more? Then call our International Information Service, toll free:

1-800-874-4000

In Florida, call 1-800-342-0400

Bell System

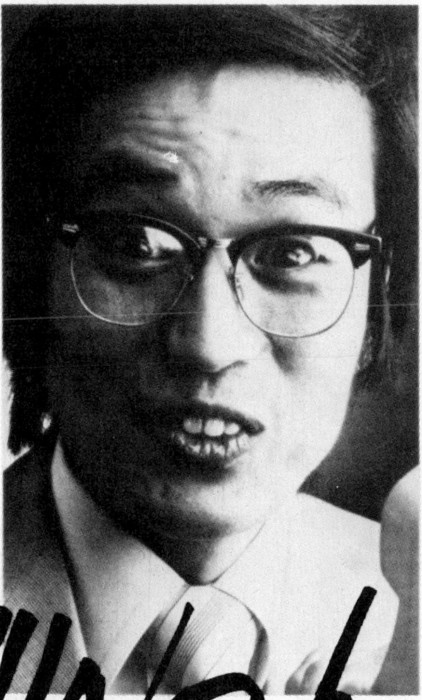

"Wah Steki!"

INITIAL 3-MINUTE DIAL RATES

FROM THE U.S. MAINLAND TO	DAY RATE	LOWER RATE
American Samoa	$4.05	$3.15 A
Australia	4.95	3.75 A
Fiji	4.50	— C
Guam	4.50	3.60 B
Hong Kong	4.50	— C
Indonesia	4.95	— C
Japan	4.95	3.75 A
Korea, Rep. of	4.95	— C
Malaysia	4.95	— C
New Caledonia	4.95	— C
New Zealand	4.50	— C
Philippines	4.95	3.75 A
Singapore	4.95	— C
Tahiti	4.95	— C
Taiwan	4.95	3.75 A

A) Sunday only (all day)
B) Saturday and Sunday only
C) No lower rate period

The charge for each additional minute is 1/3 the initial 3-min. dial rate. Federal excise tax of 2% is added on all calls billed in the United States.

Courtesy AT&T Long Lines.

meaning you can employ or reveal any amount up to 100% in 0.01s. Well short of an outright fib is a recent supposedly amusing, hyperbolized ad by the lady herself, Ma Bell. Its headline, above the picture of a Japanese gent with a glaze of amaze on his faze, promises: *Japan,now only $3.75.* (Att: typographer: there is no space between "n,n" for reasons of Creative Letterspace Perception. So please STET.)

Any idiot outside of Washington knows you dare not hope to get to Japan for (or land at Narita airport with) $3.75. So the ad is untrue in respect to physical transfer. Any idiot knows you can phone Japan. But most wouldn't know the cost of the first three minutes or—and here's real illusion—that the $3.75 is for the first three minutes but for the first three minutes *only on Sunday*. If this is a classic model for truth in advertising, I'm a monkey's uncle (as has been suggested more than once).

Why I'm Anti Anti-Advertising

What Ries and Trout in their book *Positioning: the Battle for Your Mind* (McGraw-Hill, 1981) call "The 'Against' Position" is what Kornfeld calls "Adversary Advertising." What follows, however, is derived essentially from my own experience and observation.

The best way to appreciate my general opposition to adversary advertising is to illustrate with a few examples and critiques. But let's hasten to acknowledge the manly feeling you get when you bash the competition in advertising or with your financial report card; ecstasy is what it is, Mr. President.

I've certainly had that feeling whenever I've meditated on Radio Shack's ability to compete on many levels of merchandising with GE, RCA, Sony, 3M, GTE, Japan Inc., Apple, T-I, Sears, Ward, K mart, Penney, anyone designing, making, and selling consumer electronics products (and now even school and office systems).

"It may just be the most profitable retailing outfit of any kind," said *Financial World* magazine of Tandy (d.b.a. Radio

Shack) in a 1982 issue, "with a gross margins on sales of 59% last year and a return on equity of around 40%."

Charles Tandy was delighted to be able to point out how many more "absolute profit dollars" he was able to rack up than many of the giant businesses of our generation. For example *(Fortune* 5/81), the $169.6 million net earnings of Tandy Corporation were numerically greater than those of Monsanto, Bethlehem Steel, Ralston Purina, Greyhound, Borden, Textron, Boise Cascade, Standard Brands, and other notables.

After a visit to Dearborn, Tandy once told me that he personally "told Henry Ford 'I like my business better than yours.'" However, that's as adversary as he usually got; he knew that the bottom line of being better than the next guy was reckoned in numbers, not in bleep.

For example: "Dictaphone challenges IBM to a Dual," thunders a full-page ad with its built-in pun (Dual/Duel) and rather too much space given to its un-mindblowing art. I thought a lot about oversized art when I was Superman's best editor (Chapter 5); for example I noted that comic book El Grecos seem to dump in big pix—about one to every five pages—regardless of the merit of the activity or personnel on the page. What's this, I wondered, filling space . . . or voiding space . . . or change of pace . . . or because they get paid by the square inch?

Critique. The dual/duel word play is too cute and a distraction. And since it's a foregone conclusion that Dictaphone will win its own private ad war hands down—or hands on, judging from subsequent art—the ad should be doing more telling and selling and quickly rise above its narcissism. There are always five better layouts and copy and art approaches for any given ad. If you get into a bind resembling Dictaphone vs. IBM, use this ad as your model and criticize the hell out of it. The by-product of that criticism will give you a choice of better ads that you planned and executed yourself!

Stand back when Budget Rent a Car goes after Hertz

with a two-gun fusillade! First it blasts: THE GOOD NEWS. HERTZ ADOPTS OUR PRICING POLICY. THE BAD NEWS. THEY DIDN'T ADOPT OUR LOW RATES. This is followed by a point-blank repro of what must be a regular 7″×10″ Budget ad; it promises: WE RENT LINCOLNS FOR LESS THAN HERTZ RENTS GRANADAS.

Critique. If you have to be adversary, this is probably a pretty good ad, but the primary message is actually less powerful than the secondary message; in fact, the latter used alone might have made a better ad—that you can rent a Budget Lincoln for less than a Hertz Granada (but not less gas).

> ***ADvisory.*** The Dictaphone ad exposes a major weakness of the adversary ad, namely that by resorting to this approach, you call attention—by name and also by position—to your competition, usually the cleverest ones. On the other hand, I tend to believe that some PR is almost always better than no PR, that your appearance in a competitor's ad gives you free awareness that will outweigh their putdown.

In doubt? Mention your competitor's name in your promotional piece only after you've considered all the liabilities; if you still feel *positioning your product* is a defensible reason for including it—fire when ready! I trust Dictaphone's agency did when they gave IBM its free ride.

During the annual spring advertising follies of 1981, the Sony Corporation of America went adversary on the matter of the videodisc, no doubt because they knew that RCA was in an early stage of introducing its SelectaVision videodisc system. Let me line up a few ducks in explanation:

1. Sony is in the forefront of the burgeoning video tape cassette (VCR) recorder with its Betamax models.

2. Nevertheless, the Betamax system has major competition from an incompatible VCR system developed by Matsushita and its relative, Japan Victor, whose great marketing success here is largely due to big private-label orders from RCA.

3. All through the coming of age of the VCR, other manufacturers are engineering and displaying videodisc systems, hopeful that the TV disc will capitalize on two advantages over TV taping: lower cost hardware, lower cost (and easier to handle) software. Magnavox and Pioneer are already delivering players, but technical problems are substantial, particularly in manufacturing the so-called laser disc, whose high fallout has raised costs and spread doubts, two things businessmen despise. (But what they despise most is surprise!)

4. RCA finally, by early 1981, gets its SelectaVision disc system act together, using, not surprisingly, different and totally incompatible everything. Heavy hitters like Radio Shack announce plans to join the effort. One of Sony's many domestic rivals, Hitachi, is revealed as a supplier for Radio Shack and others of hardware for the RCA disc system.

5. Sony, at least at the time, is not on the American market with a videodisc system.

Therefore, at least as perceived in this Video-Side Chat, Sony, its ad agency, or both in tandem, decide to go adversary with advertising to protect the video tape community with a bash at the obviously smaller and weaker videodisc community:

"The Story of the Videodisc [is] a rather short one. The videodisc player can play back prerecorded programming. The end." Thus Sony goes on the offensive with a double-truck ad, taking a full page to leave you with a horrid thought that, yes, a disc is (at least for now) a non-recordable medium. And then another full page to pitch the familiar benefits of VCR tape: how it records, re-records, plays back, doubles as a camera, and the rest.

My 4/14/81 copy of Sony's adversary ad was followed by Hitachi's 5/1/81 ad: "HITACHI THINKS YOU SHOULD LOOK AT VIDEO FROM BOTH SIDES."

Why not? Unlike Sony, Hitachi is already on both sides! "Hitachi believes both ways are the only way to go," the copy continues, with the coy humor that only a bigtime American ad agency can serve without notice . . . right out of the freezer.

The Tale of the Videotape.

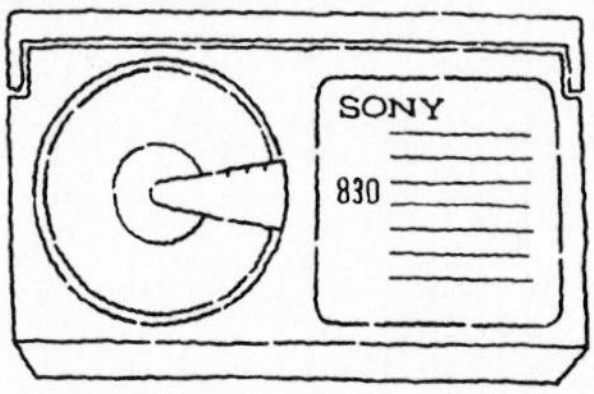

The Sony Betamax Home Videotape Recorder can also play back prerecorded programming like movies, sports and concerts. But that's only the beginning. Because it uses videotape, it can also record. And the ability to record allows you almost infinite possibilities. It lets you record television programming. And when you've finished viewing what you've recorded, you can erase the tape and record something else. Over and over again. The only thing you can do over and over again with the videodisc is watch the same show.

And even what the videodisc does, the Betamax outdoes. Because when you want to play back prerecorded entertainment, you get over fifteen thousand titles to choose from on the Betamax. The videodisc player offers barely a couple of hundred.

As our tale draws to a close, we mustn't fail to mention other wondrous feats the Betamax can perform. It lets you record a show on one channel while you're watching another. And it can even be programmed to record four different shows on four different channels for up to two weeks in advance.* Add a Sony video camera and you can create hours and hours of your own home entertainment. And with the Sony optional tape changer you can record and play back up to twenty consecutive hours. The Sony Betamax is the most sophisticated member of the most sophisticated video family in all the land.

If you're still undecided about whether to buy a videodisc player or a Betamax, remember that the story of the disc is a short one. But the tale of the tape is filled with wonder and imagination and unlimited possibility.

So if you buy a Betamax, you can live happily ever after.

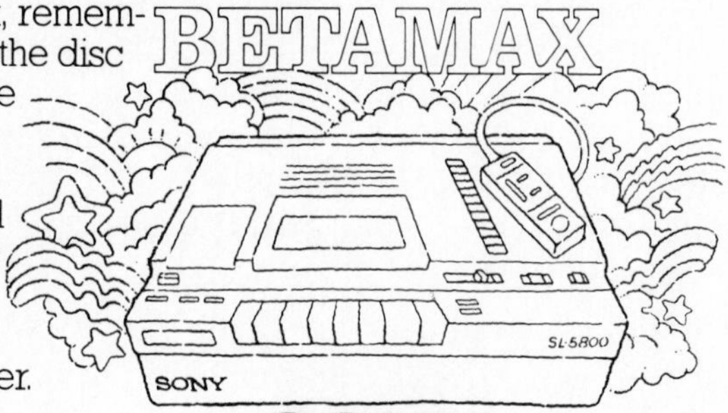

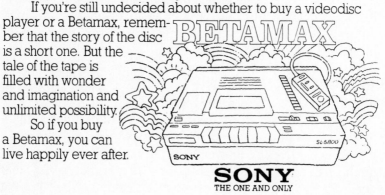

SONY
THE ONE AND ONLY

Beta

The Story of the Videodisc.

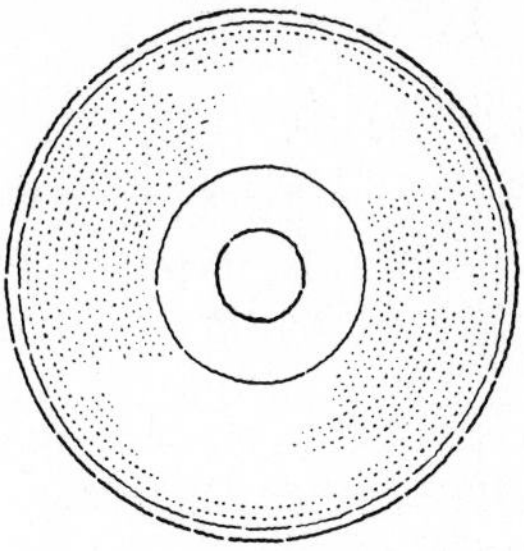

It's a rather short one.
The videodisc player can play back prerecorded programming.
The end.

Midway between salvos, my 4/22/81 issue of the useful little newsletter, *Consumer Electronics Daily*, locates sentiment from retailers and distributors for more anti-disc advertising; it also quotes two dealers whose viewpoints are a book on advertising in themselves.

One says he knows from experience that "no matter how big and well put together an ad is, one day just doesn't make a dent," even though this one ad made him "start to sweat." The other chap says "it was superb advertising, but as for effect, I haven't seen a ripple." These are guys you can admire!

ADvisory. Adversary advertising of this particular kind has, in my vintage opinion, a number of unsalutary effects, easily enumerated even if not easily believed:

1. The videodisc hadn't even gotten off the ground by April 1981, hence substantial PR for, and awareness of, the TV disc as a new medium of entertainment and education was a freebie its proponents should have been grateful for.

2. The adversary-adder, Sony, is one whose acceptance by the public made reading of those ads more likely than average.

3. It is fairly well acknowledged that more attention is given the medium than the message, hence the very existence of the availability of videodisc equipment was probably the most memorable news value in this advertising campaign. Sony's announcement thus reminds me of that famous cry "The British are coming!", which I recall as the top news story of the mid-1770s (the bottom news story of the early 1980s was that the last British MG car had rolled off the assembly line).

4. The videodisc attack ads clearly got all segments of the consumer electronics entertainment industry involved in considering the disc as a truly viable new medium, even though many had doubts until then.

Why? Because Sony implied it felt the hot breath of competition from a new source, and Sony, unlike your favorite stockbroker, is someone people stop and listen to when it says something.

By July of 1981, *Ad Forum* magazine, which also commented on the Sony mini-campaign, produced two curious predictions via the quoting of someone else: that up through the mid-80s nearly half of all videodisc buyers will own VCRs, and through 1990 nearly all buyers of projection TV sets will be owners of either VCRs or videodiscs. Since neither of those remarks casts any light, old or new, on the survival or sales potential of the videodisc, I offer some news of my own.

Flashback. Radio Shack would appear to have paid very little attention to the selling of television receivers since its initial bad experience in the 1947–1954 period. Then, the blowout of a TV set component called a "selenium rectifier" would cause your display room to smell like a yellow rain lab, and who needed trouble like that? We also noted—actually marvelled at—the way department stores and TV shops went for the cash flow of TV set sales seemingly without regard for the resulting color (red) of the ink it caused to flow in Accounting. Further, these purveyors appeared insecure without an entire wall of television sets lit up, all playing at madly varied levels of brightness, clarity of focus, and scrabbly raster—amusing unless, say, you were Zenith, and it was your half-acre of sets with vertigo and astigmatism.

Radio Shack was insufficiently capitalized to display and ship TVs, and insufficiently motivated to sell at cost-plus-10 (whether bucks or percents), and to sell non-industrial customers on credit—a glorious instinct we would short-circuit in 1963 when credit collection became an almost fatal problem.

So from the early 1950s to the early 1980s, the Shack would sell TV additives—going so far as to become a leading manufacturer of antennas, twinlead, cable and other accessories—but would essentially abstain from selling sets. But my flashback, which is so recent it's still flashing, is to the videodisc. And my deliberations and staff lectures went like this:

"From here to eternity *the video, audio and communicative arts are on a collision course*—not to come together in mutual immolation (as devoutly wished by some of us who remember life before death) but to join in permanent union. The time is NOW, in case you'd been thinking of waiting 'til 2001.

"Therefore," to continue this paraphrase of my reasoning, "Radio Shack should forget its prejudices and scars and join the Videoaudio Generation."

As good a starting place as any—since our TRS-80 computer business had already found us selling products consuming over 250,000 CRTs as video displays—was the still-virgin RCA videodisc system: the hard of it and the soft of it.

Throw Out the Baby, Save the Bath!

From all I'd learned, RCA's SelectaVision videodisc system was the closest new breakthrough in release time and had some real mass market practicalities, especially when you consider the troubles other systems were experiencing. Displays were no problem: Radio Shack stores already had color televisions on their shelves, first for demo-ing color TV games, later for selling as the video portion of its TRS-80 Color Computer. The addition of videodisc players was all we needed. So my first step into the Videoaudio Generation was to phone RCA to see how synergistic their mood was today.

That call led to meetings in Fort Worth, Indianapolis and New York City, even to the inner sanctorum of RCA's chairman's office, past its gallery of oil paintings of prior chairmen, and into a hush so deep that even the office rug seemed to have a deep philosophy of its own. I had a plan of attack to sell.

"What I want to do," I explained to the RCA folks, "is to co-introduce the videodisc player. I have a Big Bang theory."

"Which is what, exactly?" someone asked.

"That at the very moment RCA introduces this great new system, Radio Shack introduces it. When RCA breaks its ad campaign, Radio Shack breaks ITS ad campaign . . . nationwide!"

The RCA people looked at each other in what a poet once described as "a wild surmise." Was co-introduction some kind of dirty word? "Oh, we could never do that," someone ventured.

"Absolutely impossible," put in another of their execs. "It would upset our whole distribution system. Besides, where would you get your SelectaVision hardware?"

I smiled. "That's obvious, isn't it? We'd get it from you."

"Look, first you complain that our disc system isn't stereo, and now—"

"Sure I've complained," I said, "but here I am with my hat in my hand. I understand mono is all there is for the first season. It's *co-introduction* that's my main concern. Here's Radio Shack with nearly 6000 stores and dealers in the U.S.A. and 800 in Canada—nearly 7000 places we could display the merch in, say, four weeks after warehouse receipt!

"And at the same time, look: we can run ads in over 1000 newspapers . . . insert 37,000,000 4-color inserts in Sunday papers . . . mail our announcement to over 10,000,000 recent customers! That's all within 30 days of D-Day, and I haven't even thought about ads on TV or radio yet. This is muscle like you've never seen, and not one penny of co-op is involved."

I paused, looked around (no one had begun to waltz), and went on with my final reasoning. "Look," I said, "I don't care what your sales projection geniuses tell you, or how many players and discs you've contracted to manufacture. In my humble opinion *there's not a single dealer or customer out there waiting for this product!*

"Why? Because nobody needs it, or knows they need it. They've just digested video tape recorders after, if you'll recall, a frighteningly slow start. They didn't 'need' VCRs either, until prospects started talking to users, and until VCR's benefits began to be perceived; then taping became a status symbol, and the dream of a million VCR homes became realizable."

ADvisory. Consumer electronics legend has it that products don't go into high orbit until 1,000,000 customers have been sold; then the sky's the limit. (That's the supply side. Then we quickly flip to the over-supply side!)

Misadventures in Marketing the Videodisc

To prevent my readers from falling asleep during this flashback on my attempt to paint Radio Shack into the RCA videodisc picture during its breakout year (1981), here's a recap of the world according to Kornfeld:

1. The Magnavox, Pioneer, MGA, et. al. videodisc system involving optics and lasers fails over a number of years to solve its technical and cost problems and to win a mass audience, but RCA spends a reputed $150 million to develop a less sophisticated, less costly system—SelectaVision—which in 1980–1 seems ready enough to go to market and to interest Radio Shack.
2. RCA declines Kornfeld's plan to join promotional forces to co-introduce its system with RCA et. al. and supply it with RCA-built players at the same time.
3. Radio Shack then orders custom hardware made for it by Hitachi, but the timing is such that co-introduction is impossible.
4. RCA kicks off its campaign in the spring of 1981.
5. By summer 1981 the undertakers of the Fourth Estate are writing failure-oriented news stories.
6. By autumn 1981 there's a rebate program from RCA and a substantial hardware price cut by Hitachi (on its own brand of SelectaVision player), followed by RCA's price slash of a whopping *$200 off* its $499.95 1981 system list price (but tempered by a claim that owners were averaging 30 discs each).

Were time and money wasted? Undoubtedly. Was the videodisc advertising in 1981 any good? Undoubtedly not, not even Radio Shack's. Would the system get the lead out in the mid 1980s? Maybe. Does the system have merit? Yes. Will videodiscs eventually co-exist with video tapes?—Unquestionably. Why did you include this story in this book?

I included this story in this book to dramatize yet another case in which a battle was lost (or not won sooner) because the conventional thinking and practice of an industry prevented the team with the ball from putting its best 11 men on the field. We "lost" a war in Viet Nam in the same way.

If protecting dealers really demands reducing the fury and power of attack, how well are such dealers protected? Radio Shack's own 2000 dealers were certainly not protected by the weak salvos that ensued!

On the other hand, if the primary attack was weak because of lack of available hardware or software, why not wait for a more optimum moment? History is full of questions like this, all asked to get a better understanding of defeat.

You can see in Chapter 11 the sort of answers Radio Shack had for the conventional wisdom when it was its turn to introduce an exceptional new product—the TRS-80 personal computer. There's not much time left to learn our 27th Rule of Marketing:

---

27 You should give long, full, earnest consideration to the risks involved in NOT opting to go "all out" in new product sales promotion whenever you get a chance to vote.

Writing the "Fall Line" Copy

My subhead comes from many years of trying to learn how to ski under control, without fear, and without crashing. In skiing, as elsewhere, the fall line is *the natural line of descent between points on a slope,* and I have an extremely positive theory about it:

> YOU CAN'T LEARN TO SKI (WRITE, PLAY, SING, DRAW) PROPERLY IF YOU'RE AFRAID TO CROSS AND RE-CROSS THE FALL LINE.

The fall line is, to put it succinctly, the moment of truth . . . the moment of full commitment and effort . . . the try from which the only fall-back is the willingness to rise up and try again. There's no way to do anything well and properly without crossing a fall line. So whence cometh the silly idea that writing—and particularly the writing of good ad copy—doesn't follow the same law of physics?

> ***ADvisory.*** Many writers and readers think that smart-ass copy is fall line copy. I'll tell you what it is . . . it's copy that falls on its ass.

Fall line writing is as close to the trail's layout as you can get, in the opinion of this first-time book writer (who's well aware that his one robin doesn't make a spring). It's a criss-crossing of the fall line of conviction, knowledge, faith, insight, well-waxed vocabulary, syntax, poetic license. If you lack the nerve to write straight down the hill you'll probably never make it as a serious writer.

A Critique of 19 Headlines from the *Same* Magazine

Here are some examples of what I call non-fall-line headline writing. I'm not blaming anyone. I'm just saying it should be better, and I give you my reasons a few paragraphs down the hill. A weak headline predictably assures you of an ad that hasn't been run down the fall line. Why put up with it if we can do better at the same price? Good question—and it's one of the premises of this book. Now the examples:

—*Nationwide taste tests prove it! Windsor Canadian beats V.O.!*

—Nobody does it better. Winston Lights. This is your

world. This is your Winston. The only low tar built on taste.

—*Is your small copier being killed by popular demand?* (Minolta.)

—Now the excitement really begins. (Pontiac.)

—*When you decide on a Sharp SF-770 copier it's a value judgment.*

—Music lives on TDK.

—*We're out to change some Old Fashioned ideas.* (Brandy from California.)

—Introducing Ciera: the only front-wheel drive that's a Cutlass. (Oldsmobile.)

—*""The truth is, I would speak for the quality of Smirnoff anytime. Its value speaks for itself."*

—Benson & Hedges & Afternoons & Me.

—*You're looking at a $70,000 a year executive grounded by a penny's worth of paper.* (Hammermill.)

—It makes impossibel impossible. (IBM.)

—*America's truck. Built Ford tough. Space Ace.*

—Wausau. A statement. And an understatement.

—*CSX Corporation. Growth Territory.*

—Hear the beauty that is MCS. (JC Penney.)

—*Saab. The most intelligent car ever built.*

—We did it again! Three years in a row, America's favorite way to fly." (Eastern.)

—*Flex-account life. It tells you how much your life insurance really costs.* (The Acacia Group.)

What have all the foregoing 19 ad headlines got in common? Fear of fall line? Maybe. But why should I make you guess: believe it or not, *they all came from the same issue of a recent magazine (Newsweek)* which I picked up at random from a pile of publications for the express purpose of looking for quality in ad headline writing. Each of these 19 headlines (I picked the worst) fails to convince the critic in me that the love affair they suggest is more than a tease.

Fall line copy writing is *not* the slick chic(anery) of my examples. In fact no ad writing is less convincing (or more "in" today) than slick copy that can't wait to tell you what a joy it is that the whole 220,000,000 of us are able to get together for another joyous day of selling and buying, which reminds me that someone once said—unfairly, I think—that what Dinah Shore needed was "sadness lessons." (If anyone needs sadness lessons it's clients, agencies and copywriters!)

As I said a moment ago, the copy that follows such headlines usually makes things worse, and the art that illustrates or inspires the headlines is also "sound and fury, signifying nothing."

Okay, "nothing" is too strong a word; I've hinted elsewhere that any advertising is almost always better than no advertising. In fact it's our 28th Rule of Marketing:

---

28 Any advertising is almost always better than no adertising, but when "any advertising" is your best idea about what to do next, spend as little on its execution as you can, not as much as you can afford.

Put On Some Speed!

An embarrassingly large number of what I think of as "agency ads" are probably the response of my figurative agency (High Yeller, Inc.) to their client's call to "do something promotional"; the mystery is why they don't make an effort to "put on some speed" and follow the lead of their ski instructor. How can they sell if they don't ski the fall line at a speed appropriate to today's snow conditions? Can it be that nobody cares . . . that it's enough to be stylishly dressed and show up in time for class?

Now I'm going to return to my 19 slow headlines for the critique I promised you:

—"Nationwide taste tests prove it! Windsor Canadian beats V.O.!" *Critique:* Old-fashioned adversary advertising that no one believes even with documentation.

—"Nobody does it better. Winston Lights. This is your

world. This is your Winston. The ony low tar built on taste." *Critique:* See above critique and multiply by pi.

—"Is your small copier being killed by popular demand?" *Critique:* Minolta brings up a point about copiers breaking down from overuse. Fact is, most copiers don't break down most of the time. Fact is, you get bigger ones or a second one if the waiting line is too long. Fact is, Minolta doesn't start to sell itself until too far into the copy.

—"Now the excitement really begins." *Critique:* Aw come on, Pontiac, the excitement began years ago. Your adverts better show catching up and going ahead; there's a new game in town and it's no longer played by 1960 Detroit adiquette!

—"When you decide on a Sharp SF-770 copier it's a value judgment." *Critique:* Too dull, insufficiently sharp; the use of a model number in most headlines is a no-no space-waster.

—"Music lives on TDK." *Critique:* All cassettes play music. Whatever makes TDK so special is NOT this ad!

—"We're out to change some Old-Fashioned ideas." *Critique:* Brandy from California is a groupie type ad with a heavy yak . . . namely that Old Fashioneds made out of brandy are supremely drinkable. Unfortunately, before you get down to brandy you're 8½″ deep into a 9½″ ad. If that makes this a memorable pitch I'll buy you a Baccarat snifter.

—"Introducing Ciera. The only front-wheel drive that's a Cutlass." *Critique:* Oldsmobile's Toronado was the only Olds with front-wheel drive before Ciera. Oh, oh, oh what a feeling—no, that's Toyota; and FWD isn't big news any more.

—"The truth is, I would speak for the quality of Smirnoff anytime. Its value speaks for itself." *Critique:* Since the speaksperson for this ad is a lawyer, F. Lee Bailey, I'll settle for a question: I've never actually heard a bottle of Smirnoff speak. Is it English, Lee, or Russian, or Madisonave? And at the finnish (sic), who cares?

—All the rest of the cases are dismissed.

Ad Copy Made Memorable?

Let's summarize the promise of my chapter's title: *Develop a strong, credible, newsworthy point*—and *make it quickly*—without double windups and puffery! *Avoid obvious hyperbole*—let 'em feel real muscles through your shirt-sleeve. *Tell your prospects what's in store for them*—and get that benefit into the ad on time! *Write the fall line*—build up the tempo that makes all the rules work! *Write at the people;* they know the difference between a put-on and a pick-up!

SEVEN

Ad Art on a Clear Day

Not to worry. This won't be a chapter on all the many techniques of commercial art that blossom into life in our periodicals, billboards, supermarket cartons, shop windows, and on the business end of that most wondrous of modern media—the cathode ray tube, known better to most as "the picture tube" of a TV set or as a computer's "video display."

In the remote past of this book I've given you two of the four basic defects of man according to His Divine Grace A. C. Bhaktivedanta Swami Prabhupāda; now I give you the one he numbers as fourth because it deals not only with art but also art on a clear day.

Swami Sees Sabotaged Senses

"Lastly, our senses are imperfect," Swami declares. "Do you have the eyes to see God? You will never see if you haven't the eyes. If immediately the room becomes dark, you can not even see your hands. So what power do you have to see? We cannot, therefore, expect knowledge *(veda)* with these imperfect senses."

Given such undeniable imperfection, we are hard pressed to "see" anything for what it is, therefore critics are delegated—invariably self-delegated—to explain the world around them, including such physically transpicuous assumptions as soul, memory, love, glory, evil, beauty, taste. These are "somewhere" in the beholder, like it or not. And perceptions about art (Art) gambol and gyre about us much the same as radio waves, TV transmissions, x-rays, and other lethal—or at least deadly—emanations.

I offer for your consideration this statement about art in advertising: "Any direct marketer knows that pictures sell the product; photos sell the product better than does line art; full color photos sell best." This was said or written—anyway published in *Microcomputing Industry*—by Lee R. Greenhouse, director of New Electronic Media Programs at a market research and consulting outfit named LINK.

As for me, ever the direct marketer I assume Mr. Greenhouse refers to, I don't know any of those things about pictures for certain, but I do know you could bet on any of them to show.

ADvisory. Pictures alone do not generally sell the product, although I am told that it's more probable of women's wear than of other ware (sic).

ADvisory. Photos do not always sell the product better than line art or other fancy techniques and, in fact, in newspaper ads, photos can be very chancy in respect to clarity and density. I personally prefer photos, but Radio Shack has gone back to line drawings for its newsprint (non rotogravure) ads.

ADvisory. Full color versus black-and-white versus some color is a matter of cost efficiency or crapshoot. Our 29th Rule of Marketing advises:

---

29 If your ad is measurable, then the cost-effectiveness of amenities such as more color or larger size can also be measured.

Those who could "care less" about measuring ad effectiveness will use color the way they use their imaginations—with abandon.

The Lay of the Last Layout

In advertising of any sort, the "layout" is nothing more than what is referred to in capital-A art as the composition of the picture. Since the possibilities of layout are almost infinitely variable, if you're looking for waste in your ad department—or your agency's—this is a nice place to start. Ask 'em why the five layout submissions were made in colors instead of black and white. Ask 'em why the five weren't three. Ask 'em why the faces had to be drawn in such detail. Ask 'em how long it would have taken to do a minimum job, using the present submissions as maximum.

Some people say of me that I would describe Hamlet as a play in which a moody prince avenged his father's murder by getting even with the murderer—his uncle—in the course of which a number of uninvolved people, as well as most of the involved people, get terminated. They say this whenever I present the following theories about ad layout:

—that most layouts may be used repeatedly without anyone knowing or caring, and without affecting sales;
—that a little novelty in layout goes a long way;
—that you could take ten (not random) pages from any catalog and use them (selectively) for any other catalog;
—that you could take five (not random) ad layouts from any popular magazine and use them (selectively) as your own layouts for the rest of your business life.

For all that, I am a major lover and minor collector of art, and on the board of the Fort Worth Art Museum where the newest of new art is shown. No paradox. I simply know that our business is the making of measurable ads that sell products, not the making of novel and fanciful designs that gratify.

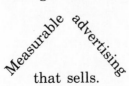

Measurable advertising
that sells.

You may not like my layout but you'd better appreciate my message or we're both wasting an awful lot of time.

Advertising artists certainly don't think they're wasting time and money by starting out with all new stuff when they could start out with, say, 50% used stuff. Haven't they read my 1st Rule of Marketing (about using used material)? Isn't the sale more important than the technique? How do they get away with it? It's because they can put their latest creation right in your little hot hand, which reminds me. . . .

How to Sell a Golden Egg

Flashback. One time in the 1940s I worked briefly for a mail order photo-processing house on the seamy side of Boston. I had what I thought was a fabulous idea for making more money, viz., to offer both regular and SUPERQUIK service, charging x-amount more for processing super quick. With a bit of quaver in the voice and shuffle in the feet, I explained my idea to the boss.

"How does it go, the SUPERQUIK?" he said with the bulbous stare of a busy man who has only so much time for trivia.

"It goes to the head of the line," I said.

"The head?"

"Well, what I mean is, visualizing the order processing as a straight line, the super-quick orders go in ahead of the regular orders the minute they're received," I said patiently.

"How do the super quicks know this happens? Oh, they—"

"Right," I summed up, "they just have to take our word for it. But of course we do try our best."

The boss looked at me for about 30 seconds. "I'm gonna tell you something valuable for the rest of your life, kid. You wanna sell somebody a Golden Egg . . . you *put it right in his hand* where he can feel it while you're selling him."

I've carried that art lesson around with me for 36 years, so what say?—let's pass it down to our sons and daughters and theirs. Because it almost never fails. You buy a pretty layout, a building model, a hi-fi speaker mockup, a computer drawing, a narrow necktie, because someone somehow put his Golden Egg where you could feel it while he was telling you how great it was. (And that's how last season's layout doesn't get used again this year at the saving of someone's salary!)

Flashback. I'll make this a quickie. An arty A/V show called "We're in It for the Music" was produced by Radio Shack for its use at projected audio fairs. It cost the company $75,000 and won a prestigious ad beauty contest, but when it didn't sell anyone anything it got mothballed. (As I said: "Besides which, everyone knows we're in it for a hell of a lot more than the music." A mere $75G worth of hindsight!)

Cullinan's "Circle Layout"

Radio Shack's cocky but insecure pre–1963 management brought on board a mail order marketing consultant named George Cullinan. By then, George was running his own consulting business and doing freelance lecturing; but a recent prior position was as boss of Alden's mail order ad group, where he formed many of his opinions.

Before I flash back to an anecdote or two, I want to share with you one of Cullinan's really solid—even if not necessarily original—ideas. It is this: *The primary layout concept of a catalog, flyer, or other ad effort must be sired in the merchandising department by the buyer!*

This by no means requires of the merchandise buyer that he be trained in composition or drawing. It means, however, that he must be able to "tell" an advertising artist his concept of the priorities of the stories to be told in the ad. The vehicle for doing this is the circle layout, a simple set of circles of varying size put down on paper by the buyer, each circle corresponding to the approximate amount of space the buyer wants for each particular merchandise offering.

In a circle layout the number of circles is the same as the number of stories the buyer wants to tell. The size of each circle tells the art department the relative importance of each story.

ADvisory. Using the device of a circle layout (see illustration) even the rankest amateur can securely communicate—even to such conscientious objectors as your ad agency art professional—the approximate amount of space you want to assign to each element of your message:

—headlines,
—pictures,
—body copy,
—prices,
—coupons or special offers,
—company logo or other identification,
—disclaimers.

You have already determined, by medium cost or other considerations of budget, the size of the message. As for the rest, if you fail to concern yourself with such individually minor but collectively major chattel as listed above, you have only yourself to blame if results fail to conform to your idea of the price of good salesmanship.

Who knows better than you the value of one element of your message versus another element—picture vs. body copy? Price vs. coupon? Who knows what *absolutely* cannot be left out? Your humble circle layout will prevent you from being faced with someone's irresistible layout which, unfortunately, lacks space for everything you need.

There's another benefit derived from forcing yourself or your people to make a circle layout for the problem: you get a reusable little checkoff list of things to be considered for inclusion or omission regardless of the project at hand.

You should never let your account executive establish the pecking order of the priority of your priorities!

Though Cullinan's circle layout was developed for catalog and flyer pages, you can see it's equally valid for the contents of any message destined for any medium—billboard, mailer, letterhead, TV commercial, radio script. Its common sense is the essence of my 30th Rule of Marketing:

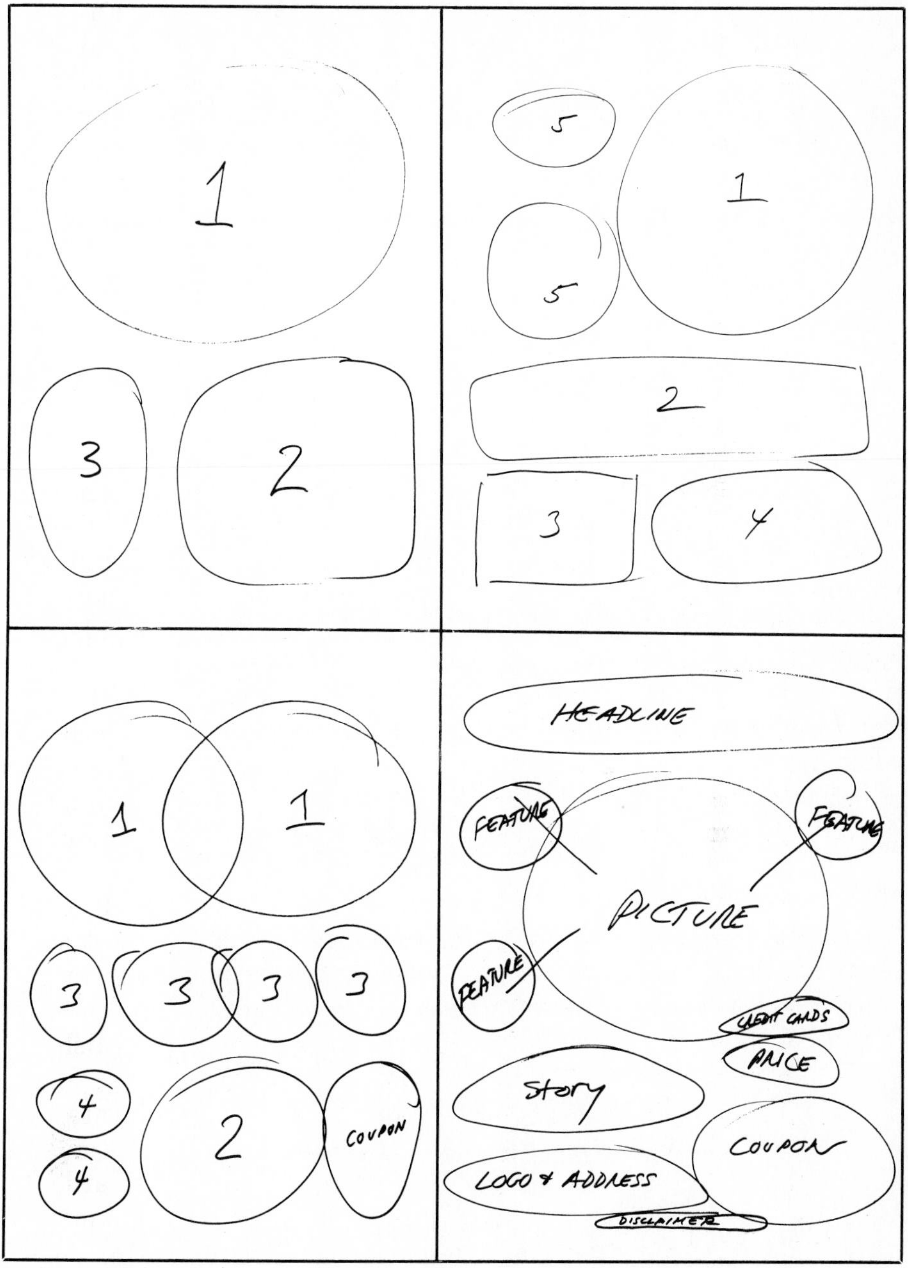
1
3
2
5
1
5
2
3
4
1
1
3
3
3
3
4
2
COUPON
4
HEADLINE
FEATURE
FEATURE
PICTURE
FEATURE
CREDIT CARDS
PRICE
Story
COUPON
LOGO & ADDRESS
DISCLAIMER

---

30 Each element of a promotional effort needs to be assigned someone's idea of percent of total available space required before the total effort is turned over to the people who will process it to its final form.

Please observe that my illustrated circles aren't perfectly round nor are their interstices filled. What you need is knowledge of what you want your ad department or agency to put into first-class working order.

Flashback. One of George Cullinan's most fearsome tests of what was going on in Radio Shack's merchandising department was what you might call the "prove it to management" session he induced us to hold before the finalization of every major piece of sales promotion, particularly catalogs, flyers and newspaper inserts.

The backdrop for these dramas was a colossal set of circle layouts and collages on pieces of brown kraft wrapping paper thumbtacked to the walls of my office. The latter was across the street from Boston University's main campus where the eds and coeds were a lot more relaxed than my buyers whenever it was their turn to "prove it to management." Drawn on or glued to those acres of paper was each buyer's circle layout for the various pages he had been assigned to merchandise, with each "circle" justified by three sets of numbers:

—the number of stockkeeping units vs. the time before,
—the number of anticipated unit and dollar sales,
—the amount of anticipated gross margin.

This may not sound formidable, but when you're explaining to all your top honchos your reasoning for each and every deed, and concerned by the implicit assurance of prompt subsequent review of your accuracy, such a session is a heavy burden . . . heavy, but a great way to get yourself seen by management. Implicit, too, is the knowledge that if management doesn't stop or alter a plan that later fails, it later becomes a judge with a sobering conflict of interest.

Naturally, there were plenty of interruptions. Once "Big George" broke in to admonish a buyer that "if you told me last year you sold 32,000 plaid skirts and this year's plan was for 38,000 skirts, I'd listen and probably say nothing. But you've just told me you're going to sell *74,000* plaid skirts at about the same price and time, and I don't buy it. And I assume and hope to God you haven't already bought it!"

As everyone knew, it wasn't plaid skirts but cadmium plated flybacks or something. But . . . point well made.

Thunder from Cloud Ten

My 31st Rule of Marketing is about sickness prevention, not sickness cure:

---

31 In business, the best time to have a post mortem is when the patient has a chance to remain alive.

This flashback goes on to show how not all of George Cullinan's advice was of the same high quality as the circle layout. One bill of goods he sold our management folks was anathema to me as a merchandiser. At one of those dreaded "prove it to management" sessions, Cullinan noted that a full half-page was given to one radio, a leather-encased transistor radio made for our Realistic brand by Toshiba. "That's no good. Impossible," said George in a tone that assured you it was Huckster the Great talking, not just some kid from the auto parts business. "There's just no way you can justify a half-page for one $50 radio."

I disagreed, saying, "It's a winner every time we run it"; George countering with the inevitability of his rectitude which, considering our disparity of age and experience, was awfully impressive.

Finally I was forced to yield to Cullinan's methodology: (1) no one radio was worth that much ad space, but (2) the whole radio category might be—he wouldn't argue that point, and so (3) the way to handle the space was to put 10 or

20 radios into that space. "Why add so many stockkeeping units?" I protested.

"Because," he thundered from Cloud Ten, "no buyer is smart enough to pick the exact one radio for this much space; he cherry-picks the entire radio line, puts in his 10 or 20 stockkeeping units, and he's *guaranteed* more business—which doesn't mean *hopes for.* Then he re-orders the fast movers and orders no more of the dogs. It's exactly that elementary."

Sadly, my top management let me down on this and similar occasions, resulting in too many stockkeeping units in our line and causing dismay among us private label lovers. We did NOT DO MORE BUSINESS by changing that layout from one circle to ten circles. And George, wherever you are in Eternity, I hope you have learned not to mess with the minds of marketers who often really do know instinctively when one item is worth an assortment of ten.

There's a macabre finale to Radio Shack's connection with its consultant and director, George Cullinan. When Charles Tandy arrived in Boston in early 1963 to take control of the company, he interviewed everyone connected with it to see how many heathens he could convert to his cult of High Marginism. In town on Tandy's first day, George was an early visitant. Just before going into Tandy's office, he stopped in mine.

"Well, I'm about to meet the Big Man," said Big George, with a crooked smile, "and when I get back I'll tell you what I think. If he's not for real, you'd better get your bags packed, but there are plenty of places you can go."

Tandy's office was 20 feet from mine. George walked from my office to Tandy's, closing the door behind him. Just as the two strong men were approaching each other, right hands outstretched for greeting, George Cullinan dropped dead.

Getting the Big Picture

Just now, at this moment, I'm looking at a two-page ad in *Business Week,* sponsored and paid for by Northern Telecom, a company that makes communications and electrical equipment all over hell and gone, Canada included. I'll describe it rather than show it, because its ad art would very likely not reproduce well.

On the left page is an old map of old Rome showing everything that was there in 747 except *la dolce vita* (which came later unless you came from the Caesarian section of downtown). It fades into the right page picture of a Northern Telecom network consisting of colored lines connecting large white dots representing Romanesque cities in America and Canada.

And my, what a tiresome point. "The road system of the Roman Empire—one of the world's earliest communications networks—took centuries to build. Messages travelled 40 miles in a day."

Opposing it is this disclosure: "At Northern Telecom we build networks that carry messages in milliseconds—and for longer distances."

Well, I should hope to hell things have speeded up over the last 1200 years. I should hope, even, that I am not alone in this perception of progress. My question is: why do ad agencies take so long to communicate the obvious to us in so elaborate a manner? Surely it's not to give their art director an opportunity to draw a map of ancient Rome?

And doesn't *someone* know that in a 172-sq.-in. ad, when you only use about 16 sq. in.—or 9.3%—for selling, you almost always end up with a lot of beauty and no beasts? Yes! Kornfeld knows or supposes, which explains my book's central point as celebrated with this 32nd Rule of Marketing:

---

32 Even with beautifully drawn or photographed cheddar in your marketing plan, you won't catch a mouse with it if it doesn't make a noise like a cheese.

There's a touch of additional bad news attached to the ad under survey, even though the boys at NT did not intend for it to be thus regarded; it's a gnat-sized-type *claimer* (opposite of *disclaimer*) that there are eight ads in this series. There ought to be a rule against ad series! But, in the barest chance that my bias is showing, write for your set of these ads to Northern Telecom Inc., Public Relations Department, 259 Cumberland Bend, Nashville, TN 37228; or call 615/256-5900, Ext. 4264. Tell them you're a serial ad major.

Elsewhere herein I again flick my whisk at ads that are not stand-alones but part of a series (I just read a Porsche ad's Part XIII). I'd even veto a series with the Beautiful People unclothed: the fact that the Lord made so many nudes is no excuse for agencies to use them in ads that are supposed to *extract lucre* but actually merely *attract lookers*. Seriality in advertising is a life sentence to limbo.

Bare Breasts Over Paris

Some will think I've sext't my text in order to build its circulation, but in fact I'm only trying to broaden minds in respect to advertising art. My source is not an ad but a news story from a 1981 edition of the *International Herald Tribune,* a marvelous daily paper published in Europe in conjunction with the *New York Times* and the *Washington Post.* The AP's copy opens in this manner: "PARIS—Bare breasts popped out all over Paris this week, and on Friday the lady turned around and bared her bottom in an advertising campaign that has disgusted feminists, delighted chauvinists and threatened to drag the government into the fuss."

All this occurred because a billboard company wanted to sell space and position *billboards* as extremely visible places to run ads. The company took its desire to the French-American ad agency CLM-BBDO and, clearly, the most artful of their group made an opportunity out of the problem.

Monday's billboard had the model, with her top and bottom bikini-clad, promising: "On September 2nd (Wednesday), I'll take off the top."

Wednesday's topless poster shows her assuring that on the 4th (Friday) she'd take off the bottom. And so she did, alas with her back to the camera, the caption reading: "Avenir, the billboard company that keeps its promises."

After okaying this campaign, "The trade association that monitors French advertising reversed itself and con-

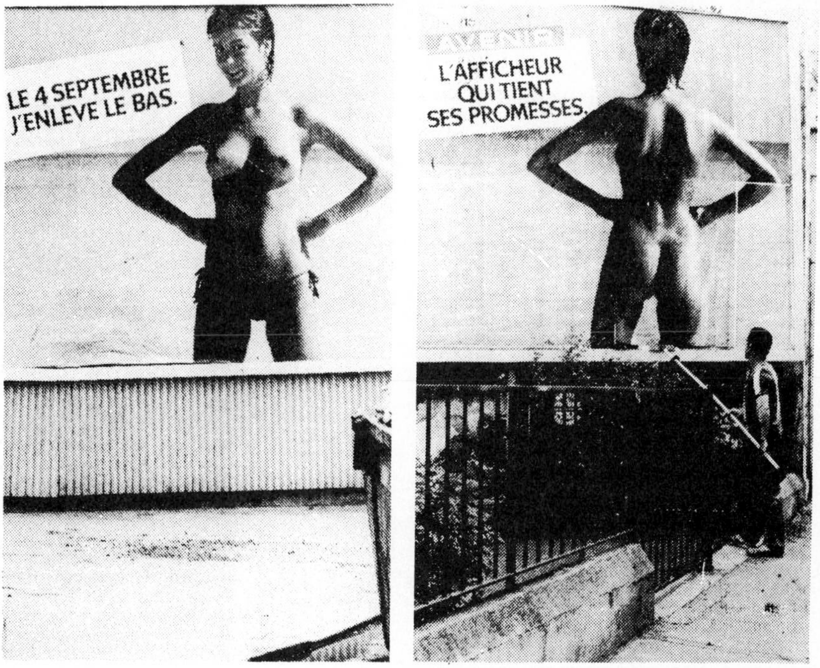

C.G. Cupic

Advertising for advertising's sake in Paris: The promising poster, before (left) and after.

Faithful French Posters Enrage Feminists

The Associated Press

PARIS — Bare breasts popped out all over Paris this week, and on Friday the lady turned around and bared her bottom in an advertising campaign that has disgusted feminists, delighted chauvinists and threatened to drag the government into the fuss.

On Monday, a smiling, bikini-clad woman on hundreds of billboards in major French cities promised, "On Sept. 2, I'll take off the top." On Wednesday, posters appeared of the same smiling woman, bare-breasted, announcing, "On Sept. 4, I'll take off the bottom."

On Friday, the advertising agency CLM-BBDO unveiled its last poster, showing the woman bottomless, her back to the camera, with the caption, "Avenir, the billboard company that keeps its promises." The agency created the campaign to sell billboard space.

A court in Lille ordered a complete coverup of the billboards after discreetly placed strips of paper were torn off the posters. The trade association that monitors French advertising reversed itself and condemned the campaign for "using the female body to promote something unrelated to women's bodies." And the Ministry for the Rights of Women said it might issue a communiqué; the Socialist government is committed to women's rights.

Courtesy The Associated Press.

demned it for 'using the female body to promote something unrelated to women's bodies,'" the story said in a final revelation.

Avoiding Racism in Ad Art

A different and more sober implication of advertising art is exemplified by a recent ad headlined, "Introducing San Antonio's new St. Anthony Inter-Continental Hotel." Its picture shows a smiling, uniformed doorman out front, looking for all the world like Coalhouse Walker (of the movie *Ragtime);* although a compliment to the model, it's also a needless continuation of the stereotype that black is beautiful so long as it's menial. This 33rd Rule of Marketing summarizes my critique of the two different but similar ads:

---

33 There is no way you can please all the people much of the time in advertising, but you can easily avoid making ads, packages, and displays that imply sexism or racism, and thereby avoid displeasing some of the people all of the time.

A little sensitivity goes a long way!

You already know of my short fuse in the matter of humor in marketing programs. I turn now to an example that is not a program, merely an ad including, by the way, another good drawing by cartoonist Saxon.

I fault the agency and the sponsor (Kodak)—not the artist—for showing me a top candidate for Kornfeld's Weakest ad of 1981 in the category of irrelevant art.

Much art in advertising is rather fine and rather relevant—much meaning 51%. And it's seldom cheap, unless it's reused or essentially a copy of someone else's art. The artmost problem is wedding picture to relevancy.

In this jumbo Kodak ad in the *Wall Street Journal,* the lady at the console says: "Good work! Two more hours, and you'll be ready to solo on the new copier!" Okay? No! Because that little whimsy is actually the entire weak main headline.

Neither the picture—which inopportunistically warns me that "the new copier" advertised may be difficult to operate—nor the headline encourages the slightest desire to read what's coming next. Says who? Says Kornfeld, who is not anti-copier or anti-advertising or anti-cartoon art, just anti another and another edition of the Little Salesman Who Isn't.

Mind if I hazard a double guess? My guess is Saxon didn't walk into an ad agency or Eastman's with this drawing, saying, "Look, fellas, I just happen to have this cartoon which I'd like to sell as the centerpiece of a good ad, and I was wondering if you could use it to advertise something that needs a good illustration to get you quality readers."

The second part of my guess is the ad people went looking for a certain kind of artist and that Saxon was the result. And in the end I find myself offering this 34th Rule of Marketing:

---

34 Whether an ad starts with a theme (copywriter) looking for a picture (artist) or a picture looking for a theme, the hardest task is to fuse art, copy and product into a positive request for an order for the advertised product or service. Attempts at relevance that are given force-fit elements result in irrelevance, regardless of their individual quality. Theme, copy and art that don't ask for customers ask for trouble.

Art Incarnate, Inc.

I certainly hope my friends at RCA won't think I'm picking on them just because they're mentioned so frequently herein, so frequently in a critical manner. It's because our companies have been in it together since radio was a pup, and familiarity breeds attempt.

But speaking of pups, as I do in Chapter 9 when I tell you how RCA's pup Nipper got booted out and then welcomed home again, there's a fairly recent RCA magazine ad I care enough about to criticize merely in respect to art, copy, relevance, illusion, and unwarranted assumption.

Art Critique. The use of reverse copy (white type on a solid background) is less dangerous than when used on a dotty process-color background, but still runs a chance of being unreadable, especially where insufficient spacing between the lines makes the reader quit before he's through.

Copy Critique. The headline reads: "The next revolution in the science of home entertainment is brought to you by the same company that brought you the last one." Who can buy that when the "last one" was the video tape recorder (VCR) and it was brought to *them* by Matsushita? Further, as just noted, the use of reverse type and minimal line spacing makes the copy—citing 1981 as the year of the RCA SelectaVision revolution—well nigh impossible to tolerate. Incidentally, if the videodisc is actually "the next revolution in home entertainment," who'd be needlessly embarrassed in public if the winner turned out to be a disc technology other than RCA's?

Relevance Critique. The lengthy disc-player picture in this ad becomes vaguely relevant only at the bottom of the ad, but I question how relevant it was to the 219.3 million Americans who hadn't seen such a system before. A large outline sketch of Nipper is also barely relevant as logo or even a design.

Illusion Critique. In my second chapter I quoted Swami Prabhupāda as saying that illusion is one of man's four basic defects. His Grace insists that "illusion means to accept something that is not." Consider, as I point out in my copy critique above, if you think the last few revolutions in home entertainment were incited by RCA. I wish they had been! But, for example, the audio tape cassette in universal use is a Philips patent. The source of magnetic tape is Germany. Edison had a bit to do with disks; others marketed TV on them before RCA.

Unwarranted Assumption Critique. I consider it a guiding principle of advertising copy and art to assume nothing, or as little as you can. In the referenced ad, RCA apparently assumed (a) that people would understand and be captivated by the SelectaVision player depicted on the left side of the ad, and (b) ditto by the attentive dog on the right side. Since I've already disagreed with both theoretical premises, I'll say no more, but try to soften all my critiques with this lengthy 35th Rule of Marketing:

---

35 Material created for sales promotional purposes—whether painted, printed, photographed, spoken or fabricated—should make few if any assumptions of prior familiarity on the part of the intended audience. Be leery of presenting hard-to-recognize objects unless their use can be presented with extreme clarity. Avoid making the audience guess your message (paradox) or laugh at it (humor). Shun technical specifications if they are obscure to your least-informed customer prospect. Avoid abbreviations; it's a "given" that many words which are commonly abbreviated in your industry will have different meanings in other industries. Consider if unincluded data on product size, weight or color will encourage inaccurate anticipation by the audience. The road to inattention is paved with unwarranted assumptions!

I know without a doubt that some messages are memorable precisely because they violate that 35th rule. So fizz-fizz plop-plop all you want to, Alka-Seltzer, but remember what this modifying 36th Rule of Marketing says:

---

36 When you make an exception to a Kornfeld or any other Rule of Marketing, make your exception EXCEPTIONAL!

I have one final commentary on assumption, warranted or otherwise; it's presented because of my assumption that it could prevent or help us win World War III . . . that's all.

In a newspaper article on the hostility of the Vietnamese to Russians, a Vietnamese is said to have remarked: "You can always tell the Russians . . . they're never alone, they never spend any money, they never smile, and they never wash."

Just right for a chapter on advertising art is a Pin Craft Corporation ad that regularly appears in the *Wall Street Journal*. Minimal art, hand drawn for clarity without loss of detail; no surprises when the mail-ordered wallet comes. Minimal layout and space—used again and again, so ob-

---

THE WALL STREET JOURNAL, Thursday, July 30, 1981   5

ADVERTISEMENT

Thinner Wallets

Until recently the thinnest wallets were made from expensive seal skins. Then a new material was developed — Oxford Nylon. Pin Craft Corporation patented a unique line of wallets out of this durable woven material. Consumers' Research Magazine did an extensive study on wallets and concluded by giving their top recommendation to Oxford Nylon wallets. Oxford Nylon does not have the thickness of leather, yet it is more durable, lighter, longer wearing, flexible and very thin. Thus the Oxford Nylon wallet is more comfortable to wear, and your clothes look better without a wallet bulge.

Available in 3 popular styles, all have window cases for 16 or more credit cards. Try an Oxford Nylon wallet with the understanding it can be returned within 31 days for full refund. Three year guarantee. Great gifts for friends and associates. Give yourself a 10% discount when ordering 3 or more. Send the coupon or the equivalent information to:

Pin Craft Corporation   Dept. Q78SW
16 N. Mentor Ave., Pasadena, CA 91106

Sportser—Smallest and thinnest. A cardcase and billfold, for hip or shirt pocket. $7.00

Classic — Thinnest hip pocket wallet, with a separate section for your money and notes. $9.00

Executive — Coat or hip wallet with a handy stacking rack for six additional credit cards and a 3½ x 5 inch picture window. $11.00

Put the model letter **S, C,** or **E,** and quantity after the color(s) you want:
Black_____ Brown_____ Navy blue_____
Burgundy_____ Dark green_____ Tan_____
Add $2.40 for embroidered initials_____ in gold□ or silver□ gift wrap□. Made in USA
Name (Print)_____
Address _____
_____ Zip_____
Check□ M.O.□ Cash□ MasterCharge□ Visa□
Carte Blanche□ Diners□ Expires _____
Card#_____
To speed credit card orders, call free (800) 423-4541. In Calif, AK, HI, toll call (213) 793-2101.

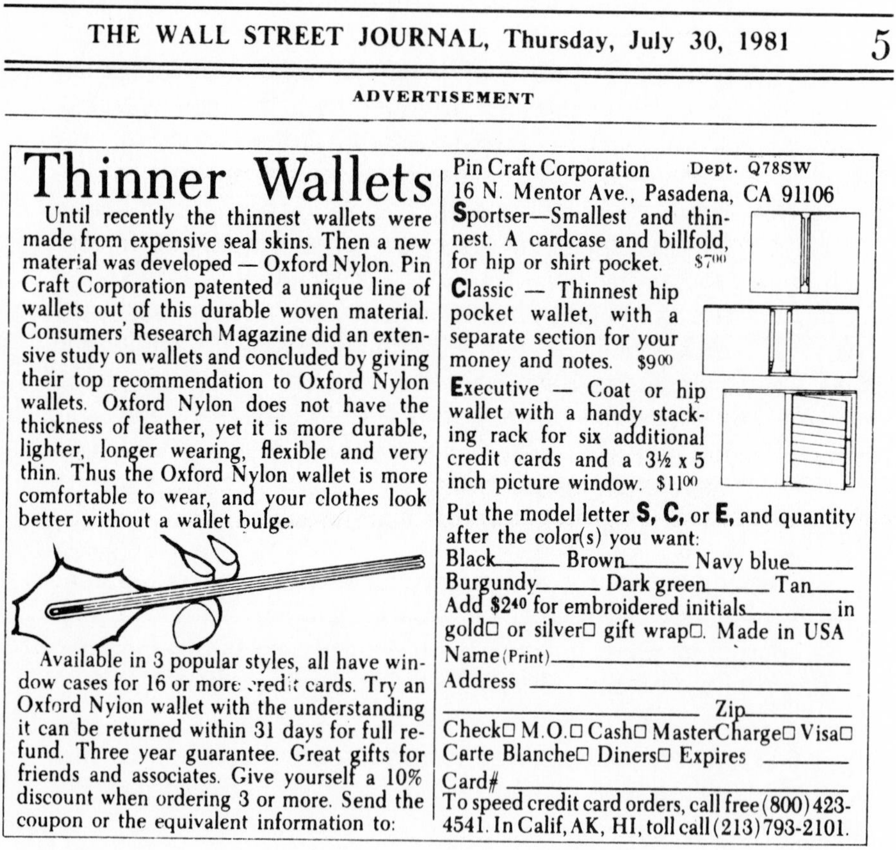

viously a winner (and remember my advice on using used art).

Why don't they leave enough space between the lines of the coupon for writing? Simple! Blank space in ads costs money. If you want their product, you'll figure out how to write for it. Consider why they use the word "ADVERTISEMENT" to make way for their pitch. Do they ever run it anywhere but at the top of a page? Never.

Any assumptions? You bet! Theirs—we all want a thinner wallet than the one we have. Mine—it's all we'll need if interest rates, prices and unemployment remain high.

The Artful Dodger

The foregoing subhead is neither Charles Dickens nor Ebbett's Field remembered, but a small sheaf of things about ad art that didn't find a home anywhere else. For example; the in-house corporate Art Director. If it's a she, I've no experience; if it's a he, I've got news for you.

Art Directors I've known—present company always excluded—have generally wanted to run the whole department but rarely exhibited the talent for binding wounds and mending differences that regular, uncreative executives are supposed to have in lieu of souls. When shout comes to yell, it may be that your Art Director would rather direct than draw. Just remember who told you.

Art Directors I've known are the exact opposite of color blind; given four colors, they saturate first and blanch later (after being criticized). So now you know why the overuse of color by many commercial artists is like Dr. Pepper in Texas—it's the thirst that doesn't quench!

ADvisory. Less is more in ad color; more is what you get unless you're fussy and persuasive.

As noted, Art Directors, both industrial and graphic, dislike reusing anything they or the company have used before. Why? Maybe it's, "Look, you hired me to design, stir, spice, blend, have taste, improve our image; how can I make you a meal out of yesterday's garbage?" Or, "I never promised to make you great ads with a pair of scissors." (Complain and pay. Frequent complaints will eventually save you money.)

Our 37th Rule of Marketing is a good clue:

---

37 Everything you have to say about and be wary of in respect to commercial art directors, you can also say about plumbers, decorators, and architects.

(Regardless, I've yet to meet one I didn't enjoy working with and knowing.)

Don't think or a moment that I am against creativity; I'm gung ho for creativity; but when you're working in one dimension (as on a page) you don't try to work it out on a ceiling (as in a Vatican). What you do is pay heed to our 38th Rule of Marketing, because it applies to every phase of marketing—not just advertising art:

---

38 When facing any marketing problem, face to the rear first because it's the end result that matters. Once you have honestly and fearlessly determined the desired effect—more business, improved awareness, better positioning, new converts, greater visibility—you then face forward and determine how to initiate a process for achieving it.

It's no different than retaining a law firm to WIN a case rather than to defend one; if they can't *think back* from "win" to "how," you've just rented yourself another epiphenomenal esquire.

Make the relevancy test—is it? or isn't it?

Make the productivity test—win? place? show? or scratch? Don't think this means only the productivity of ads, billboards, cartons, face-plates and dashboards.

At Fort Worth's Tandy Center we have several elevators that could run faster and be better interfaced with others; we have garage entrances some trucks can't enter or leave without incredible acrobatics; we have variable lights for ads and PR down the sides of our buildings but all their hundreds of light bulbs have to be changed by hand. Why? Because the amateurs who ordered the work assumed the pros who designed and built it were untouchable in respect of productivity.

ADvisory. Being creative often means *not* letting it happen!

Last, there's the matter of male/female and young/old human models in display advertising. If Radio Shack shows a boy building a kit, it gets two phone calls and nine letters from mothers saying Shack is against girls. If the kid on the carton is white, they hear from blacks; if young, from old consumerists who never die. If beautiful, what about respect for us homely souls? If in violent combat, it's total war.

If you want to make a buck with models in your advertising art, be prepared for flak, marching parents, threats of boycott, maybe even injunctions. Most of it is consumerism, a do-good disease that occasionally does good when an exceptionally large pickable nit is isolated.

ADvisory. Don't make love, don't make war, don't make merry; just make it to the bank on time.

EIGHT

The Big Bad Ad (Author's Opinion)

Time now for an interlude of comic relief to change the pace, even though this intermission will be perceived by most readers as more tragi-comic than comic. When the Teacher and Leader—as Stalin was nicknamed by his intelligentsia during his reign—calls out a big ad, its purpose and quality should be superb. Right? Sorry, but the record indicates that when it's time to go public with your communications the result is something you (a) lack the precedence or desire to review, (b) purposely don't get shown, or (c) don't believe is your affair (i.e., to mess with what goes on in that "department"; you let Dick or High Yeller, Inc. do it).

I've assembled a handful of large ads for the purpose of demonstrating that big, primarily institutional ads are rarely good ads or even money's-worth buys; that this sort of waste is rampant in the world of advertising—needless waste, not the iffy kind I earlier called "Wanamaker's Conundrum" (when you don't know which half of the ad dollar is wasted, but know one is). Here there's no question of 50% waste; it's total. My message?—doing better than "bad" is not only not difficult, it's also not a moment too soon to save the media's ecology.

If one of my "big bads" happens to be YOUR ad, please remember I'm just a critic at work reviewing another opening of another play. In proof of fairness, I also include at least one Radio Shack ad I find big and bad.

Naturally, many ads—particularly the king sizers— are faulty due to having been sired "between a rock and a hard place," products of lower level folks executing compromises between client and agent.

The Client—Not the Agency—at Fault

ADvisory. Even so, did you know that in ad matters THE CLIENT IS AT FAULT when fault is found? Then read my 39th Rule of Marketing and be better informed:

---

39 In matters between the client and the agency, the client is at fault when fault is found.

This hadn't occurred to me until I read about NBC's new letter N, said N being part of a new (agency) logo which proved to be the N the Nebraska ETV Network was already using; not a similar N, an identical one! But in a newspaper article, the N-finding agency's respected president, Walter P. Margulies (Lippincott & Margulies), absolves his firm. "It was the network's task . . . to search out such duplication," he says.

Thus it follows logically that if your ad is bad—big or small, pretty or ghastly, and a failure at winning friends and making sales—it's *your fault* for accepting it. You may be surprised, but that's a premise I can live with.

One of the reasons why I went to the trouble to do this book was to make sure you read two memos: (1) it's your fault when the ads are bad and/or don't pull; (2) it's your fault when you accept the mistaken notion that you can't tell good from bad ads *as investments* until after the dice are rolled. Show me the buyer or manager in any other part of your enterprise whose similar thinking would be acceptable to you!

When pondering those memos, I reached for the nearest

big ads in whatever I was reading at the time, and dropped 'em in my Pendaflex file for use today. Frankly I was surprised at the number of big ones that were bad ones: it could be that as many as 90% lack the news value, courage, clarity, conviction and magnetism warranted by their size and cost. After looking over my samples and notes, you should be—MUST get to be!—better prepared to search and destroy on your own.

Even a Big Dab Won't Do Ya

The Commercial Credit Business Services Group is a Control Data Company, and yet, for all the dough and savvy those two fine names represent, they chose to run a big ad that is an almost perfect example of what I say NOT to do if its intent is to persuade people like me to follow their lead.

Start with the headline: BLACK INK. Each letter measures nearly 4¼″ by 3″ wide, or 58 × 42 agate or 160 × 72mm. Each letter is about the size of a Radio Shack Pocket Weatheradio (cat. no. 12-156, $12.95). The space consumed by this two-word headline is 114.7 square inches, and its cost—per a recent *Wall Street Journal* rate card for the national edition on a one-time-run basis—was $21,712.74, the cost of a secretary for a YEAR! Message value so far: zero (red ink).

What could have saved the day would have been a headline in agreement with my 40th Rule of Marketing:

---

40 The headline of every ad must challenge or lure the reader into reading further, or risk his skipping to the next headline written by the next advertiser.

If BLACK INK is a big dab that won't do ya, remember that the Brylcream ad says, "A little dab'll do ya," and save most if not all of that $21,712.74—say $18,000; for those savings you could hire a fledgling in-house ad copywriter for a year!

The first sentence of Commercial Credit's body copy—body copy is what follows headlines when sub-headlines don't—reads, "It's a pretty precious commodity these days." What's a pretty precious commodity? BLACK INK? Right! It obeys to the letter our 41st Rule of Marketing:

---

41 The point made by the main headline of every ad must always be reinforced in the first line of the body copy.

But alas, instead of plunging on to another point, the copy settles down to the sort of redundancy Madison Avenue must have patented in 1938. "BLACK INK. It's a pretty precious commodity these days. Or to put it another way,* red ink is sure a lot easier to find."

ADvisory. The asterisk (*) is to remind me to tell you that THEY ALWAYS PUT IT ANOTHER WAY, the copywriters; that's what happens when the original way gets bogged down at High Yeller, Inc., and what to say next has become unclear.

ADvisory. Redundancy in copy is what I call the Double Windup. It occurs when the pitcher is so delighted with his windup that he continues winding up until ordered to release the ball. (Game called because of darkness.)

That high repeat factor inspired my 42nd Rule of Marketing:

---

42 Unless redundancy is seen to be an essential repetition of what's already been said, ad copy should proceed directly to its next new point—that is, from made Point A to new Point B.

"Red ink" is not a new point, only a new color!

"The fact is," the ad next says, "a company has got to have smart financial management to make it through today's economic obstacle course." May I call this a smartass observation, please? (They and we have already made it through to here.)

"Cash alone won't do it," says the next sentence. Won't do what? Not only a non sequitur but a clear violation of my 43rd Rule of Marketing which insists:

---

43 When advertising copy says something WON'T DO, it must quickly say either WHY IT WON'T DO, or WHAT WILL DO, or preferably both.

To shorten this critique, I can assure you that at least four essential points of this ad have yet to be established:

1. They say we'll get more than cash when we come to them for assistance, but fail to say why we need cash (or more).
2. They say we'll get "smart money and meet smart people who can provide the financial management [we'll] be needing," but fail to say why *their* management is needed or smart.
3. They fail to identify us as their chosen customer.
4. They fail to identify *themselves* by name or place.

Ultimately, at the bottom of the body copy, comes this final weak suggestion: "Maybe our people and your people should get together. It could mean black ink for both of us." And at long last we get the full implication of the headline: BLACK INK. But why not have come right out with it, why the sudden subjunctive "could" instead of a more manly and assertive "would" or "will"? The question inspired our 44th Rule of Marketing:

---

44 Never ever say "maybe" in an ad—say "yes" or "no."

Altogether a conspicuously consumptive ad!

Love That Whatchamacallit!

I realize it's difficult to follow the specifics of ad copy and art as I asked you to do with Commercial Credit's entry, so take a breather, courtesy of Armco Industrial Credit Corporation—another credit company effort I found both big and bad—not bad credit, just bad salesmanship. I found it when I took a random walk through *Dun's Review* and read:

When was the last time
you talked to a finance company
that knew its
widgets from its
whatchamacallits?

Thinking it appropriate to call in a guest critic, I sought out Ambrose Bierce via his 1906 publication, *The Cynic's Word Book,* satanically retitled (in its 1911 edition) *The Devil's Dictionary*. Only Mr. Bierce could do justice to this Armco ad; it was that stunning an achievement.

"Achievement," Ambrose noted, is "the death of endeavor and the birth of disgust." Too strong? Well, something at least on the order of dismay was certainly awakened in me on catching grown men and women of the marketing profession in the act of seeking to reduce salesmanship to whimsy. Whatchasay, shall we forget about sticky widgets? Okay, but first, ever the devotee of equal time, I want to give Armco another chance to sell you something: call them at 1-800 527-2202 (in Texas -442-3824); mention Dept. 41—it's a code, proving at least they tabulate ad responses.

Aetna Life & Casualty doesn't talk your language very well when it runs a large ad asking you to "hitch your portfolio to something almost as sure as death and taxes."

It just takes them too long to say you can hedge against inflation with one of their Participating Mortgage Separate Accounts, after coaxing you to think through a cartoon that takes too long—75% of the ad's space—to illustrate inflation.

In the middle of their plea I dozed off and dreamed I spent my hedge ($350) on a Krugerrand that went to $1350 without help from anyone outside of government. What's a Participating M- S- A-? Write Aetna at 151 Farmington Ave., Hartford, CT 06165, and tell 'em Kornfeld said to tell you, but quickly. . . before it's too late.

Ready to "Enter a New World of Pleasure?"

Even in the best of times, who'd imagine someone would run a six-page ad in a news magazine that would need two pages just to say, *"Enter a new world of pleasure,"* and later to say, *"Vantage pleasures . . . when you want good taste and low tar, too"?* Imagine: six pages . . . full color . . . 17 words; and then guess the cost.

I checked the *Newsweek* rate card: $381,348 on a one-time rate basis; $22,432 a word. Even in better times, my word for such extravagance is "overkill." No illustration needed!

Today, the cigarette people seem to have little, aside from pleasure, to advertise. There's not much pleasure in printing an even larger Surgeon General's warning, or claiming reduced accidental fire-starts by careless smokers under 14, or giving out hints on easy ways to repair polyester damaged by dropped butts. So what's in it for the advertiser or even the smoker when a Barclay ad claims, "The pleasure is back"?

Barclay's pleasure-world is not a new one but the old one returned to. The good news is Barclay describes it in one page, not six like Vantage, and what I say is: "The hell with the results, Barclay pleasures quicker."

ADvisory. If you're going to be big and bad, be quick!

New subject: even if no one asks, "The Shadow Knows," chortles Taster's Choice, a Nestle entry in the Pleasure of Drinking Coffee world. "There's no mystery here," says the ad I recently read about Taster's Choice being "100% freeze-dried coffee. So it looks, smells and tastes like ground roast." Go easy on the redundancy, Taster's; you said that just two sentences ago: "Ahh, the fresh-perked ground roast flavor. . . ."

But to be contentious, I do find a bit of mystery here, aside from not knowing what it is the Shadow knows: how does freeze-drying make frozen stuff taste unfrozen, and what's so great about ground roast? (More husbands than wives read the magazine in which this ad ran; if husbands are not as familiar as wives in grasping the mysteries of gustation, culinization and chill factor, they need to be told.)

Pan-Fried Apple, Porsche, and Xerox

"When we invented the personal computer, we created a new kind of bicycle," reads the headline of an impressive full-page ad run by Apple Computer, Inc., violating a number of my strictures on advertising matters. The first is the matter of making news, which I say all ads must do one way or another. Make news. Provide benefits. Sell goods and services.

Even if it were important news to single out one bonafide inventor of the personal computer, you'd be hard-pressed to find agreement in the industry on who it was.

How much of whose claim is history and how much hyperbole if, as author Donald D. Spencer writes: "The first *microcomputer* (Altair 8800) was introduced in early 1975. . . . The Altair 8800 microcomputer was based on the Intel 8080 microprocessor. The introduction of the Altair 8800 was the beginning of the present wave of personal computers." This appeared in his book *Exploring the World of the Personal Computer,* published by Howard W. Sams.

Then there's the headlined bicycle's mysterious (even after explanation) analogy; the bicycle is certainly not Apple-invented or re-invented (a trendy verb used more creatively than reliably by Sony in some of its heady product ads). I have a 45th Rule of Marketing that speaks to the point of translating analogies and claims into advertising lingo:

---

45 When making analogies and claims in advertising, clarity of intention is even more urgent than relevance or accuracy.

In my later remarks about spokespeople in advertising, I particularly stress the liabilities incurred when ads feature the picture and statements of an employee of the advertiser. Why? Because it's not a benefit and often irritates the others on the team. Apple's ad uses the chairman's picture a record five times. (No, not a record—Johnson Controls used a chap's picture *six times* in an April 1982 ad!)

"When we invented the personal computer, we created a new kind of bicycle."

#1 of a three-part series.

Steve Jobs and his partner, Steve Wozniak, developed the first personal computer in 1975. Today, Steve Jobs is vice chairman of Apple Computer Inc., based in Cupertino, California. Apple has grown to be a leader in personal computing.

What is a personal computer?

Let me answer with the analogy of the bicycle and the condor. A few years ago I read a study ... I believe it was in Scientific American ... about the efficiency of locomotion for various species on the earth, including man. The study determined which species was the most efficient, in terms of getting from point A to point B with the least amount of energy exerted. The condor won. Man made a rather unimpressive showing about ⅓ of the way down the list.

But someone there had the insight to test man riding a bicycle. Man was twice as efficient as the condor! This illustrated man's ability as a tool maker. When man created the bicycle, he created a tool that amplified an inherent ability. That's why I like to compare the personal computer to the bicycle. The Apple personal computer is a 21st century bicycle if you will, because it's a tool that can amplify a certain part of our inherent intelligence. There's a special relationship that develops between one person and one computer that ultimately improves productivity on a personal level.

"There's a special relationship that develops between one person and one computer that improves productivity on a personal level."

Today, most people aren't even aware that the personal computer exists. The challenge of our industry is not only to help people learn about the personal computer, but to make the personal computer so easy to use that, by the end of this decade, it will be as common in our society as the bicycle.

That's one of the reasons I wanted to do this interview. I wanted to explain what a personal computer is, how it can help all of us make better decisions and how it will eventually impact all phases of society ... from training dolphins to glaucoma research to growing a more nutritious crop of soybeans.

What's the difference between a personal computer and other computers?

The key difference is that one-on-one relationship between man and machine I was talking about, because the emphasis is on a *personal* interaction.

The whole concept is this: for the same capital equipment cost as a passenger train, you can now buy 1,000 Volkswagens. Think of the large computers (the mainframes and the minis) as the passenger train and the Apple personal computer as the Volkswagen. The Volkswagen isn't as fast or as comfortable as the passenger train. But the VW owners can go where they want, when they want and with whom they want. The VW owners have *personal* control of the machine.

In the 60s and early 70s, it wasn't economically feasible to have the interaction of one person with one computer. Computers were very costly and complicated; 50 people had to share one computer. Back then, you could have the passenger train but not the Volkswagen. But with the advent of micro-electronics technology, parts got smaller and denser. Machines got faster. Power requirements went down. Finally, electronic intelligence was affordable. We finally had the chance to invent the personal computer, to invent the "intelligent bicycle."

"When we designed the Apple, we wanted to offer the benefit of a $15,000 computer or a $100,000 time-sharing system with a computer that costs as little as $1,500."

Basically, Steve Wozniak and I invented the Apple because *we* wanted a personal computer. Not only couldn't we afford the computers that were on the market, those computers were impractical for us to use. We needed a Volkswagen.

People like us were the initial market for the personal computer. After we launched the Apple in 1976, all our friends wanted one. By the time Apple II was on the market in mid-1977, the demand for the personal computer had already begun to skyrocket.

Today, we've sold over 150,000 Apple personal computer systems. That's because Apple recognized this passenger train/Volkswagen relationship about 2 or 3 years before anyone else. When we designed Apple II, we wanted to offer the benefit of a $15,000 computer or a $100,000 time-sharing system with a computer that costs as little as $1,500. Obviously, one of the differences between a personal computer and other computers is price. Another difference is size.

I'd like to use another analogy here: the huge motor and the fractional horsepower motor. When the first motor was invented in the late 1800s, it was only possible to build a large and expensive motor, just like it was with the early computers. Those motors were used to power entire shops, with pulleys and belts running throughout the shops to drive the individual machines scattered within. Only with the advent of the fractional horsepower motor could horsepower be brought *directly* to where it was needed.

With the portable Apple, you could say we invented the first fractional-horsepower computer. The Apple is small enough to go where you need it. You can get the information you need on your desk, in your office, in the lab, the school or the home. In other words, Apple broke down the huge monolithic computer into small, easy to use parts. We made the computer friendly. So, like the fractional horsepower motor distributed horsepower to where it was needed, the personal computer can distribute intelligence to where it's needed. Ultimately, it will be this distribution of intelligence that will *change the way we all make our decisions.*

You've stated that the personal computer can increase productivity on an individual level. How so?

Personal computers will increase productivity because personal computers are tools, not toys.

For example, in the last 15 years, there have been only four tools that actually have increased the efficiency of the office worker: the IBM Selectric typewriter, the calculator, the Xerox machine and the newer, advanced phone systems. Maybe that portable cassette player you're using could be number five. Like all those inventions, the personal computer offers its power to the *individual*.

In the 80s, the personal computer will do as much for the individual as the big computers did for the corporation in the 60s and 70s. Today, Apple's putting the power of computing into the hands of people who might never have had the chance to use it before.

"In the 80s, the personal computer will do as much for the individual as the big computers did for the corporation in the 60s and 70s."

We at Apple call our personal computer a third-wave tool.

Toffler, in his latest book, writes that the first wave was the invention of agriculture ... made possible by the tools of agriculture. The second wave embraced the tools of the industrial revolution. The personal computer is a third wave tool to help every individual deal with the complexities of modern society.

You know, about 10 million bicycles will be sold in America this year alone. When we start thinking of a personal computer as a bicycle, a Volkswagen or a fractional horsepower motor, we start to realize what kind of effect 10 million of these typewriter-size machines is going to have in our own lifetime.

This is part one of a series where Steve Jobs talks about the personal computer, and the effect it will have on society. To find out more about the Apple family of computer products, see your authorized Apple dealer. For your nearest computer store, call (800) 538-9696. In California, call (800) 662-9238. Or write: Apple Computer, 10260 Bandley Drive, Cupertino, CA 95014.

apple computer inc.

Another of my violated no-nos is Apple's use of "Part 1 of a series," etc. Why? Because no one's interested or impressed. When I last looked, Porsche was beyond No. 17 "in a series of technical papers," lost in the slipstream of elegant advertising. (This, too, may be a record number.)

Finally, the subject Apple ad seems to me to typify High Yeller, Inc.'s odd couple: good-looking and at the same time boring. In being boring, Apple shares the limelight with most other computer advertising, personal or commercial; for proof see the computer ads in any airlines inflight magazine; yes, I include Radio Shack's attempts at making its TRS-80 more exciting or anyway more fun than Hawaii.

> ***ADvisory.*** The theory about long body copy like Apple's is that once you've hooked the reader with your headline and product and offer, he'll read anything you want to tell him. But when, like Apple, you vanish into such fog as "you know, about 10 million bicycles will be sold in America this year alone," it won't get you there, Steve, although your popular product already has. (Steve's the big apple at Apple.)

Kill That Coy Ad!

"Introducing the Xerox 828. You tell us what you do, we'll tell you what it is," is how Xerox trumpeted a new small computer at about the same time the above-cited Apple ad was making me glad it wasn't one of mine. The Xerox blockbuster offers us a classic case of coyness, another of the marketing profession's life-threatening diseases.

It almost immediately gave birth to our 46th Rule of Marketing:

---

46 Kill a coy ad before it gets to print if you can catch it. Few readers will be entertained or appreciative; a majority won't stay sharp long enough to get the point.

The "majority" are the people you try to reach in ALL your ads, even if your majority is simply people to whom you want to sell a Rolls Royce and they number only four thousand head. When you multiply my theoretical 4000 people × 90,000 dollars and get sales of $360,000,000, you've got you a deal that's as far from coy as Main Street is from Madison Avenue!

In Chapter 6, "the Double Windup" emerges as my name for a phenomenon in ad copy that means the writer and ad never seem to release the ball (= message), though they threaten to do so every time the arm intersects home plate. In addition to coyness, the Xerox ad's 22 lines of copy provide us with a whopping 12 Double Windups . . . Ivy League reluctance to make a pitch?

> "So you're a businessman . . .
> "You own a . . .
> "Oh, you're a secretary . . .
> "No matter what you do . . .
> "Best of all . . .
> ". . . and if you have a . . .
> "Okay . . .
> "What does it cost to own . . .
> "We'll be happy to tell you what it is . . .
> ". . . as soon as you tell us exactly what you do."

Did I forget a few double windups? See: that's a part of the problem. I waited until line #18 to find out the product's cost. I waited indefinitely to find out if the 828 was available now; the hint I got was mention of an 800-number and it has become obvious that 800-numbers are mostly only good for getting dealer addresses, many of which aren't current. Did you catch what a Xerox 828 is? Their cuisinartful definition says it's an Information Processor.

A *what?* "Listen, Ethel, if you don't have any information to process you may never make it into the 21st Century," is what I told my wife when she asked, "What's an Information Processor?"—looking over my shoulder at the one I was using, which she thought was some sort of typewriter.

Lest Xerox and Apple think I've singled them out for special AD-versity, try this large Radio Shack ad that, yes, actually asks you to look before you leap!

I happened to be in a plane with that same Ethel when this newspaper ad suddenly competed for tray-table space with my second Tanqueray on the rocks.

"What do you think?" I asked her, splashing with my stirrer at this waste of corporate funds.

"I think it's a lousy ad," she said. "Whose is it?"

Without a moment's hesitation, she too knew that an old saw like "look before you leap" won't cut the mustard!

Yes: a headline made for skipping, and custom made at that!

The ad's picture of someone looking before leaping is graphically more Prudential than prudent; nix pix like this when your in-house or agency genius tells you it's a winner.

> ***ADvisory.*** Ad people also tell you another thing which, like the 1982 convergence of the planets on the same side of the sun, is true only about once in 167 years: "What you're looking at now"—in proof or other pre-publication form—"will look even better when it's in print." It won't. It will almost invariably look worse.

The five sub-headed TRS-80 services are presented redundantly: "All at Your Radio Shack Computer Center" and they're "only at Your Radio Shack Computer Center" and the same as shown in the picture and the same as mentioned in third line of body copy, 17th line of body copy, 29th line. . . .

My 41st Rule said: "The point made by the main headline of every ad must always be reinforced in the first line of the body copy." But "if you've searched high and low for a reputable full-service computer store," as our ad asks, it still fails to advance the cause of "Look Before You Leap."

At the same time, we get introduced to an allegedly awful problem: the location of a good computer store that isn't a Radio Shack. Surely, five years after the coming of the little computer, there's quality competition somewhere out there in the top 50 major SMSA markets?

In summary, the many fine and bonafide Radio Shack territorial imperatives are far from clearly enunciated in this jerky, redundant plea for your business. And the moral is clear: when in doubt about how to get an ad into gear, ask your reader to buy something; say: "Buy here because—." Don't fight the problem by asking your reader to waste his mind and time in on-the-ad training caused by your inability to "find it (the logic) with either hand"—another Tandyism.

Genstar's Anonymous Donation

"$65,000,000 FROM AN ANONYMOUS DONOR," is how a challenging full-page ad opens in the Forum of the

2000 Caesars (my name for the NYSE member list). Its manufactured news consumes 17″ of depth of the 20″ available: 85%. You guessed it—the next revelation was a letdown, nothing less than a dazzling Double Windup: "To most people we're anonymous."

Why the constant need to be reminded that *headlines must be reinforced* by what comes next in the ad, not diminished?

Not until the third paragraph of body copy do we learn what line of business Genstar is in: building materials, land and real estate development, financial and marine services.

But then that feckless coy offer: learn more about Genstar, let them send you their verbal etching, it's "one of the most interesting success stories you never heard of."

And right below their logo—a linear five-word advertising slogan I call a "sub-logo-logo"—is this super unfunny coy claim: "Our success is unheard of." Rum, what, for a $2.3 billion company with a net 1980 income of $154 million?

Back to that headline—"$65,000,000 FROM AN ANONYMOUS DONOR"—well, that turns out to be the amount of dividends Genstar paid out to its stockholders. The rest of us readers . . . we're anonymous? No, we're identified non-owners. So who's anonymous? Not the client; he's identified as Genstar. Hmm, only one unknown left, Podner: the agency.

Contemporary with that Big Bad Blockbuster was a slightly different full-page magazine ad by the same Genstar, still exhibiting a problem in getting its success across: "WE RANG UP $2 BILLION, BUT NOBODY HEARD." (No? Where was the IRS?)

Negative advertising themes should never be used before thinking twice, particularly themes that explore the fine art of belittling one's own company or product. This 47th Rule of Marketing goes right to the point:

---

47 Advertisers who belittle themselves or their products in their advertising, whether seriously or in jest, can expect little result.

$65,000,000 FROM AN ANONYMOUS DONOR.

To most people, we're anonymous.

To our shareholders we're famous, because last year they got $65,000,000 in dividends. The payout per common share was up 32% from 1979 and was double the rate in '78. In fact, we've raised our dividends every year since 1970.

We're Genstar, a company with revenues of $2.3 billion and net income of $154 million in 1980. Over the past 10 years, our revenues and earnings per share have both grown at a compound rate of 30% a year; net income, at an average of 39% annually.

We're in building materials; land and real estate development; financial and marine services.

We're active in the United States and Canada. And on the New York and Pacific Stock Exchanges.

Find out more about us through your broker, or call 800-648-5600 (in Nevada, call 800-992-5710), ask for Operator 153. And we'll send you one of the most interesting success stories you never heard of.

GENSTAR

Our success is unheard of.

(Dollar amounts are Canadian.)
Executive Offices, Three Embarcadero Center, San Francisco, CA 94111

WE RANG UP $2 BILLION, BUT NOBODY HEARD.

Last year, our revenues were $2.3 billion with a net income of $154 million. That probably makes us the biggest company you never heard of.

Over the past 10 years, our revenues and earnings per share have both grown at a compound rate of 30% a year. Total net income has risen an average of 39% annually. We've increased our shareholders' dividends every year since 1970. And doubled them since '78.

We're Genstar. We make building materials. We're in land and real estate development. We provide financial and marine services. We're active in the U.S. and Canada. And we're on the New York and Pacific Stock Exchanges.

You can find out more about us through your broker or call 800-648-5600 (in Nevada, call 800-992-5710), ask for Operator 153.

And we'll send you one of the most interesting success stories you never heard of.

GENSTAR

OUR SUCCESS IS UNHEARD OF.

(All figures in Canadian dollars.)

Executive Offices, Three Embarcadero Center, San Francisco, CA 94111

"Little" means anything from a zero to a seriously negative effect.

My next subject is a vast example of what I call Post-Evanescent art, and don't ask how much it costs for a Madisonangelo to create such a canvas: if you have to ask the price you can't afford one, as J. P. Morgan said about yachts. The way I make it out, old man Noah's in trouble again. And advertising's ecology is going down the drain again, naturally at the expense of someone who thought he was buying immortality.

"We wouldn't have cancelled his flood insurance," touts our most spectacular Big Bad Ad, the sort I've been teaching you how to search and destroy. Its very next sentence violates my rule about instant development of the headline theme: "Disasters sometimes run in pairs." Score it one more excellent Double-Windup avoidance of theme development if you will; but here's a tip: "Disasters sometimes run in pairs" can be saved and used again when High Yeller, Inc., needs a great headline for a hosiery ad.

And the end of this ad, there's one last forlorn shot at developing the Noah theme, when they talk about ". . . filling our client's needs. And not leaving them high and dry."

Look, Podner, it's what the advertiser, the AIG Companies, a.k.a. American International Group, says they want to do, so don't knock it. My raised hand means I will try filling my needs with another Tanqueray on the rocks with five olives. It's so I won't be left high and dry, and to fortify myself for the coming of AIG's next big ad.

Ask Your Little Caesar

One cannot but hope that the typical American CEO sees Big Bad Ads like the foregoing only after they've appeared in print and someone such as your faithful critic complains. So don't get me started on institutional advertising unless you want to hear some four-letter invective. I feel that a boss who turns his back on approval of institutional ads which don't fly also loses his right to complain about employees taking the Concorde instead of Icelandic.

We wouldn't have cancelled his flood insurance.
Disasters sometimes run in pairs.
Because after the victims lose their property, they've been known to lose their insurance. All because their insurance company decided that type of business was too risky to write.
We don't think that's playing fair.
At AIG, we believe stability is important.
If this sounds too good to be true, look where it's gotten us.
We've grown into a multi-billion-dollar corporation with more people in more offices in more countries writing more kinds of commercial insurance than any other American insurance organization.
All by filling our clients' needs.
And not leaving them high and dry.
The AIG Companies.
Let us take the risks.

Ask your Little Caesar to judge two semi-institutional ads that ran simultaneously in *Forbes*. See what he thinks about them and you'll get a better idea of his grasp of the realities of salesmanship in today's world. I'll give you my judgment in advance: one ad was run to please (or avoid) the boss, and one to please (and try to better inform) the reader. You won't have to guess which is which; you'll be told!

Honeywell's office automation ad is what I think of as a typical agency job. It depicts a crowd of actors paid to admit ignorance. It's a takeoff on the series of commercials where similar dodos await the coming of the Hutton: "When E. F. Hutton speaks, everyone listens."

The headline asks, "OK, who doesn't understand Office Automation?" And once again, the first sentence of its body copy fails to expand upon the headline, a fatal weakness.

Instead it says: "With so many vendors clamoring for attention, Office Automation has become a confusing subject. For everybody." Not only not advancing the headline, it repeats the theme of the picture of people admitting they don't dig office automation. Double Windup? You bet!

Toshiba's headline, on the other hand, in an ad exactly the same size as Honeywell's, instantly reads us chapter and verse: "Toshiba offers you a realistic way to start automating your office. It's as easy as ABCD."

No questions asked by Toshiba's ad. No street full of ignoramuses. No confusing subject. No mention of others in the field (Honeywell says there is "a handful of vendors" offering compatible gear and advises sticking with those that do); it forced me to compose a rule about NOT mentioning competitors in your paid promotional efforts unless you're anxiously seeking to position yourself. It's our 48th Rule of Marketing:

---

48 Never mention competitors by name or industry in your advertising unless your intention is positioning for parity or better status, or for adversary purposes.

The Toshiba ad winds up most impressively. "These machines represent a new level of office automation. Toshiba is one of the very few manufacturers with experience in the three essential fields: Business Machines, Communications, and Data Processing. That's why, where other companies are only talking about the theory of office automation, Toshiba is ready to deliver advanced office automation equipment today."

Compare this articulate frontal attack to Honeywell's pussyfooting! And remember: it's imminent total war between all the electronic gladiators for control of your office!

There's also a significant difference in the description of the technology. Honeywell calls it Stand-alone, Administrative, and Multifunctional. Toshiba calls it a Line of Business Machines, a Line of Communications Systems, and a Line of Data Processing Systems.

Whatever an automated office actually is or will be, given only two sources and asked to judge them from their advertising, the choice is obvious.

Toshiba's serious approach to communicating tomorrow's business systems is a clue, however small, to the reason for Japan's mastery of most of the new areas of commerce into which it has entered since WWII. A side-by-side comparison of these two marketing efforts underscores the contemporary American dilemma: if advertising is not a science, it's at least an uncommonly revealing mirror!

The art of making a marvelous claim that it has no intention of delivering is personified in a recent BMW ad whose headline takes 80% of its space to claim "THE CLOSEST A CAR COMPANY CAN COME TO A MONEY-BACK OFFER." In these times of big discounts and special deals, such a promise probably made a lot of luxury car prospects read farther, even as I did.

The opening lines of body copy—in fact the opening two paragraphs of it—fail to advance the headline's cause an iota, merely chattering about the inevitability of the value of most things falling once they're bought and used. The other shoe falls, so to speak, from paragraph three on, when we learn to our dismay that BMW's big deal is to point out that

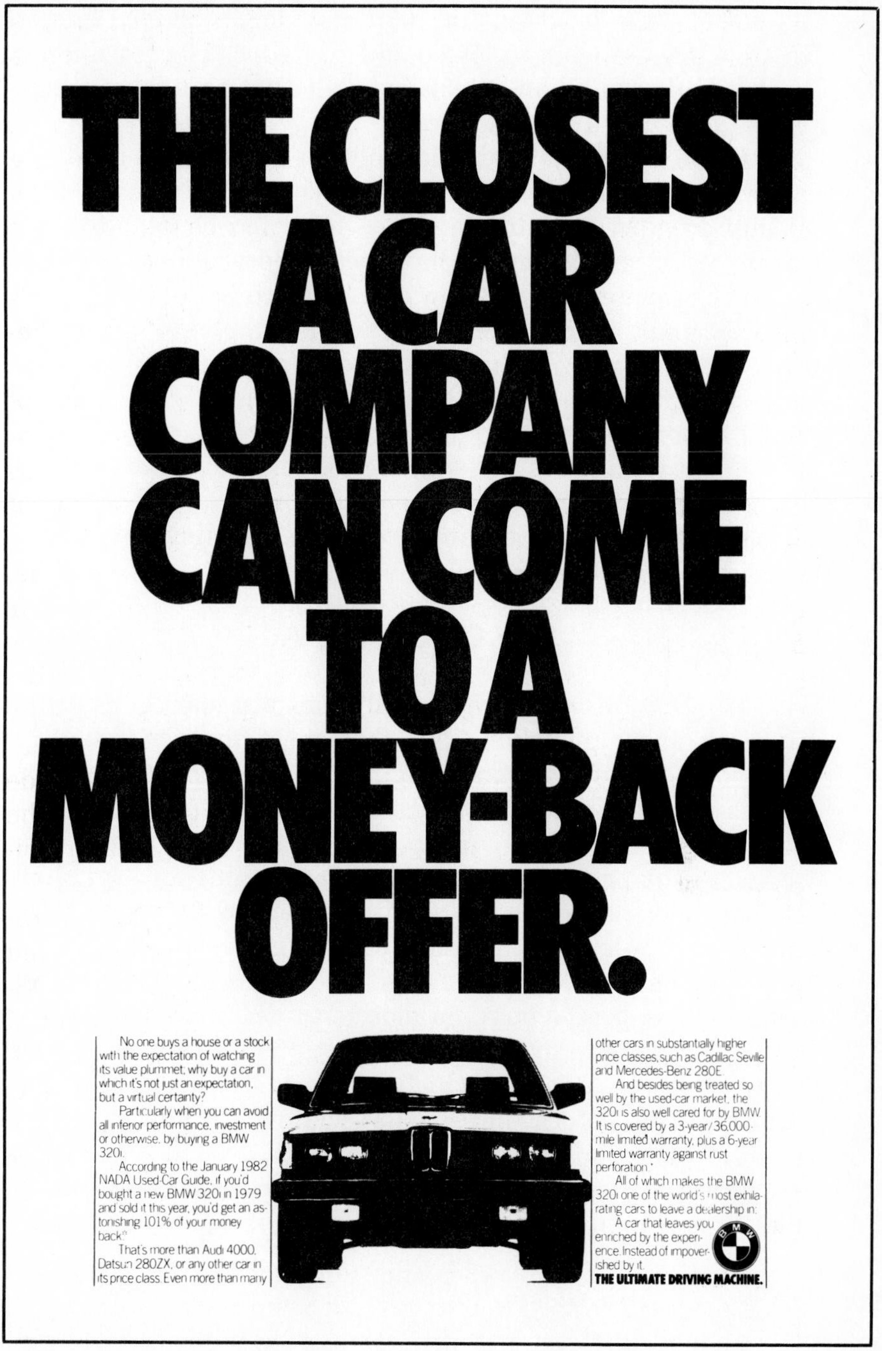
THE CLOSEST A CAR COMPANY CAN COME TO A MONEY-BACK OFFER.
No one buys a house or a stock with the expectation of watching its value plummet; why buy a car in which it's not just an expectation, but a virtual certainty?
Particularly when you can avoid all inferior performance, investment or otherwise, by buying a BMW 320i.
According to the January 1982 NADA Used-Car Guide, if you'd bought a new BMW 320i in 1979 and sold it this year, you'd get an astonishing 101% of your money back.*
That's more than Audi 4000, Datsun 280ZX, or any other car in its price class. Even more than many other cars in substantially higher price classes, such as Cadillac Seville and Mercedes-Benz 280E.
And besides being treated so well by the used-car market, the 320i is also well cared for by BMW. It is covered by a 3-year/36,000-mile limited warranty, plus a 6-year limited warranty against rust perforation.*
All of which makes the BMW 320i one of the world's most exhilarating cars to leave a dealership in:
A car that leaves you enriched by the experience. Instead of impoverished by it.
BMW
THE ULTIMATE DRIVING MACHINE.

its model 320i, if bought in 1979, now has a book value (in the NADA used-car guide) equal to "101% of your money back"—followed by an asterisked callout of an almost illegible bottom-line disclaimer.

Come on, BMW! Anyone who has ever sold a used car knows that, unless it's a collector's item, breaking even isn't even a dream worth dreaming. As for yours being close to a money-back offer, it might have been had you dared to offer a sticker-price trade-in allowance after three years of driving. Get your "money back" by having it applied 100% to the cost of a new BMW. That, lads, would make BMW an ultimate driving machine and I might turn in my 1979 Mercedes 300D for one tomorrow.

What we have is a new definition for a familiar category of marketing device: *the bait and no switch ad.* Are so many ads like that simply because advertisers believe making a noise like a cheese is all cheese is good for?

The GOOD Big Ad

Big Bad Ads are exceptionally conspicuous because they so often show up where the elite meet to exchange machismo, to parade columns of figures, to disinform the enemy: such arenas as the *Wall Street Journal,* the *New York Times, Business Week, Forbes,* the principal news magazines, the television at prime times, and wherever things are publicly shaken and moved. Every so often, the handwriting on the wall becomes legible thanks to some big ad that's good simply because its message is legitimate and useful—not the graffiti most people have no motive to decipher.

I'll run some by you with a critique, beginning with a large ad from Amax in which you're told, "If you own one share of Amax stock, here's what you own," followed by the amount of eleven different minerals you own. Ownership is expressed as "reserves per share"; for example, 1.2 tons of potash ore.

Critique. I find it refreshing to be shown how a piece of paper—a certificate of common stock—can be translated into the ordinary language of ownership: a thing visible and tan-

If you own one share of AMAX stock,

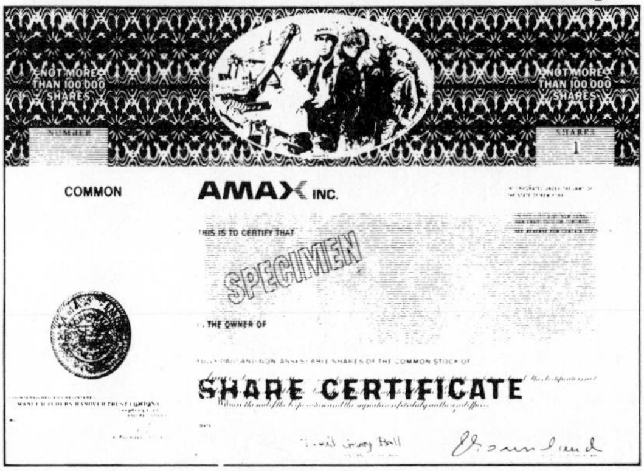

here's what you own:

Reserves per share*

Molybdenum	12.5 tons of ore
Coal	53.6 tons
Petroleum	0.2074 barrels
Natural Gas	5,315 cubic feet
Phosphates	9.1 tons of ore
Iron Ore	7.4 long tons of ore

Copper	3.7 tons of ore
Potash	1.2 tons of ore
Lead and Zinc	0.3704 tons of ore
Tungsten	0.0377 tons of ore
Silver	0.1278 tons of ore

*A composite investment for each share was created by dividing the number of common shares issued at December 31, 1980 (62,084,114) into the relevant reserve data for each mineral, as stated in the AMAX Form 10-K Report for 1980.

Behind each share of AMAX stock are significant known mineral reserves. Although reserves are constantly changing and we can't predict the future, our experience has been that a number of our reserves have expanded as a result of new discoveries, improved technology or economic conditions. In fact, throughout the history of AMAX there are important examples of reserves proving to be far greater than the original estimates.

For instance, the 1918 estimate of the Climax molybdenum mine placed reserves at 6 million tons of ore. Since then, 426 million tons have been extracted. And today, there are still 433 million tons of *proven* ore reserves down there.

Similarly, when AMAX began mining potash at Carlsbad, New Mexico, in 1952, ore reserves were estimated at 60 million tons. Today, over 75 million tons have been brought up and there are still 77 million tons of reserves down there.

When you put these facts together with $4.6 billion of capital expenditures and investments by AMAX over the last 10 years, it adds up to a very bright outlook. And that means good news for us, our stockholders and America. Because of our outstanding position, AMAX will continue to be in a leadership role of supplying minerals and energy to meet the demands of America throughout the eighties, and beyond.

You can find out more about AMAX in our special report, "Mineral Reserves: Investment in the Future." We'll also be glad to send you "AMAX Update," a summary of pertinent financial data, updated monthly. For your free copies, write to Investor Relations Department, Box A, AMAX Center, Greenwich, Connecticut 06830.

Or if you prefer, you may call (203) 622-3000.

Today, AMAX is in a unique position for growth and prosperity, backed by our assets in the ground. A very comforting thought for our shareholders. And for our country.

AMAX MINERALS ENERGY

© 1981 AMAX Inc.

gible. Since the least informed among us sees daily changes in prices in the marketplace, such a translation helps us accept an otherwise mysterious, malignant specter: losses of anywhere from fractions to whole points of worth on a day when "nothing happened."

How much better an ad it might have been if Genstar, for example, had discussed share ownership (and dividends) in the sensible English of portions of acres, trees, ocean frontage. Amax has found something institutional to sell and broken it down into desirable parts, and merits a "Bravo!" from anyone who has swapped—or might be considering a swap of—hard cash for soft certificates.

"Vin blanc vs. white wine," headlines a slick full-color ad sponsored by Food and Wines from France, Inc., which is probably an association—you can find out by writing P.O. Box 986, Dept. W (that's the media code), New York, NY 10101. I already know enough to say that this is a good ad for anyone interested in white wine; today that might mean anyone but me, the Man from Beer and Gin.

What makes this ad even more remarkable is its source. Most ads produced by associations (or pseudogroups assembled simply to share costs) collapse into either silliness or symbols—avocados, bananas, steel, wool, come to mind.

Critique. Without mentioning California, Italy, Germany, Spain, Portugal, Chile, Roumania, or Australia once (remember what I said about NOT mentioning the competition?), this ad makes its pleasant case for French wine both interesting and credible.

It recommends that you follow up by consulting your neighborhood wine merchant for "prices that are sure to suit you [and knowledge] that between white wine and vin blanc there are oceans of difference." The main such ocean is, of course, the Atlantic, but the copywriter, in rare form, was content to stop just this side of making waves.

It's tough to make an institutional ad actually beneficial to the reader. This exceptional example ran in the Sunday magazine section of the *New York Times,* an ideal place to start influencing people whose taste is in their minds!

Now visualize an A. B. Dick ad that is less than totally good by my definition, but certainly not a Big Badder. Careful analysis reveals it to be a copier ad (the Lord must love copiers because so many are being made by so many makers), but I advise copying its execution only after modification.

Critique. Dick gets right down to business, asking the question all advertisers should ask all readers who are not their employees or ad agents: "What's in it for you?"

Any time you can't answer that one intelligently, pull your ad or polish it. (The answer here is far from brilliant.)

The first line of body copy reads: "The new A. B. Dick 7200 is much more than just another high-speed copier," quickly identifying the product, the manufacturer, the model number, and the fact #7200 is a new item. The facts that it's new AND a high-speed copier are essential to justify the headline. Use of the model number is an error (non sequitur) we all make: *a model number is rarely beneficial or memorable in ads!*

Its vast blob of a picture has six needlessly obscure call-out numbers which identify features itemized in the body copy. It consumes about 50% of the total space instead of the preferable asymmetry of 66% or even 33%; other ways of making art like this better are simple, obvious, and numerous.

The slogan below the logo is, like most of the tribe, trivial and boring. "We're putting frustration out of business," says A. B. Dick with the faint smile of an auditor who has found a nickel boo-boo. Not Dick's smile, of course; it's High Yeller, Inc.'s observance of Madison Avenue's divine right to snicker.

NINE

The Corporate Identity Game

When I read about famous old Allied Chemical Corporation—the same Allied C. C. that has been one of the 30 stocks comprising the Dow Jones Average for many years—changing its name (in 1981) to Allied Corp., I groaned quietly to myself. When I read their ad explaining this earth-shaking move, the one that simpered, "We've changed more than our name [but] dropping 'chemical' from our name doesn't mean we dropped chemicals from our business," I decided that this chapter's theme was a tale that really needed telling. Its publication might be just in time to save a lot of companies a lot of money. Too late, though, for Allied.

Flashback. When I came to Radio Shack in 1948, I knew electronics was a real comer, but oh . . . that name! Mortifying. Embarrassing.

Radio Shack's "shack," in case you didn't know it, comes from the early days of marine wireless telegraphy. When the new-fangled equipment had to be added to ships designed for such meager communications as wind and calm, the question was where to put it. The answer was to house it in a makeshift structure topside, which, because of its shabby appearance, was promptly nicknamed "radio shack." Soon radio amateurs ("hams") would call their transmit/receive room "the radio shack." And the name has only grown stronger with age.

In WWII the word "shack" acquired another meaning which made matters even worse: the verb "shack up" was added to the American language. Fortunately, as I saw it then, I found that Radio Shack was legally able to add the sober and majesterial word "Corporation" to its name in advertising, although, as noted elsewhere, acquisition of the company by Tandy in 1963 made us a division instead of a corporation, and the "shack" problem returned to haunt many a sensitive employee and customer.

Most of Radio Shack's existing trademarks were devised to avoid using the word "shack"—Realistic, Science Fair, Archer, Micronta and others. Paradoxically, since the company's rise to fame as a division of Tandy Corporation, none of the company's monikers, with the exception of TRS-80, has captured and held the public's awareness the way "Radio Shack" has. (Pride cometh after the rise!)

ADvisory. The letter/number word "TRS-80," one of my more fortunate creations, is the name of the breakthrough personal and business computer line Radio Shack began making and selling in 1977 (see Chapter 11). As with most trademarks, its greatness is perceived only after the product succeeds. (As my wife Ethel says: "All princesses are pretty.")

Logo-rrhea and Other Nominal Follies

Sometime in the 1960s, I wrote to the then chairman of RCA, Robert Sarnoff, complaining both as stockholder and customer that RCA's newly instituted logotype (logo) changes were unsatisfactory to me. The traditional, encircled-RCA logo has been replaced by a hard-to-read trio which seemed to be, I wrote, more Russian (Cyrillic) than readable. Also I noted with extreme dismay the sudden disappearance of RCA's "Nipper" logo—Nipper is the name of the dog shown listening to His Master's Voice via a loudspeaker.

ADvisory. The 1980s saw the return of the Nipper logo, but now that the company is substantially out of the audio business, the logo is far less relevant than it had been.

It was clear that things at RCA post-Sarnoff (David) were undergoing critical cosmetic surgery when its Vice President in Charge of Corporate Identity (sic!) responded to my complaint approximately as follows:

> Dear Mr. K: things are different up here on the farm than they were when Radio Shack first started doing business with us. Regrettably, the old order passeth. As regards the letter A in RCA, which you described as Russian-looking, it was created for us by one of America's leading designers. But thanks for thinking of us. Sincerely, VPICOCI.

ADvisory. I have found that when the old order passeth, you can make way for the new disorder.

I have also created this 49th Rule of Marketing:

---

49 No one should be put in charge of corporate identity except in a review capacity, and never full time, and never with a title.

You can now better appreciate the simplicity of one of RCA's competitors, the larger (and recently better-managed) General Electric. Although a.k.a. GE, it has remained free of what I call "Logo-rrhea" (a violent urge to change names and, in consequence, logos); in fact GE's health is remarkable for an outfit accused by my late father, L.K. Senior, of manufacturing products which wear out at precisely the moment their guaranteed lifetime elapses.

When Lucky Strike green "went to war"—the theme of a WWII ad campaign theme alleging a higher need for the war effort of something in the green ink of its package—it went white and never changed back. (Lucky Strike is a cigarette.)

The creation of such delicacies as new names and logotypes is a form of modern art that appeals to the amateur in executives who imagine that slogans and intricate name designs are what make the customers come and the banks lend with amazing grace. This does not appeal to executives who are founders; founders remember!

The appeal of this art form to the more seasoned professional is more difficult to explain unless you buy the idea that new identity gives you a great rallying point for all the forces within and without the Camelot. (I don't.)

It is said that Exxon spent $150,000,000 for its namelift. They say Arco spent a bundle not to be Atlantic Richfield any more. Should it survive, I hope and pray Chrysler won't pay through the grille to become actually (and not merely advertisingly) "the New Chrysler Corporation"; the odds on both happenings are 1-2 and 2-1, respectively.

How Radio Shack Got Its New Logo

After adding "Corporation" to "Radio Shack" in 1949, I was obliged to shed it when The Shack became a division of Tandy—already a corporation. When I became its president in 1970, I went through a period of nominal disenchantment. But silence on the subject of logos was interpreted as disinterest; now every one of my honchos felt free to diddle with the company name in print. Radio Shack's nominal art suddenly ranged from neo-cubism on our giant truck trailers to post-expressionism in store posters and something like revanchism in our foreign locations (we had begun to expand into Canada, Australia, England, and Europe).

I noted with horror that every manager had a different logo and that these logos were getting into print and neon even before our resident geniuses had customers to serve. It was a genuine crisis and I went to work on it with a plan to create a new logo in two weeks or less.

I quickly went down the hall to our in-house ad agency. "Give me a new Radio Shack logo," I said, "one that is as readable in six point (1/12") type as it is in letters six feet high. It must look well on store fronts, cartons, forms, letterheads, and product escutcheons. It must be easy to execute in any medium or color. We have a ten-day deadline."

I warned against logos requiring multiple or special colors, or using fadeaway lines and other greasy kid stuff. I scribbled ideas, talked concepts, examined magazine ads; and I waited. Finally desperate for a quick fix, using the "make or buy" principle discussed earlier, I made a few outside calls to ad agencies and independent art studios in Fort Worth and Dallas.

It didn't take long for what I'd thought of as a small project to become a pronounced pain in the bibby (a Charles Tandy *ipse dixit* which I always presumed to be located somewhere south of sacrum and north of soprano).

As over a period of months I found myself rejecting expensive and unsuitable offerings from outside the company, cheaper disasters from within, and designs much too close to logos used by others, I began to think of settling for art right out of a type stylebook.

Any printer will be glad to show you his typography sample book. You'd be amazed at the number of type faces "in stock" and not only ready for free logo use but also amenable to such modifications as you or your artist desire—uneven alignment, altered letter spacing, reverses, photographic distortion, thickening, widening, extending, personalizing.

We had "fought the problem" by over-intellectualization and under-rationalization. Trying to be tricky and original is how you get yourself up Logo-rrhea Creek without a paddle. (How else do you get "CSX Corp." from the recent merger of Chessie System Inc. and Seaboard Coast Line Industries Inc., one of the great Logo-rrheaic events of our time?)

An *I* for an *ER* at Western

Shortly after the epidemic at Allied Corp., I became aware of a new outbreak of Logo-rrhea on Madison Avenue. A full-page ad revealing this appeared in the media under the auspices of Western International Hotels. As it happened, I'd just returned from an invigorating first-time visit to the island of Maui, where I had stayed in a hotel next door

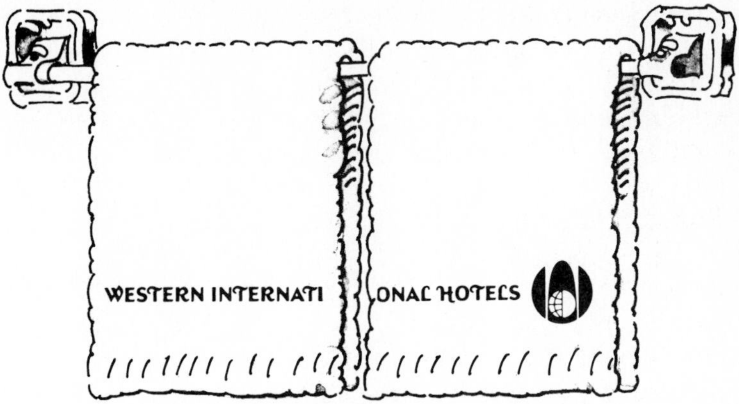

Our great name had one small problem.

So we made it smaller.

We have the kind of great hotels people don't forget.

Unfortunately, we had the kind of name people didn't remember.

So we changed it.

Of course, the Century Plaza, the Houston Oaks, the Camino Real Mexico City, and each of our more than 50 other very individual hotels will still have the very same style and personality that made them famous.

That doesn't change. But together they'll be known as the Westin Hotels. A name destined to be as memorable as the hotels themselves.

And there's one more thing that hasn't changed.

For reservations call your travel agent, company travel department or 800-228-3000.

to one of theirs. The reason for my remembering the Western International was that it had better food. Little did I realize their name was perceived as being so forgettable that it had caused them to want to make it smaller by 14 letters—1 smaller by changing Western to "Westin," and 13 more by totally eliminating "International."

> ***Special ADvisory.*** Elsewhere, at the same time, another well-established company was *adding* International by changing its name from Household Finance to Household International!

Westin-nee-Western expands on its position like this: "Unfortunately, we had the kind of name people didn't remember." This really surprised me since I'd always carried their four-color brochure in my attaché case to keep track of their many useful addresses and phone numbers. For example: the Peachtree Plaza; Continental Plaza (Chicago); the two in San Francisco—Miyako and St. Francis; the Chosun in Seoul, Korea, first of that country's full-amenity hostelries; Las Brisas in Acapulco; Shangri-La, once the only four-star hotel in Singapore with a tennis court; and others.

It was hard for me to believe that no one knew much about them and remembered even less. It was easier to believe that nice brochure's claim: "50 years of service and the best is yet to come."

As you would have guessed from tracking my skepticism this far, the W-I logo also had to go to the final resting place of all disinherited logos, the circular file. The new Westin logo turns out to be a transvestite W in the middle of a circle, and it's the only portion of this magazine ad that isn't basic black. It's vintage burgundy, and it may be the costliest W in advertising history. What follows, in consequence, is this 50th Rule of Marketing:

---

50 Since the addition of even one color to a black and white ad costs money, don't buy even one extra color unless you perceive an overwhelming justification for it. If perceived, then execute it brilliantly.

Later, still curious, I ran down the ownership of the former Western International—now Westin—Hotels. It is UAL Inc., formerly much better known as United Airlines. My reference book said UAL (nee United)—hotels notwithstanding—was still 88% an airlines company. And I say it suffers from Logo-rrhea, though my reference book doesn't say.

What's *Logo-rrhea?* A disease of the imagination that costs time and money. Even if it leaves no scars, its contribution to the bottom line is zero. So? Make your old logo 25% bigger if change isn't mandated for legal reasons; in lieu, give your in-house Ad Manager a 15% raise for coming up with such a great way to cut expenses.

The Company Spokesperson: Famous, Anonymous, or Non-Existent?

Agencies love to use spokesmen in advertising, and so, apparently, do in-house agencies, if Radio Shack's is a typical example (Arthur Fiedler, Paul Burke, Peter Nero, Isaac Asimov). The agency we hired and fired after our first maladroit meander into TV commercials (see Chapter 2) sold us on the likes of Rod Serling and William Shattner.

Endorsement of a product or service by famous persons is supposed to provide authenticity and luster to the endorsed (and lucre to the endorsee). Like every other supposedly good thing, this one can have as many liabilities as it has assets.

Liability #1. In many examples, the more visible the spokesperson, the more liable he or she is to distract instead of attract; and anything that distracts the audience in a 30-second TV commercial can blow your whole message.

Asset #1. But if your company or product or service needs more awareness or distinction, there's something to be said for getting exactly *the right* spokesperson.

Liability #2. Sometimes the spokesperson gets more out of appearing for you than you do, or moves up another career notch during your association. This almost invariably results in a demand for more recognition during the commercial—"This is Lud Beethoven for Radio Shack"—and for more money.

Asset #2. Smile if your long-time contract has three years left on it.

Liability #3. All too often a catch-phrase becomes catching. "Hi, I'm Pat Summerall," is joined by, "Hi, I'm Arnold Palmer"; pretty soon you can't remember—as audience—whose "hi" to hie to.

Asset #3. To escape the crowd, consider getting yourself a bright new personality like Roger Staubach: watch the papers for somebody who has just retired; stars in transition should cost less than stars in firmament and may surprise you with their skill at a new game.

But don't get me wrong: I'm not 100% sold on the need for spokesfolks; at heart I like to let the product and the price do the talking. As proof, I offer this 51st Rule of Marketing:

---

51 If your company needs a spokesman, it's probable the idea came from your ad agency, reinforced by your Yes Man of advertising; and that the person selected will be unsuitable, possibly a large stockholder, probably the Chairman or CEO; and it's certain that a favorable effect of this on your business will be undetectable.

Radio Shack has used a number of unnamed announcers in recent years when it seemed better to embellish the product being offered on TV with a warm, articulate body, and a highly placed one wasn't deemed essential. The benefits of anonymity in spokescasting versus big name talent are worth noting because it's almost a cinch your Mr. or Ms. No Name will be:

—much less expensive, also more available due to proximity and more flexible career commitments;
—easier to control, less likely ever to insist on personal identification (name) in your TV commercials;
—less likely to detract from your message by inducing

the audience to look at him or her instead of the product, or due to media overexposure;
—at least equally capable of handling the presentation of a product as actor/announcer;
—eager to please you because of the realization that he or she can be replaced tomorrow without wrecking your ad series.

Famous endorsers are often suspected by the audience of not using the product they so proudly hail. Rest easy in the case of pianist/conductor Peter Nero. It so happens Peter is an electronics buff first class and really does use Radio Shack's Realistic audio gear and TRS-80 computer hardware and software. (His front doorbell, however, rings in the inimitable dit-dit-dit-Dah of Beethoven's 5th; I'll have to take the 5th on whether it's a Radio Shack dit-dit-dit-Dah.) Novelist Isaac Asimov, too, is a devoted user of Radio Shack's TRS-80 as word processor (see Chapter 14).

But in many cases the company spokesperson or endorser is chosen for reasons other than actual use or preference, a practice that severely weakens the credibility of personalities as marketing aids.

ADvisory. If you can't find a famous user or convert a prominent person into an actual and satisfied user, look for a better idea. When you elect to use one, strive for total credibility on the endorsee's appearance with your product or service and synergism between product and spokesperson with respect to age and character. But remember your first duty is to keep your product "on camera" and up front.

There also our 52nd Rule of Marketing.

---

52 Before employing a spokesperson as salesperson in media ads, first you should have examined and discarded all other selling techniques. Try to resist using either the boss or other executive as your spokesperson as it causes internal resentment among those who actually do the work. And always be believable.

(Why kid me with "I'm Nancy, Fly Me to Noumea"? She wouldn't be caught dead with me, and I've even heard it might be the other way around!)

Why Religion and Advertising Don't Mix

I do have plenty of reservations about spokesfolks, and this is a tale of one of them. "It all started in 1975 with Brother Dominic, the Xerox monk," says the *New York Times,* fittingly in a Sunday issue. At about the same time, the writer noted, "Volkswagen was trying to figure out how many nuns could fit into a van."

There was a sudden rush to use religious figures in advertising; and advertisers do lean toward copying other advertisers when the scent of victory is detected; we're always sniffing for new (or born-again) ad hoc trends.

Was it a new ad-venture when Xerox promoted Brother Dominic saying paper-copying is so remarkable "it's a miracle"? And was it a good idea? This 53rd Rule of Marketing is part of my reply:

---

53 Religion and religious figures in secular product advertising should be faithfully observed by 100% omission.

Aside from questions of taste and improbability, for denominational reasons the use of such spokes- or silent-people excludes too large a segment of advertising's audience.

> ***ADvisory.*** But products such as Blue Nun wine and St. Pauli Girl beer are exempted from that rule by reason of their Grandfather Clause (providing for the continuation in use of something now in existence; newer things don't qualify).

From the same story we learn that Brother Dominic, the Xerox monk, "is played by 50-year-old . . . comedian Jack Eagle." And that Mr. Eagle said: "I'm probably one of the most famous monks of all time, and I'm Jewish."

I can't help but feel that via such monk-y business, Xerox and/or its agency have spread illusion and irreverence where neither was needed.

Item. A friend has assured me that the Xerox/monk ad campaigns—they are plural—were very successful. I remain unconvinced: principle before interest. (There's no disputing, of course, the enhanced awareness of Mr. Eagle to the world of advertising and the theater. Mitres off!)

Olivetti vs. IBM

While I was writing this chapter, I observed, from its advertisements, that the Olivetti people had developed a very strong urge to take away from IBM as large a part of the "smart typewriter" business as they could, and subito! Since it's "when in New York, don't do as the Romans do, do as the New Yorkers do," Olivetti got itself a famous spokesman. (For trivia fans, Olivetti's home is not Rome but Ivrea, a town near Turin.)

Enter Ed Asner, as a "show me, I'm from Armonk" character who demands specifics on Olivetti's crushing superiority over IBM on points selected by the company and the agency.

It should come as no surprise that every question Ed asked in the Q&A-type ads resulted in the answer—Olivetti wins again! (For the same trivia fans, Armonk is IBM's New York State home town.)

> ***ADvisory.*** Question and answer type ad copy should be avoided. It makes too many demands on the reader. Long check-off lists in ad copy—for example, AT&T recently ran an ad headlined "56 ways to manage better" followed by 56 check-off suggestions divided into eight groups of seven questions each!—should also be avoided for similar reasons.

The matter of *positioning* (see Chapter 10) is obviously the reason for selecting IBM as the target, and of *awareness* (see Chapter 11) in the selection of Asner as spokesperson. Olivetti is well known in Europe and Asia; to make it

56 ways to manage better.

This check list may surprise you.

Modern communications has capabilities undreamed of a few years ago. Every one of these electronic short-cuts can be applied to your business by means of a Dimension PBX from the Bell System. Check those that interest you. Then check your Bell Account Executive, a specialist in your industry and head of a team that will work with you to develop a Bell business system exactly suited to your needs.

Gain Control 7 Ways:

( ) Have total, centralized control over all company communications.
( ) Assign calling features according to workers' needs.
( ) Transfer unanswered calls after a predetermined number of rings.
( ) Tally all chargeable calls by individual, by department.
( ) Control both energy and communications with a single system.
( ) Add or subtract specialized features as your needs change.
( ) Use traffic printouts to fine-tune your communications system.

8 Keys to Cost Management:

( ) Make sure toll calls get automatic least-cost routing.
( ) Install an effective energy system at a fraction of the usual cost.
( ) Make long distance calls from outside phones over company lines.
( ) Back up every billable phone charge with full details.
( ) Rearrange phones and features without help from outside.
( ) Increase your business without adding console attendants.
( ) Limit which phones have access to WATS lines.
( ) Cut down on travel expenses by encouraging teleconferencing.

6 Management Aids:

( ) Let those using available lines know when you have to get through.
( ) Hear a special signal whenever a call is urgent.
( ) Secure your private calls from accidental eavesdropping.
( ) Have special phones and features for your busiest people.
( ) Depend on remote maintenance to detect and correct most problems.
( ) Get periodic reports on your system's efficiency.

Protect Yourself 7 Ways:

( ) Restrict usage on phones available to visitors, maintenance people.
( ) Lock and unlock security areas on schedule, anywhere.
( ) Direct after-hours calls to whatever desk happens to be manned.
( ) Make certain that machines are turned off nights and weekends.
( ) Detect any attempt to remove office equipment.
( ) Have your communications system checked every 24 hours.
( ) Be sure to have strong, local service backup for your communications.

8 Productivity Boosters:

( ) Re-dial busy numbers automatically.
( ) Recoup the time workers lose by repeatedly trying to complete calls.
( ) In place of several calls, have one three-way conversation.
( ) Eliminate the need for communications auditing at each location.
( ) Be able to reach your key people instantly.
( ) Discover new ways to reorganize your office, based on Bell technology.
( ) Spread the work evenly among phone order-takers.
( ) Reduce phone chores so the work of secretaries can be upgraded.

7 Energy Savers:

( ) Use regular telephone lines to control heating, cooling, lights.
( ) Reduce energy usage as much as 20% with a simple added feature.
( ) Keep an accurate record of energy usage, company-wide.
( ) Set up your own ON/OFF schedules, and change them at will.
( ) Shed peak loads to avoid exceeding utility's rate limits.
( ) Start with least-needed equipment when cutting back power.
( ) When areas become vacant, shift to more economical cycling.

8 Ways to Save Seconds:

( ) Add a third party to any two-way conversation.
( ) Have your calls follow you when you're office-hopping.
( ) Ring a buzzer in the mail room when you want a messenger.
( ) Transfer calls without help from the operator.
( ) Be able to answer calls to other desks from your desk.
( ) Use your phone as a direct intercom with other phones.
( ) Page people with the touch of a button.
( ) See instantly when a busy outside line is free.

5 Image-Builders:

( ) Give customers direct lines to your sales and service people.
( ) Answer customers' questions while they're on the line.
( ) Put customers on conference calls with up to five people at once.
( ) Silence your phone during meetings without missing calls.
( ) Have all outside calls answered or forwarded within 4 rings.

The knowledge business

equally well known here, position it with our biggest . . . sure!—IBM.

With Ed Asner as "Lou Grant" in a highly rated TV program about newspapering, Olivetti gets instant awareness, although we mustn't ignore the point that Olivetti is pushing typewriters and today's journalists us terminals instead of typewriters. (To use ex-newsmen who visit our old haunts, the silence of copy blooming on the business end of a cathode ray tube is shocking when compared to the thwacking sound of newsrooms in the days of paper and platen.)

Another larger problem with the Olivetti/Asner ads seemed to me to be their use of too many technical specifications and features. Too many specifications in ads can easily turn lookers into applauders, but we want buyers, not fans!

ADvisory. How many buyers should we hope for from our ads? Enough to bring home $10 in sales for $1 in cost. Or enough to bring home as little as $5 plus measurably increased awareness. Why settle for "adverts," as they're called in our Birmingham (UK) in-house ad department, that don't do as the Romans do?

In the Eyes of One Beholder

Advertising makes such intensive use of physical beauty that there are times when I've felt a Pretty Face Is Like a Malady. If you haven't got one, if you emulate those who do . . . beholders may become believers; so goes the irrationality of otherwise perfectly rational people.

ADvisory. When the old idea machine runs out of gas, one of your outside or inside ad geniuses will offer you a pretty face in a layout you can't refuse. Yours!

Beauty was in the eyes of the beholder who saw the ad hoc advertising technique of using the clergy as a beautiful way of creating illusion for a client. At least that was my reaction to an ad for the Dallas Hilton hotel.

At the same time as the appearance of the aforementioned Xerox and VW ad campaigns using religious figures, my copy of *Dun's Review* arrived. Thumbing through it, I quickly spotted the Dallas Hilton hotel ad (in which a nun was featured) as a classic example of the "mea culpable" ad.

75% of its space is occupied by the beatific clasp of hands and saintly smile of the lady in black, our least-likely hotel room renter. This three-line headline can cause you to lose faith in ad copy (see and sin no more):

When Sister Mary Agnes held a
conference, she chose the most
heavenly place she could find.

Two things occur to me: (1) if you believe this you'd believe anything, and (2) the copywriter may win this year's Kornfeld Processed Words Prize for limp finales.*

*The ad ends by assuring you: "*There's only one word to describe a meeting at the downtown Dallas Hilton . . .*"—but I don't tell you; you'll have to guess that one word by taking my alternate-choice test. (Note clue.) Check only one word:

( ) Kinky
( ) Luverly
( ) *Divine!*

TEN

Let's Look at Positioning

Position is everything in life . . . or is it? When I lived in Boston you talked about "position" only if it was a social place (and if you didn't have one). With "-ing" added, position becomes *positioning,* advertising's favorite word for (1) locating the client's business in the competitive pecking order, (2) determining where it should be in x-number of months or years, and (3) making strategy to get it there.

Flashback. For my book and chapter's purposes, this marvelous remark was recounted in *Time* magazine during the last Karpov-Korchnoi world championship chess series (the game of chess being the epitome of position and reposition). We are reminded that mystery-writer Raymond Chandler once dourly observed: "Chess is as elaborate a waste of human intelligence as you could find anywhere outside an advertising agency."

Regardless, we must study positioning as if our livelihood depended on it, because, in fact, it does. Why did Radio Shack run an ad with a headline asking readers to "compare Radio Shack's TRS-80 Word Processor with IBM and Wang," if not to position itself as manufacturer and purveyor of products of allegedly comparable, similar or better value?

Before 1977, furthermore, anyone comparing Radio Shack with IBM or Wang would have been looked upon with

Compare Radio Shack's TRS-80® Word Processor with IBM® and Wang.®

You'll See That Radio Shack's TRS-80 Does More and Costs Less!

When you buy Radio Shack's TRS-80 system, you get a very powerful word processor. It's complete with a faster printer and SCRIPSIT—the finest word processing program available for a personal computer. And unlike dedicated word processors, a TRS-80 can process your text *and* your data.

Designed for Office Workers, Not Computer Specialists

A TRS-80 Word Processing System lets your secretary prepare your memos, letters and reports electronically. Text is corrected and revised right on the video screen. Then, as many correction-free "originals" can then be printed as needed —at almost 500 words per minute!

At the heart of our TRS-80 system is our exclusive SCRIPSIT™ word-processing software. Virtually anyone can use our word processor, because instructions are displayed in plain English, not "computerese." Hard-to-remember codes have been done away with, because most features are accessed with just two keystrokes.

From the chart, you can see that Radio Shack—and only Radio Shack—includes a self-paced training course on audio cassette tape. That, and our superb manual can quickly turn typists into word processing professionals!

Feature	TRS-80 Model II SCRIPSIT™	IBM Displaywriter®	Wangwriter™
Block Move/Duplicate	✓	✓	✓
Full Headers and Footers	✓	✓	✓
Automatic Decimal Tab	✓	✓	✓
Automatic Word Wrap	✓	✓	✓
Automatic Centering	✓	✓	✓
Automatic Pagination	✓	✓	✓
Background Printing	✓	✓	✓
Disk Storage Capacity	350K chars./disk	264K chars./disk	240K chars./disk
Daisy Wheel Printer	43 chars./sec.	40 chars./sec.	20 chars./sec.
Display Format (Characters per Line x Lines of Text)	80x24	80x25	80x24
Optional Applications Software	Acct.,dbms, Stat. & more		
Audio Training Course	✓		
Approximate Price	$6297	$8995	$6400

Other TRS-80 Word Processing Systems Start as Low as $2932.95

We Make Spelling Errors Obsolete

Your TRS-80 word processor can even "proofread" your text to catch spelling mistakes—automatically. Just add our new Spelling Dictionary (available soon) and an extra disk drive. Features over 100,000 words with hyphenation points. You can even add 2,000 words that are common to your profession!

More Than Just a Word Processor

With our optional software packages, your TRS-80 can also streamline your accounting, provide fast and accurate sales projections and much, much more.

The World's Best Support, Too

When it comes to microcomputers, no one offers better support than Radio Shack. Our TRS-80 Model II is available at over 550 Computer Centers and selected Radio Shack stores nationwide. Leasing plans are available, as are two service plans.

For a no-obligation demonstration, call any Radio Shack store for the location of the Computer Center nearest you. And be sure to take your secretary!

Radio Shack®
The biggest name in little computers™

Order Your TRS-80 Today!
Because our TRS-80 word processing systems are so popular, there may be a slight wait for delivery. But at $6297, it's well worth the wait!

☐ Call me—I want a demonstration.
☐ Send me more information.

Radio Shack, Dept. 82-A-248
1300 One Tandy Center
Ft. Worth, Texas 76102

NAME ______
COMPANY ______
ADDRESS ______
CITY ______ STATE ______ ZIP ______
PHONE ______

A Division of Tandy Corporation Retail prices may vary at individual stores and dealers
Displaywriter is a trademark of IBM Corp Wangwriter is a trademark of Wang Laboratories, Inc

pity; who could image that—from then to now—there are even times when its (Tandy's) P/E ratio is better? Even so, a new position must be established and re-established by various marketing techniques until the minds of those who need to know are firmly tilted in your direction. And conditions must continue to warrant the holding of that position. If you don't believe me, ask the man from General Motors, Alfred E. "Happy" Goodwrench.

Some businessmen don't give a hoot what their position is so long as there's cash flow, good credit available, and better numbers every time they're added and compared to prior times. Others are quite intense about their status in the rating game: they would go to any extremes to preserve and improve status, regardless of cost or theoretical value.

Then there's the type who's dead sure of his position where it concerns what he possessively calls "my customers." I cannot identify with him. Brand or store-name loyalty is in a weaker "position" today than ever in the memory of any living American. You don't *have* customers; you *get* them; you *make* them come back as often as you can, and you never stop trying.

ADvisory. If you don't run scared you may run last.

I furnish this clipping for the opposing view. "What we're really saying," a Sony sales manager told his interviewer, "is that Sony's customers are brand-loyal. They don't shop on price. Price would be the last reason for our competitors to cut into our market share."

Despite the fact that Sony has a deservedly fine reputation in this country and Europe for design, technology, and ability to command what's known in the trade as a premium price, such a mindset is what I might nostalgically call "Philco thinking." Loyalty is also "nice and would suffice" if only it could be put on auto-pilot!

We keep advertising, positioning, cleaning house, smiling welcome, because loyalty is a gardenia in the corsage of positioning; when it turns brown, it's just a memory.

How Radio Shack Answered Its $600,000 Question

Many job-makers in the private sector have a better developed notion of where they would like to be positioned in respect to competition than of (a) if it's achievable or (b) if it's a practical goal. I have a really useful anecdote on the subject.

Flashback. When Radio Shack's new owner, Tandy, began opening lots of new Shacks after the 1963 acquisition, the Tandy concept was that those new stores should do $600,000 per annum in sales. That was the volume of the typical audio electronics retailer of those times, although Radio Shack was never the typical audio dealer most people thought it was.

But there was this one problem: the new stores we were opening were averaging under $300,000 a year. Half!

One day when Charles Tandy was questioning me about the 50% shortfall of his program—"M'progrum," was how he said it—I responded as I always do to actual or implied criticism: peevishly.

"Because *we're opening $300,000 stores* the way we locate and fixture them, and with our present product line," I said.

[Pause.] "You know you're *right,* Kornfeld," Tandy said, conferring on me the utmost compliment of his assortment of two. Then, after brief communion with his muse: *"And what's wrong with a $300,000 store?"*

The answer to that question—nothing!—was the most fruitful conclusion we could have drawn to get the modern Radio Shack into condition to make a race for first place. We knew we could structure a system of profitable stores at that level; we simply agreed to position the mid-1960 Radio Shack as a $300,000 store, taking the odd bigger fish as exception instead of rule.

Now we could surge ahead with armies of new stores as opposed to standing around hoping to change reality into something it was trying not to become (as so many fixated businessmen do).

I've watched some pretty big outfits try to change reality in consumer electronics manufacturing and distribution in my time: Sylvania, Westinghouse, Philco, Columbia (CBS), Motorola, Revere, Ampex, and others. The list of hardware "victims" of the post-war "war" between the USA and Japan is embarrassingly long.

The Case of the Knocked-off Radio

I discovered a use for positioning quite by accident, when pondering how to introduce a new radio of ours on the back cover of the 1969 Radio Shack catalog. Before that time, the idea of positioning had seemed a bit out of our class.

The radio, called the Realistic FM Concertmaster, was inspired by my urge to emulate the brainchild of an old friend, Henry Kloss, who had innovated it for his then founder-run company, KHL.

I was often "inspired" by Henry. As you may know, his latest feat of innovation is the big-screen-TV revival, first at Advent and now at Kloss Video. He is the only person in the audio industry to whom I ever wrote a fan letter (although I should have written one to the industry's most notable business success, Avery Fisher).

Flashback. My singular fan letter, however, was not inspired by the magazine article which quoted Kloss as saying something on the order of this: "The road to profits is paved with good engineers, not good salesmen."

"You're all wet about that," I scolded him one day at a hi-fi show in Chicago, only to be answered with Henry Kloss's articulate mumble and his whimsical look (of an owl regarding a rodent that has strayed too close).

The KLH radio was not difficult for us to be inspired by, or to improve in cabinetry and price. We also felt our sound was better. Another entry in the FM-only quality table radio contest was "The Fisher" interpretation of that masterpiece. Still another was fielded by a competing retailer, Lafayette.

I decided to position Realistic's entry with both the KLH and Fisher radios, and to omit the Lafayette (remember my theory about *not* mentioning the competitor?). I'd capitalize on an unprecedented chance to position the Shack with two of the foremost music equipment companies of the 1960s. A

The Realistic "FM-Concertmaster" is NOT the world's first high-fidelity FM radio, merely the newest. And by far the least costly. Take the $20 to $30 you save and buy yourself something nice. You worked hard to earn it. And we worked hard to save it for you.
RADIO SHACK'S audio engineers decided Realistic should attempt a better-sounding, better-looking FM radio than Scott, Bogen, Fisher, Harmon-Kardon, KLH, Zenith, well—really *anybody*.
We said "OK" but only if we could legitimately say three things about it: (1) that it *was* better-sounding, and (2) that it *was* better looking, and (3) that it *was* lower priced.
At $69.95 nobody can debate the fact that our new Realistic "FM Concertmaster" is $20-$30 below competition.
The three unretouched photographs at the right sort of substantiate our claim to greater beauty.
So the problem of legitimacy boiled down to how we could say our set sounds better without adding a new dimension to the credibility gap.
After pondering this subjective problem, we emerged from our smoke-filled lab with a momentous decision. To wit: *we would GUARANTEE better sound!*
Now most guarantees are as elusive as mosquitoes in a dark room, and often as shady. Ours isn't. It goes like this: if you truly believe that ANY one of the better one-piece FM radios on the market sounds better than our "FM Concertmaster", just state your case to any one of our 300 or so Radio Shack store managers and he'll give you a tongue-lashing (tongue in cheek) you'll never forget.
If he's as smart as he said he was when we hired him, he'll also give you a hearing test for free, because he'll have proof-positive that you don't know the sound of better sound when you hear it!
— see page 45

cover page of our annual catalog was the positioning arena; it allowed me to develop five significant points:

1. *Don't stretch credulity* in your haste to position. Beginning with the headline, I acknowledge there are other fine FM table radios and that Radio Shack's is not the first.
2. *Shift gears quietly.* While acknowledging that our entry isn't first on the market, I take advantage of the subliminal assumption that recency is better than initiation by saying ours is "merely the newest."
3. *Embellish savings if real.* Why merely report savings if they can be dramatized? Our copy tells the reader: nice things can be bought with those savings, and empathizes . . . how hard we both have to work to produce important "found" money like our promised $20 or $30.
4. *Consider artistic initiative.* Our picture shows our radio larger and in more detail; but by perspective, not by making the other sets look ridiculous.
5. *Challenge the prospect.* Near the end of the body copy, I decided on another way to impress our position: since claims of superior sound can be made by anyone and are extremely subjective, let's (nicely) challenge the reader. So our ultimate point was: if *you* can't tell the difference between Realistic versus Fisher/KLH . . . maybe "you don't know the sound of better sound when you hear it"?

Hectoring Ajax—or Out of the Kitchen, Into the Can

Suppose you're a soap manufacturer with an outstanding cleaning powder for kitchen use. You've called it "Hector" because there's an "Ajax" leading the pack and you'd like to mount an Homeric challenge. Instead of a head-on challenge, you consider taking a different position; in this case you designate it as a bathroom beautifier instead of a kitchen cleaner. As you gain success in your marketing, its advertising component continues to seek territorial initiative until "Hector" cleans just about anything cleaner than clean (whiter than white having already been claimed by another product).

Hopefully, your R&D is as productive as your efforts in the marketplace, or "Hector" will have hectored more than merely in vain. Every failure of the merchandise to match the marketing is another nail in advertising's coffin. Not only that, a lot of creative and hard-working people will have given you a piece of their one and only lifetime . . . and you will have, to use the wonderfully descriptive vernacular, trashed it.

Suppose it was the DeLorean car you were given to position? Obviously you'd consider taking prompt aim at the existing luminaries: Ferrari, Jaguar, Mercedes, BMW.

But suppose it—the DeLorean—came across to the public as an overpriced Corvette or as a Caddy Seville in stainless steel? Now you'd need repositioning; and it can be done quickly with a good car, as Audi has shown us with its 4000 and 5000 series, at the same time helping us forget its quite miserable series 80 (also known as the Fox).

Those neat little Audi 5000 ads quoting neat little German engineers saying neat little things (that were a cross between engineering acuity and love for the American hamburger) did a better job than Ford and GM may ever have the vision to try to do. Which is what? To position their new entries and simultaneously exorcise the sorry recent past.

What if you labored in your lab and emerged with a lotion that was a spray deodorant better than anything Chanel or Lauren had in their lines? Aside from hoping to change America's habits in regard to how you "stay fresh" all day, there are lots of positioning options to consider:

1. *Price.* Offer four ounces at the price of two?
2. *Package.* Both contained and container offer you a chance to position yourself with the leaders; "with" is good enough in areas where it's hard to be "better."
3. *Chemistry.* Create a scent with a sensible benefit, and never stop promoting it *comparatively.*

4. *Mystery*. Add something that has has a unique appeal such as a special formula or (not musk!) allure. Maybe here's a spot for a spokesperson who uses it because. . . .
5. *Display*. Create a better (because useful to the store) counter display.
6. *Sweetener*. Most dealers understand the benefits of more gross margin, liberal return and exchange privilege, floor plans, dating, co-op advertising. Sweeten your pot with something different: difference that's memorable is remembered!

In summary, consider our 54th Rule of Marketing:

---

54 When positioning your product or plan, identify other similar products or plans with which you'd like yours to be judged in the sense of parity or better, then tilt your advertising and PR implacably in that direction.

And consider as well this 55th Rule of Marketing:

---

55 Even if you elect to show your positioned or repositioned product in a more favorable manner than your competitor's, or as being technically superior, use carefully selected specifics and avoid aggressive adversary advertising.

In other sections of this book I've warned against using adversary advertising, but when your idea of positioning is to get a rival to move over (or move out), it's hard to advise against taking a hard-line initiative.

The technique is to "do it your way, but nicely," as the song says. The recently cited ad in which Radio Shack suggests comparison of its TRS-80 word processor with that of IBM and Wang refrains from initiating anything like the total war that comes to mind instinctively when Hamlet's uncle's only concept of taking the throne is murdering the king.

Radio Shack, being more civil than that, is peacefully willing to settle for a chart showing enough equals and superiors to win customers and influence future sales. Its attempt at positioning its TRS-80 product with an IBM or a Wang really comes as a free ride.

> ***ADvisory.*** There are lots of "free rides" available to any advertiser in any ad! "Find, remember and use them," is what I've always preached, rarely with lasting effect.

But position is borrowed, never owned, seldom a unanimous conception. For example, read the sobering complaint of this recent letter from a Radio Shack customer:

"Our company has been doing research into computers and word processing equipment, and it has been my recommendation . . . that your Model II TRS-80 would be our best buy. I thought you might like to know [what our people] said . . . each of them was put off merely because of the brand name Radio Shack which has some very unfortunate word associations . . . your product is good but it sounds tacky."

> ***ADvisory.*** Even if you're the world sales leader in your business, and even when you're over 60 years old and $2 billion in sales, you can't expect to convince everyone that your sound is the sound of music. And so? So don't waste money in the attempt. There are worse situations than being rich and ordinary.

Perceptions of Parity

Recently someone sent me a book on positioning, knowing I was trying to make noise like a literary cheese. When I took a peek at the table of contents I found something of immediate interest—commentary on what the authors call "The 'Against' Position" and I call "Adversary Advertising." Here the subject was Avis' famous "We Try Harder" asault on Hertz' dominant position, a classic tale of positioning (with all due attendant myths).

"Many marketing people," say co-authors Al Ries and Jack Trout in *Positioning: The Battle for Your Mind* (McGraw-Hill, 1981), "have misread the Avis story [assuming Avis] was successful because it tried harder.

"Not at all," they continue. "Avis was successful because it related itself to Hertz. If trying harder were the secret of success, Harold Stassen would have been President many times over," is their amusing analogy.

> ***ADvisory.*** In my opinion, the day you don't get there by trying harder is the day you learned you were a principal beneficiary of the will of J. Paul Getty.

Flashback. Coincidentally, after the surprising victory of Mitterand over Giscard D'Estaing, a French friend told me, "It was as if Stassen had won over Carter."

The "We Try Harder" theme referred to by Ries and Trout is what Avis' legendary boss, Robert Townsend, got by toughing it out with his advertising agency. As he tells it, he selected Doyle Dale Bernbach, one of Madison Avenue's biggest ad agencies, on the condition that DDB would get Avis $5 million worth of advertising for $1 million. Why 5 for 1? Because Hertz was five times better off than Avis. And Hertz—like Mt. Everest, I guess—was there to be climbed.

When I first made noise like the writing of this book, I was told: "Read Townsend's book *Up the Organization* and see what a million-seller business book looks like." I did. And I enjoyed its alphabetized list of macho maxims.

But the agency story, hmmm, is THAT what Bernbach said about the 5-for-1 challenge?—"If you want five times the impact, give us ninety days to learn enough about your business to apply our skills, and then run every ad we write where we tell you to run it." Well, well.

My reaction was this 56th Rule of Marketing:

---

56 Don't give the keys to your kingdom to ANYONE inside or outside the company unless you know for sure that a preemptive nuclear strike is now in progress and it's D + 10 minutes.

It will not be of the essence to know whose strike it is.

The desire by Avis, at least initially, was to achieve parity with Hertz: equivalence in the marketplace where vehicles are rented and leased, and in people's minds. Parity for Avis vs. Hertz, as for K mart vs. Sears, would be a nice—but scarcely endgame—position. With the momentum of your struggle for parity comes the impetus to pass and stay ahead.

And thus my 57th Rule of Marketing comes into relevance: It warns:

---

57 If the position of your product is seen as parity with others on the market, repeat "vive la différence" aloud until you've worked out a strategy for making it higher and less vulnerable. It's not good enough to be Just As Good.

Don't Try to Sell Me Any!

From *Ad Forum* magazine we get a window to the mind of jingle king Spencer Michlin on this matter of parity and how to avoid it via the technology of advertising. "Today, advertising is so heavily censored: networks, the FCC, the SEC, the Food and Drug Administration . . . it has become harder and harder to say meaningful but good things about your product or service. Besides—[my italics]—*the vast majority of products are at parity.*"

And so? "You cannot say one headache remedy is better than another. But you can make 'em feel good about it. You can make your advertising memorable. You can surround your product with an 'emotional gift wrapping.'" (Like a jingle.)

What a dismal position, parity! Accept it at your own risk. Don't try to sell me any; I'm the guy who has described his business for years in this manner: "The only catalog (store) (product line) that isn't Me Too." My pet jingle is a one-noter: the cash register ringing up sales.

Lena Horne's grandmother early in life told little Miss Horne how to overcome the conventional parity of a white/black world with remarkable clarity, saying: "You will look people in the eye, and speak distinctly, and you will never let anyone see you cry."

If you accept "me too" as your position, you perish, twisting slowly in the wind of time. Don't! Instead, sample these tidbits of current real-life refusal to accept parity as position:

Small cars compared: "The best way to appreciate an Isuzu is to test-drive a Rabbit." (Newspaper ad.)

We advertised, you didn't: "If you live in this rapidly growing region, we want to be YOUR Discount Broker!" (Ad in regional edition of financial publication.)

Similarity rejected: "Penn began its campaign with the slogan: 'Goodbye, Gatorade, new Pripps Plus is here.'" (Magazine article.)

Couldn't care less about Hyatt-Regency: "Happy birthday, Chatsworth. I couldn't get you a reservation at the Americana Hotel in Fort Worth, but I got you something almost as nice," says tycoon showing butler new Rolls Royce outside window. (Ad run in newspapers and magazines to position new luxury hotel.)

Brands have unique personality (and to hell with generics?): "How people feel about a brand rather than what the brand does" is terribly significant, says Young & Rubicam, the largest U.S. agency, advertising advertising's best friend: the brand manufacturer. *(Wall Street Journal.)*

> ***ADvisory.*** When you start feeling ordinary and equal, fight back with repositioning and originality!

Soup's on, but not just anybody's: Although it'll be difficult, says a securities analyst who follows Campbell's Soup Company's progress, they're going to start yet another drive to make more folks hungrier for more soup. *(Wall Street Journal.)* You can be sure, Sir Thomas, the drive won't include your brand name; parity's not canned at Campbell's!

Along the cereal circuit: Despite "a strong brand name and good consumer awareness," Ralston Purina's Chex brand cereal has a "stodgy image" and anyway somebody in the front office knows things can always be better; they're creating some new advertising and reformulating the cereal. (Opus cit.) In positioning, things like reformulation help you put parity in its proper place—slightly east of Poland.

Pringle's fights back: Proctor & Gamble's alleged losses on the formed and canned potato chip, Pringle's, are of "Edsel proportions," but P&G are going back to the drawing board and the lab to prove they can change drain to gain. (Opus cit.) Not parity, not even a commodity, says the munching crowd; but the people in the Ivory tower don't believe in not trying to convert alleged failure into actual opportunity.

Once when a Radio Shack buyer told me "our CB antennas are just about the same as others," he was startled at the emphasis of my disagreement. Having started my own antenna factory with $80,000 after a midwest firm rejected my million buck offer for theirs, my pride was involved, but so was my common sense. As Charles Tandy used to say, "When you put your name on a product, the product is *yours* and no one else's."

Genereal Disease, Anyone?

Business Week magazine tells us in a recent article how "generics and house brands are moving in to reduce the number of name brands on the shelf." In the case of food marketing, "the merchandising schemes now under way may change the face of grocery selling forever."

What's "generic?" Is it a position? Not exactly. It's an adjective used to modify product—i.e., a "generic product" is one that is brandless. We can make it a noun, too, by saying "a generic" is any unbranded product, regardless of whether or not your dictionary knows it (mine didn't).

The brand people see generics as a disease for making them sick. Some business people see it as a way to get well. I see it as a road to nowhere, a marketing plan for an increasingly impoverished but commodity-rich society whose fear of profits makes creativity a witch for burning. (Their reward will be endless standing on line.)

Where they sell generics you buy coffee that is simply labeled COFFEE; no capitalistic reek of advertising, none of the trickiness of maker's mark. You buy PANTYHOSE, TOOTHPASTE, BEER, YOGHURT, WHITE WINE. Neat or drab, tasty or tasteless, but cheap. Carried to its extreme, however, this interesting new game of commodity poker won't be dealer's choice; it'll be state's rights, and neither fun nor games.

As we read along in *Business Week* we learn that PAPER TOWELS and disposable DIAPERS outsell Pampers in a Denver supermarket chain.

Calling this merchandise "No-Frills Food," a monicker not even an in-house ad agency would be able to sell its management, the article claims No-Frills creates "anxious moments for packaged food and household product brand managers." It claims savings to consumers of up to 20%. And credits those elusive experts lazy writers call "many observers" as saying they smell a 25% takeover of the grocery biz in the 1980s.

The real crusher is a grocer with the bad case of what I've dubbed "genereal disease." He says that "when people shop [his store] they remember the buck—not the brand advertising."

Depression (recession) is mighty hard on advertising claims, but a great fertilizer for generics. And the threat to the position of national brands isn't really generics; the latter will typically be located near the branded merchandise and when the economy sours or the Have Nots have even less, they'll get sold. The advertising for generics is for the store, not the merch.

ADvisory. The real threat to conventional merchandising is Private Label. Not only in my opinion but in my experience as well.

Today you'd be hard pressed to find a drug store, food

store or department store without a slew of house-brand goods. I've made them my position for 25 years. My position, but not my threat. I like the business and I've succeeded in it. There are 1000 other ways to say "Open sesame."

Privacy as Position

Radio Shack's detour from public to private label dates back to the mid 1950s when the just-founded hi-fi audio manufacturing firm of Harman-Kardon offered to make us an FM tuner and a matching amplifier. The success of that tuner and that amplifier, at $39.95 and $29.95 respectively, whetted my appetite for more.

In 1955 I went on a "fishing" expedition to Japan to see what we could find. We found plenty. Plenty of skillful and dedicated workers, plenty of manufacturers eager to export and, above all, eager to please. We opened a trading company in Tokyo in that same year, and stayed with it even when other importers told us it was too high a price to pay to have profit centers on both sides of the water.

By 1963, when our new owner (Tandy Corporation) came to Boston to see what adversity—mostly poor credit collection—had done to its new acquisition, you may imagine my delight at finding Tandy so gung-ho on private label that he couldn't wait for me to close out the national brands that had co-existed on our shelves with our own Realistic, Archer, and Micronta imports.

The difference between old and new Radio Shack managements was simple. The old came from the "We Have Everything So Nobody Has to Walk" position of merchandise assortment, and Tandy from its obverse: "We Have Only What We Have and It's All Ours." We dropped our stock-keeping units from 15,000 to 2500 and, as Tandy liked to say, "never looked back."

Flashback. A Mr. Murao, at Toshiba's headquarters in Tokyo, once asked me to come over and gives his sales-samurais a lecture on The Radio Shack Way. "For you I'll do it, Murao-san," I told him, "but I guarantee nothing I say will make sense to your people."

I put on my professor's hat and went downtown to teach for an hour. Winding up my remarks with full details on how Radio Shack now sold *only its own brands* as the key component of our success story, I asked for questions. Hand raised. Questioner recognized.

"Do you carry Sony line?"

"No," said I, emphasizing it by adding a loud "ee-YAY," which is sort of Japanese for NO.

"Soooo," replied my questioner, smiling, "then how you be success in retail store without Sony line?"

Get the picture, Shirohige? I'd talked for a solid hour on how our basic strategy was NOT to carry other brands, and gotten nowhere!

Even when presented a fact like a Radio Shack, it seems beyond the faith and experience of the average retailer or supplier to believe stores can succeed without a strong position in brand products. Even though privacy assures you these four initiatives:

1. *Exclusivity:* Outlets you control won't arbitrarily alter your price on YOUR product; if you do it, it's at your own discretion!
2. *Satisfaction:* Don't tell me you and your group don't have more pride in the work when the brand is YOUR brand!
3. *Creativity:* Privacy offers you glorious opportunities to do really creative things—for example, one of my own pet projects was the million-seller Realistic cube "Weatheradio"—and match your skills with the rest of the industry, not as a test of machismo but as a fact of business life.
4. *Commodity avoidance:* What's worse than to have your hottest product—and the hot ones are the first to get hit!—become a commodity? How? By discovering in the morning newspaper that, once again, you're selling at the wrong price.

My 58th Rule of Marketing tells you exactly what it meant by the word:

---

58 A commodity is a product whose retail value is reduced to its lowest common denominator by having its value known and agreed on and changed at the whim of the Market. To make your product a product instead of a commodity, ADD VALUE to it, and CHARGE FULLY for the value added.

It must be a reflex action at Gucci.

PR's Place in Positioning

PR is the accepted acronym for Public Relations except for those who prefer a fancier description such as Repository of the Official Position on Man and God.

Townsend's *Up the Organization* cold-bloodedly advises: if you have any PR practitioners around you should "fire this whole department [and] if you have an outside PR firm, fire them too."

Though I seem seldom to agree with quoted sources, in this case I would indeed fire the outside PR agency. But I'd retain one or two PR types and *train them to do it your way.*

Radio Shack spent all of its childhood and most of its adult life without a PR person and without either a Marketing Manager or a Marketing Department. Our public relations stuff was produced by the advertising or treasurer's department.

The dissemination of new product releases, new plant and store opening news and the like were duck soup for our ad people. The more our own-brand program took hold, the more obvious it was that we were on our own in the electronics industry; national brand PR was meaningless to the born-again Radio Shack.

I have a 59th Rule of Marketing about that:

---

59 After thorough discussion by management, including observation of what others do, your company should prepare and disseminate its own PR in house, accepting PR as important positional advertising; even if unmeasurable, it is worth doing well.

This Little Piggy Had None

Aside from our "poor boy"—also a Tandyism—treatment of PR, Radio Shack ran until 1978 without a department or person titled Marketing. One reason may have been the fact that we were actually poor for so long, and another that supervision of both merchandising and advertising had been my plural duty for so many years I'd gotten us involved in marketing without having observed a need for its conventional bureaucracy. What we needed was manage*ment,* not mana*gers!* (The only other practical explanation is ignorance.)

Flashback. During one of many trips to Wall Street, I was asked about marketing, and used the foregoing as my excuse for not having any. Once I even overheard a guy misquote me, saying "The arrogant S. O. B. says they don't need any."

Maybe it was the same guy who asked me to identify our major competitor? When I said "Sears," he made a noise like "Funneee." There are those to whom the truth is anathema owing—I have always imagined—to its lack of duplicity.

Radio Shack now has PR and Marketing departments, but not large ones. And I have no rule about not having them. Insofar as marketing is concerned, most of the data is generally available n/c, including the data on your market share.

Market share? It's all too often a "big nothing" number that goads into furious activity the shakers and movers of this chapter's central theme—positioning. If the size of the market is x and your share of it is x-y, what's the difference so long as x-y is a satisfactory number? But have fun with the What-Ifs. Get them to sell you a TRS-80 with VisiCalc and play with market share; like "bottom line," it's "only a number."

A pal at Sylvania (before Sylvania became Norelco along with Philco and Magnovox in a triple-header of what went wrong with American business) once told me Sylvania's TV set market share (by rank) was #10 and they'd better move it up or else.

"To what?" I inquired.

"To #6," he said.

"Or else what?" I asked, knowing he'd say "or we quit the TV business," and knowing we both knew they wouldn't.

Recently I read where Panasonic was going to enter the ranks of Japanese electronics manufacturers in the rat race to see who could sell the most paper copiers in the American market—that colossal sponge that's universally expected to docilely absorb whatever's spilled near it.

Panasonic guessed it could get a 30% market share, which shows you how well they do their homework while reconfirming the presence in our competitive Garden of Eden of a new man-eating flower—the chrysanthemum with the gargantuan appetite. How different was it when America was in charge? Well, if it wasn't market share then it was market penetration or some other formula; the difference was that we meant it and that it would almost undoubtedly work.

Flashback. "The hell with that Market Share noise," Tandy said once on a clear day, "just give me a Number One in Profit Share and I won't care what you call it."

Final Thoughts on Positioning

As adverse to the corpus delictus as over-concern with market share can be, over-concern with PR can be even more of a problem and embarrassment in the hard, cruel world of seeking, locating, and setting up a position worth having and worth defending. The remarkable 1980s front office casting problems demonstrated by RCA, Bendix, ITT, CBS, Columbia Pictures and others show you the nasty color of adverse PR.

How, you wonder, with clever professional publicists lurking about, did the bad genie of hiring, firing and sexism get out of the bottle? Once again I blame it on nagging incompetence in the vicinity of those Louis XV corner offices. *The Boss can and must get involved* in sensitive PR situations, even if 'tis himself that's down the proverbial tube.

Many so-called news stories we read—even in our finest journals—are actually planted, albeit with a tad of re-writing, by PR agents and other consultants. But they do say some readable things in print. One I noted recently was to the effect that home-brewed PR is too frequently amateurish.

They fault the poor writing, the puny significance, the excess of space given to I. B. Honcho's latest benign irrelevancy. They find the important news in the release buried in the compost heap. Granted!

> ***ADvisory.*** So just don't sign on a PR-ist whose nose for news has a deviated septum, and don't hire a pleader instead of a peddler when *selling the company* is the project.

As I have often said about this aspect of advertising, the duty of all public relations is to MAKE NEWS, NOT WAVES. Another thing, Mr. Honcho: be careful about hiring a backslapper. *The Wall Street Journal* says a Search Firm—who else?—advises that "corporate writers can go far by making the boss sound like a star [thanks to the PR-ist who] generates ideas and acts as a sounding board for the boss." That far is much too far indeed!

And then later we read of academe's conception of public relations as position when the dean of a business school observes, poetically, that PR can be crucial to any enterprise because its fortunes float "on a reservoir of good will."

Nice metaphor, dean, but I think that that particular reservoir is usually frozen over solid. If you can't sink a Las Vegas gambling hotel whose bosses are tainted daily in our press, or a government whose elected gentry often seem to merit or attend prison, how can you expect to sink Firestone for a measly few million bad tires? Or Ford for Pinto?

> ***ADvisory.*** Good will is phoenix to commerce's ashes, yea, to the bitter end. The most ripped-off customer can be persuaded to love you the moment you pick up phone or pen and say: "This is the Boss speaking. What can I do for you?"

I'm about to say bye-bye to this chapter with a little anecdote about not being able to provide for every little contingency when it comes to positioning. Not even in that nine-figure (multi-hundred-million buck) contract you've just been asked to sign, replete with the customary booby traps and legal paraphernalia, and your corporate fate in the balance.

Flashback. One time when such a contract was laid out on Charles Tandy's desk for signing, he asked our lead lawyer: "Does it say what I expect to get out of this deal?"

Told that it did, "Then I'll sign it," Tandy said, picking up his Cross pen and inking the paper in his familiar left-hand scribble.

"You haven't even read it," complained counsel, alarmed and disturbed that his weeks of hemstitching and foxtrotting were being treated cavalierly.

"Hell, I haven't got the time or the patience or the smarts," Tandy replied. Then, looking around at his customary audience of bystanders, invited guests, and employees on their third hour of waiting for a still unkept appointment, he said of this and all contracts:

"If it's what you want, sign it. There's no contract you can write that'll dot the i's and cross the t's and be 100% perfect and binding if someone wants to break it."

So it is with PR, as I've prepared in a manner suitable for framing as our 60th Rule of Marketing:

---

60 If an event has occurred within your company that you think the world should know about, decide how to tell it, who should tell it, what should be told, make it an in-house project. Stick to the central and hopefully only point. Choose your media and addressees as carefully as you can. And then let it fly . . . FIRST!

If you fret and haggle over each little potential effect in terms of positioning, awareness, advertising, good will, you'll fall on your keester.

"Keester?" Well, that's yet another Tandyism. I think it means something like the aforementioned "bibby"; and I've always assumed it was the place that comes just an instant before the fall.

ELEVEN

Marketing the TRS-80

Every extraordinary event has its diversity of witnesses, all saying "but I was there!" in defense of the reliability of their account. Rashomon had--- was it seven? Watergate had perhaps ten times that many. Soviet Russia claims almost every important scientific invention of the 19th and 20th centuries.

Some agency-type ads claim their client has "re-invented" an already invented invention like the transistor radio, an item that Regency, an American firm, more likely invented than a Japanese company. If you think Betamax is the first video tape recorder, I'm told that Ampex, another inventive American manufacturer, was first on the VCR scene, though certainly not with one for home use like Sony's Betamax.

So it's not exceptional—in the brave new world of advertising—if someone proclaims invention of the personal computer or if others have different versions of its parentage. I view the Large Claim as one of Madison Avenue's recipes for feeding client egos while simultaneously feeding the public what it believes to be nourishing; actually it's a means for getting the client his ad without sweating out hard-sell copy and art!

Despite the verifiability problem of claiming creativity (small c), I claim fustest with the mostest for the leastest for

Radio Shack. It was probably the first company in the world to design, manufacture, and self-mass-market through its own store group a $600 personal computer system with integral 12″ video display: our chapter's hero, TRS-80 Model I.

And it was your claimant correspondent who authorized the design and manufacture of the TRS-80 Model I, and who selected its nomenclature, general appearance and first system selling price, even if reconstructed history evokes different claims for different names as time goes by (as created by newer pressures on business journalism).

Fortunately for you, however, this chapter does not dwell on the petty reality of initiative, but on this very large one: how the marketing of the first of the now extensive range of TRS-80 models and related products was carried out.

Surely this is one of the all-time All-American marketing successes in electronics history! Not many products can vindicate so extravagant a seigniorage, but, as the man said when his best friend found him in close quarters with his wife and asked him what he was doing there: "Everybody's got to be somewhere." How did Radio Shack—of all companies—get to be in that particular "somewhere" at that moment in history?

Ten Elements of a Cosmic Conjunction

What some call luck, I call fortunate circumstance when describing the evolution of the TRS-80; certainly a fairly large number of discrete events and situations had to be in apposition almost simultaneously. These included:

1. By the mid 1970s, Radio Shack was an established presence in both the design and the manufacture of electronics products and accessories, with 17 factories and 3000 employees busy churning out goods, mostly for its own resale purposes.
2. The traditional manufacturers of computers were seemingly preoccupied with mainframe and mini systems; at any rate, they were looking the other way when others visualized—and materialized—comput-

ers at 1/10th to 1/100th the price, and found ready customers for their little computers.

3. Computers were considered a rare species of creation requiring an extremely cool and clean zoological environment, special handlers, special financial arrangements; the cost of selling and maintaining them was believed irreversibly high.
4. A group of hobbyists was tinkering with computative hardware much as the old-time radio amateur whose chief thrill—aside from pinpoint communications without benefit of the Bell System—was building his own equipment.
5. Certain semiconductor companies were delivering a relatively new device, favorable in size and cost, called a *microprocessor,* also called a CPU—acronym for *Central Processing Unit;* essentially it's the heart of a computer and fabricated on a single silicon chip. (Computers may have hearts, but they do not have souls, even at Cray or IBM size.)
6. Two critical computer components—the CRT (Cathode Ray Tube) for displaying, and the keyboard for manipulating data—were available at surprisingly affordable prices.
7. RCA had a useful basic patent and circuit concepts for what is known as a *character generator,* which was also available at a suitable price. The character generator allows alpha-numeric data (letters and numbers) to be displayed on a cathode ray tube as contrasted to, say, pulses displayed on oscilloscopes or picture-images displayed on television sets.
8. Radio Shack had a need for showcasing its technological design and manufacturing capabilities to continue the process of upgrading its image—*improving its position*—from its 1960 reputation as "Nagasaki Hardware" to something as figurative but ambitious as a retailing Texas Instruments, or a manufacturing Lyon & Healy. (Note: actually I never bought anything for "Shack" that came from Nagasaki.)
9. Radio Shack's management structure was such that

long deliberations—or even short market surveys—were about as rare as oranges in Moscow; for merchandising projects costing under one megabuck for tool-up plus initial inventory investment, GHQ was seldom consulted unless (my favorite ploy) it was felt desirable to have an accomplice to share blame.

10. The company already had employees who enjoyed putting computer jigsaw puzzles together, including one who, by virtue of being a merchandise line buyer, regularly prowled the electronics industry for things to add to Radio Shack's unique "Parts Place" category of goods for resale.

These are merely ten examples of planetary conjunction in 1975, give or take a year, which made possible all that follows within the purview of my narrative. So you can now see more readily that for Radio Shack to do what it did, the ground had to be incredibly fertile and all the divining rods dowsed in a unanimity of direction.

Imps, Intels, Scamps, Zilogs

We're not quite ready for the marketing story . . . first there's some more background material required; I'll try to make it entertaining. Imps, Intels, Scamps and Zilog—while there's a community of interest between these particular names—reveal the computer industry's quaint way of messing up the Queen's English so outsiders may keep their ignorance intact.

When some of us at The Shack began going overt in our plans for a low-cost microcomputer, one of our factories, called Tandy Instruments, had just run out of something to build because its last two products, an LED alarm clock and a pocket calculator, were "too rich for our blood" in the U.S.A. and had to be transferred to the thin, pale hands of our brothers (most of whom are sisters) in the Far East to be made competitive in cost and sell.

Selection of the microprocessor (CPU) itself became a vital task for our Systems people. Imps and Scamps were CPU chips from National Semiconductor; the so-called 8080 was an entry by Intel; and after a time, Zilog—another semiconductor company from "Silicon Valley" near San Francisco—showed them its Z-80 microprocessor which ultimately became the one chosen for TRS-80 Model I.

Key feature of the Z-80 was that it was designed with what high-techs call "automatic RAM refresh," which, although it sounds formidable (and actually is), I can sort out for you in this manner: it took many more parts in support of microprocessors that *weren't* Zilog Z-80s to keep the RAMs remembering what they had "in mind" and should have ready for you to manipulate without a lot of ers, ums and worse.

One of our tech-execs recalls having lunch with a buddy at Mostek, a Dallas semiconductor maker. When the buddy said he'd like to get some business, our man Jack said:

"Okay, just tell me how many 4K dynamic RAMs you'll sell me for $1 a pop."

(Two things about that. First, RAM is the acronym for Random Access Memory; in use it's a memory chip whose contents can be written-in or read-out on demand by the CPU. The word random means simply [ha!] that access to the stored memory is independent of its location—doors wherever, so to speak. The 4K means 4000 units of memory. But most important, the $1 offering price was perhaps $4 under the going price.)

After lunch, the buddy met the price, to our man's great surprise, and presto! the soon-to-be TRS-80 with 4K RAMs had a jump on others planning to use 2K units. This epitomizes a jump The Shack has always felt it had on rivals . . . a genuine dislike of paying more than less for everything. Part of this is due to the late C. D. Tandy's revered trinity:

> "*Pay less, but*
> *pay cash, and*
> *pay promptly,* none of that 60/90/120-day jazz."

Many people, including Zenith, were approached to see if they would make us video monitors in lots of 1000 (our first estimated TRS-80 order quantity). That only one of them showed any interest is not surprising; when Radio

Shack went all private brand from 1963 forward, our manufacturing friends in America were mostly too large and too rigid to think of stooping for a little peanut like us. Seems they forgot how dearly huge elephants are supposed to love little peanuts (which explains in part how they lost—maybe forever—their radio, hi-fi and tape recorder business).

But one domestic TV maker listened to our pleas . . . the same RCA who was deaf to my pleas in respect of the videodisc player (see Chapter 6). Not only did RCA agree to supply us with TRS-80 video monitors—12″ b/w TV receivers without tuner, speaker, and certain other circuitry—but also the RCA silver-gray cabinet we selected served as a style guide for the rest of the system, while saving us the cost of tooling our own.

The computer itself—Zilog Z-80 and support parts—was located in the separate keyboard case, which we had custom made for about $50,000. Cheap?—you bet, and proud of it. You'd better "think cheap" if you're just getting going and you want to make a noise like an IBM.

Flashback. During this period, actually from 1970-1977, my GHQ was located in a raunchy-looking former factory a few blocks west of downtown Fort Worth. My office was private only if you overlooked a stained ceiling that leaked, a rug that remained ever-mushy from the leaks, a never-found hideaway for Texas-sized rats, and decor that resembled parts of a display thrown out by Georgia-Pacific on V-E Day. My homely office was far from displeasing to everyone. An industry pal from somewhere north and east of St. Louis visited me, looked around, and said, "Um-huh, umhuh, now I can see why Radio Shack has such a good earnings record, Kornfeld; it's because you didn't go fancy-schmancy when you moved down here."

"Listen," I shot back, "my dump on Commonwealth Avenue in Boston wasn't fancy-schmancy either."

True, he agreed, but I wasn't president then; possibly a hint that presidents are expected to waste conspicuously and want for nothing, so that the overall impression of Zerodefects Corporation is not equated with the rickety outhouses some private sectarians call factories.

My 61st Rule of Marketing got born, right there and then:

---

61 If there is too much discrepancy between the commercial housing of your officers and your troops, don't be surprised when the corporals don't behave like captains and if you are occasionally referred to as some kind of fink (because in a lot of ways you are).

During the 1975-6 period, Radio Shack had begun in earnest its push to get a small computer designed and made. Eventually, 15,0000 square feet of space and seven employees were designated as the Where and the Whom, formalized by a memo from the then vice-president of manufacturing, now chairman, John Roach, dated March 1977. We already had on our board our chief engineer for the project and a software specialist.

Whenever I'd see the breadboard that was turning into an equipment, I'd say: "We'll order it the day it can play chess with me and nobody from engineering has to hold the wires together or tell me 'it was working just a minute ago, but—.'" (I was planning a Queen's Pawn Gambit opening, if you know what I mean.)

One day they said it would, that in fact there'd be a microcomputer to be approved for putting into production early that afternoon.

Confessions and Blessings

As I crossed over the stairhead separating my grungy office from our grungy, windowless conference room, a distance of not over 50 feet, I noticed that Mr. Tandy was getting into or out of his black Continental. Aha, I thought, as I ran down to intercept him, just the accomplice I'll need when I tell the world we're going to try to sell something for many hundreds of dollars beyond our alleged inability to sell a single unit of anything for over $399.95.

"Charles," I panted, "I need you to come upstairs to bless a new project we're going to release for manufacturing today. I'd like you to see it and know about it on the bare chance it might be an exclusive winner."

"What is it?"

"A computer, a little desktop computer."

"COMPUTER!" Tandy said. "Who wants a computer?"

I spelled out what was unusual in the idea of Radio Shack's building such an item and my wanting to do it:

1. There were no known customers asking for one;
2. so it was impossible to identify typical buyers, also we'd ruled out thinking about doing a home computer;
3. thus we had no opening order quantity set beyond what would be needed to buy parts economically, but not less than 1000 were being considered;
4. and since all we had was a very rough idea of parts and labor costs, a selling price had yet to be firmed up, though "I guarantee not to give away the gross margin to prove any points."

As we walked toward the stairs, I offered one last admission of innocence: "Charles, it's the first product I've ever been involved with that had so many fundamental unknowns. And there's also this known: if the project does succeed it would be like inheriting a Boeing 747 and deciding to keep it . . . you'd need spare parts, aviators, crew, hangars, extra long landing strips, the works."

Confessed and blessed, the world's first mass-marketed personal computer inched toward its destiny with marketing.

I named it "TRS-80"—T for Tandy, R for Radio, S for Shack, 80 for the number of Zilog's "computer on a chip." I decided to use Radio Shack instead of our usual brand for serious technical items (Micronta), or our corporate name; here was a golden chance to make Radio Shack a manufacturing name in addition to its established retailing name!

Though the silvery-gray cabinet color came from our video monitor deal with RCA, I strongly approved its selection on the principle that we didn't want something as serious as a computer to sport racing stripes, funny colors, or kinky names like Peaches or Cream.

"It has to look sober, dignified and impressive," I noted, and "it must be marketed only as a 100%-wired *system*—not a kit." If we were zeroing in on business and school buyers, a kit was the last thing to consider; and while we courted hobbyists and welcomed their patronage, there were more people in commerce and classrooms than in workshops.

The pressure of current events such as electronics shows where rudimentary small computer projects were being shown or discussed, our beginning awareness of Commodore's PET, Apple, and others as contemporaries, and the need to "get off the pot" now that we were on it, caused a demand for a firm TRS-80 kickoff date. New York's Hotel Warwick and August 3, 1977, were selected; plans were made, invitations sent, and TRS-80 included in the annual catalog we would release to the public before Labor Day.

I-Day was now a reality, where *I* stands for Introduction of a hitherto well-kept secret. But D-Day was illusory, where *D* stands for Delivery. I'd been promised 50 off-line units in June, but the line hadn't started to run, and it was June 10th!

Flashback. There's another amusing but wistful story about the second week of June 1977. The opening of a big computer show in neighboring Dallas prompted a visit to me in my office by a top honcho from (then) rival Lafayette Radio. He was in Texas, he said, to take in the show and "see what this computer business was all about," which by deduction revealed to me that Lafayette had no plans for anything even remotely resembling a personal computer in its '77-'78 plans.

Would I tell the man from Lafayette—a nationwide competitor since just after WWI, headquartered in Long Island—what we had on our front burner? There was no way they could whip up a Lafayette-brand microcomputer before our grand introduction exactly 47 days later. The hell I would! They never told me anything.

"Yeah," I agreed."Anyone who isn't interested in knowing more about computers is some kind of ostrich."

Since that time, but surely not because of computers, this lifelong competitor shrank from 300 or so stores and franchises to about 8, from $100-a-million-a-year sales to about $12 million, ultimately to be folded into another company and all but vanish from the contemporary scene as a major force.

As with Allied Electronics before it, Lafayette was wry testimony to the never-ending saga of rise and fall in business in a country that's tough on losers unless they're in the multi-billion sales class. And sometimes even then.

To Market, to Market!

As part of the package prepared for TRS-80's introduction to members of the press and financial analysts who followed—or might now care to follow—Tandy Corporation, I included a four-page self-created "Interview with Radio Shack's President Regarding the Company's Microcomputer Business," to pre-answer many of the questions I felt I might be asked to answer 10 or 20 times. On looking it over after an interval of many years, I find still enough meat in it to pass some along to you:

> *Quote.* The image Radio Shack seeks is one of higher-than-average technology and innovation [and to let] the whole world know that our capability goes far beyond $100 CB radios and even $500 hi-fi receivers, things we also make ourselves.
>
> *Question.* Why have you called the TRS-80 "the most important product" ever made by your company?
>
> *Answer.* Because it opens all sorts of future horizons for related sophisticated products and spin-offs from microprocessor know-how, and may very well lead us into new marketing fields.
>
> *Question.* What about home users?
>
> *Answer.* Well, every user lives in a home, but we can't immediately hope to see products like TRS-80 used widely there although we'll do our best to interest the Average Man in our system.

Quote. We're not out to undersell anyone but to give value and reliability. That's what Radio Shack is all about.

Question. How does Radio Shack intend to market the TRS-80?

Answer. Our basic plan calls for one immediate method—via selected company-operated stores worldwide, plus franchise and dealer stores. There are at least four alternative methods, several of which might eventually be tested: mail order, direct-selling by salesmen, wholesaling beyond our established system, and discrete "computer stores."

Quote. The TRS-80 if nothing else should bring us the extra glamour you can't buy with advertising and sales promotion, or with claims and promises. Radio Shack as a technical company, a techniques company, a state-of-the-art company—that, quite aside from potential profits, is one of the fundamental aims of our microcomputer division. . . . So you may rest assured that we did not approach this project opportunistically, as, for example, a lot of companies did with things like electronic watches and CB radios. Again aside from profits—how much is image worth? Millions, we think. And how much is a new business venture worth? I think "incalculable" is a proper word. And why microcomputers instead of something else? Because, without any question, this device is inevitably in the future of everyone in the civilized world . . . now and for as far ahead as one can think.

Tandy Corporation's Annual Report for the year ending June 30, 1977, was able to carry a color photo of the TRS-80 on its cover because publication trailed the Big Apple (sic!) kickoff by eight weeks. In my "Industry Perspective" inside that report I wrote that its introduction demonstrated our "faith in the inevitability of such products, established a price point at or below the scant immediately visible competition, [and provided a vision of customers who were] businesses, schools, services and hobbyists [but that] home use is a later generation happening." Timely, free PR!

Tandy Corporation Annual Report June 30, 1977
Radio Shack
TRS-80

Massive free PR came when we bound an insert into our 9,000,000 circulation annual 164-page catalog showing two men and a gal playing with the TRS-80, and a price list indicating that while the separate parts of the system came to $649.85, the system price was $599.95.

It also let the world know four other important things: that it was (1) wired and tested, (2) NOT a kit, (3) UL listed, and (4) e-x-p-a-n-d-a-b-le.

If I scarcely knew a computer from a tv set with a typewriter in front of it, I knew enough to insist on those four details. And I'd enough experience selling audio in parts to understand that the pitch for a whole system is a lot easier for the pitcher to deliver and the crowd to see than a pitch of separate parts.

Meanwhile, back at the farm after our sensational New York launch, the orders started pouring in and the phones never stopped ringing. But our team of seven builders and designers had only grown to 15, and the first off-the-line TRS-80 was a breech-delivery on September 15. They came out one a day until the 20th, when 21 computers got built, but the month's grand total was a measly 130. October was better by a factor of 3X. Nevertheless, there was queuing room only, and back orders were growing like sunflowers—a new experience for Radio Shack ever since its frustrating but turbulent mail order days. Now, just to get on our waiting list you were asked to ante up a ten percent deposit as a token of your good faith and sincere desire to become an owner!

Chat-33 and Chat-35

A familiar problem was the threat of firing promotional salvos with only blanks in the guns, meaning that from the first day TRS-80 burst into being as a $600 computer system, we had many times more orders than systems.

Nevertheless, in my column "Flyer-Side Chat #33," which arrived at over 10,000,000 customer addresses on August 31, 1977, I told this vast army of potential readers and buyers to look for the TRS-80 insert in our new catalog, that its "importance goes far beyond [the fact of our] mere design, construction and sale of a fine piece of electronic merchandise; it signified the dawn of the microcomputer age in respect to availability and affordability to ordinary people, schools and businesses. There are plenty of cameras and TV sets that cost more!"

Eight weeks later I was back with November's Chat #35 which was mailed to the same 10-plus million recent customers, and, even though our cupboard was bare, they read: "A naval officer writes me saying [TRS-80] was an 'historical breakthrough' and will be remembered for all time to come. Meanwhile, we're oversold and flooded with inquiries. Orders are being filled on a first-come first-served basis. To get (or give) one for Christmas will take fast action on your part and . . . this isn't a come on."

Not to be outdone by the rest of us, Charles Tandy put his own little show on the road by causing to be opened in the basement of Tandy Center a store called "Tandy Computers." By God, they'd stock everything available, put out their own catalog, and even if it didn't succeed (which it didn't) it might show us what things aside from our own would sell and in what quantity (which it partially did).

Eventually, when I saw that it wasn't a moment too soon to open Radio Shack Computer Centers in the top 50 markets (more on this later), we converted Mr. Tandy's store into one of our Centers and sold off all the non-Shack merchandise.

Tandy's was an exciting idea: open test stores in the still unfilled Tandy Center mall and run them as working laboratories. He opened a telephone store. I opened one, called "Safehouse," for selling burglar alarms and other protection devices and systems. Later both were combined into one fairly decent store, but even by 1982 not enough oomph was evident to warrant going nationwide with a chain of Safehouses.

ADvisory. Oomph is 20% pretax profit plus 25% p/a sales gain, and oomph is a gross margin you don't give away! And if you don't have a better definition for oomph, better learn mine before you roll out your first or next pushcart.

By Christmas 1977 I had already felt the wrath of parents who were offended when I suggested in an ad that if they didn't spend the $599.95 for a TRS-80 for Junior or Junie, the world might just pass them by.

After muttering to myself about how it hadn't been my idea at all to insult people who didn't have $599.95 to buy the kids something smart to make the kids intelligent, I changed my mind. After all, if those angry parents were smart enough to read and believe my siren call, they were smart enough to realize that today's kids would either be marginal idiots (or heirs) in 20 years without computer knowledge.

It resulted in this 62nd Rule of Marketing:

---

62 If you can create advertising that is adversary in the sense of offering to sell something quite expensive, but complimentary in the sense of being an intelligent purchase, don't hesitate to be frank and hurt a few feelings. The "hurtable" individual is a person who is much easier to convert into a customer than one whose basic response is "show me."

Well, what do you do when you know these four things:

1. that you have a product that's a real winner,
2. that you have backorders like crazy,
3. that relief is not yet in sight,
4. that common sense tells you you can't stay as far ahead of the pack as you are now?

The clarion answer is this: *you start selling harder!*

Pricing and Blitzing

How the price of TRS-80 Model I in system form got to be $599.95 instead of $799.95 or $999.95 or even $1199.95 is a short but interesting marketing decision which, like so many others, is a smart call only if (a) the product moves at the price, and (b) the price hasn't come out of your hide.

I can guarantee you (a) + (b) is a winning formula, whereas the formula (a) − (b) tells you why the selling of television sets at "commodity" prices has been both snare and delusion for so many for a mere 1.3 generations.

After discovering that Radio Shack's company gross margin would not be torpedoed at $599.95, and on being assured by our factory that further cost reduction would emerge from mass production, I froze the price-point against all temptations, including one suggestion from an eastern computer-parts retailer that $1000 to $1200 was not only attainable but also reasonable in view of the scarcity of competition.

On or near the market in modest quantity were Commodore; Apple, which had color but lacked a video display and was more money; Compucolor whose 8001 was being advertised at $2750 as "America's lowest-priced personal computer system with color vector graphics"; and Processor Technology's Sol-20—advertised as "the small computer"—at $995 kit and $1495 fully wired (also less monitor); and one or two others.

My reasoning for $599.95 vs. other numbers, given it was not at a cut in normal gross margin, was just this simple:

The $100s or more per system that we MIGHT make if the business was out there, MIGHT be just enough to kill the product; and why risk killing a product when it was so rare, so prestigious, so far above our median $29.95 sales ticket?

There was also another point which had been demonstrated to me again and again in consumer electronics: whenever anyone produced a rabbit (winner) out of his hat, ten other companies would display their bunny at the next industry show, and two would claim to have fathered it.

Hence the rest of my rationale for $599.95: given the hard costs and high technology involved in making TRS-80s, our down-on-the-deck price would help discourage the typical loft-operator and low-balling importer from taking a ride on our bandwagon until the late 1980s, if ever.

To be sure, opportunities for such high class ratiocination as this are few and far between for most of us. When they occur—even from outright provocation such as Detroit had when the first VW tootled at them 30 years ago, and the first clean Toyota 12 years ago—they're often muffed.

We had another marketing tool at our disposal aside from exclusivity, good design, appearance, and price: the people. We had already begun to tap the multitudes through our flyer, our catalog, our other massive media programs, our annual report to shareholders and employees, our shows for the press and for the Street, our steady PR efforts.

By Christmas 1977, only four months after we had announced TRS-80, a mere 90 days after production had risen to more than one a day, we were ready to drop, as they say, another shoe. We'd decided there would never be a better time to really go public with the personal computer than ASAP.

Radio Shack was determined not to overlook the obvious, and the obvious was that very few people in the entire country had ever seen or touched a computer, much less thought of owning or using one—at $599.95 or at any price.

So we took the TRS-80 and a cadre of handlers and talkers on the road—to the people—beginning in March 1978. By then, six months after the assembly line had begun to churn in earnest, our number of computer-manufacturing employees had grown from 7 to 385; the factory size from 15,000 to 85,000 square feet; the backorder pile from a hill to a mountain.

Our road show, internally nicknamed "computer blitz"—we were advised not to use "blitz" for shows in England!—was originally planned for the 50 largest American SMSA markets. We began with Phoenix which, though only the 28th largest in terms of metro ranking, had the advantage of being a good Radio Shack city: close enough to Broadway for an out-of-town trial run and re-write, blessed with predictably warm weather so snow couldn't postpone the show.

The problem of simultaneously trying to sell TRS-80s in Phoenix even as the waiting list was growing was solved in an ingenious manner. We'd fill all the Phoenix backorders and have enough on the local shelves to fill all new Phoenix orders by the time our advertising program began.

City by city, we'd blitz, fill, stock and sell on a local basis, while the national program continued on its back-ordered way.

By March of 1978 another piece of our marketing puzzle fell into place when production and forward delivery schedules allowed us to announce that TRS-80 could now be sold by all 4000 American stores, dealers and franchisees. We might as well "let it all hang out," because the demand was such that in most cases we didn't even need display units. Surely this decision brought the computer into the grassiest of the nation's grass roots five or ten years before it would have occurred without this Radio Shack product and its marketing.

The original TRS-80 "blitz" promotional budget was based on an arbitrary per-store basis—something like $600 per store in Phoenix-size cities to $1000 per store in the biggest markets. In round numbers, Phoenix in 3/78 had 36 Radio Shack company stores, so about $21,600 was spent on media, travel and entertainment ($600 × 36 = $21,600).

This is the lineup of our media program:

1. Personal invitations were mailed to 5,000 Phoenix customers, selected on a basis of recency and frequency, as well as to our stack of mail inquiries from the area.
2. We now had an eight-page TRS-80 catalog, so 500 copies were sent to each store.
3. Mailgram invitations were sent to press and certain other influential persons, followed later by phone calls.
4. The company's in-house ad agency placed newspaper, TV and radio advertising, and created direct-mail literature.
5. A press kit was prepared by the agency, including a TRS-80 brochure, catalog, my interview and welcoming speech, the Tandy Corporation annual report, and one of Radio Shack's famous five-cell flashlights.
6. The stores got demo computers, window and ceiling

To the Doctor, the Lawyer, the Butcher, the Baker, the Candlestick Maker, and Everyone Else

Radio Shack introduces the most important, useful, exciting, electronic product of our time. The $599 personal computer. The new TRS-80. See it today!

THE SURPRISING TRS-80 CHECKLIST

- ✓ **EXPANDABLE?** *Yes, no hassling with major modifications. Just add from a variety of peripheral options.*
- ✓ **EASY TO USE?** *You don't have to know a thing about computers. The user's manual makes it simple.*
- ✓ **LANGUAGE?** *TRS-80 uses BASIC, a simplified computer language.*
- ✓ **REAL KEYBOARD?** *Yes. A genuine 53-key professional type.*
- ✓ **12" VIDEO DISPLAY?** *Included! High resolution screen with brightness and contrast to adjust to lighting variations.*
- ✓ **SOFTWARE?** *Programs for home, business, personal finance, education and entertainment available now and more to come.*
- ✓ **PERIPHERALS?** *Available! The hardware you need to make the TRS-80 into the system you want!*
- ✓ **SERVICE?** *Fast TRS-80 service is available through any Radio Shack store — we service what we sell!*
- ✓ **DEPENDABLE?** *We're famous for reliability and have been in business since 1921.*
- ✓ **INSTRUCTIONS?** *Our instruction manual has been acclaimed by our customers — both novices and pros.*
- ✓ **CREDIT PLANS?** *Yes! Master Charge and Visa (most stores).*

PROFESSIONALS? TECHNICIANS?	BUSINESSMEN? EXECUTIVES?	HOME OWNERS? HOBBYISTS?	STUDENTS? TEACHERS?
Yes, they're using it to keep records and save time.	They think it's the best thing since the cash register.	They've been quick to find uses we didn't dream of.	TRS-80 is the quickest way to grasp data processing.

It's true. TRS-80 is on demonstration and available from stock now at every Radio Shack store in this community!

LEVEL-I WITH 4K RAM	**$599***
LEVEL-II WITH 4K RAM	**$698**
LEVEL-I WITH 16K RAM	**$889**
LEVEL-II WITH 16K RAM	**$988**

Until the world's largest electronic chain designed and built the TRS-80 microcomputer there were only two ways to go: Build a computer from parts and pieces as a hobbyist. Or buy or rent a computer for your business or activity. The cost was often in the tens of thousands of dollars. And what you got was probably more than you required. Radio Shack had a different idea: to take the mystery out of computers AND dramatically reduce their cost, without sacrificing the essentials. The result is TRS-80. More TRS-80 computers have been delivered to satisfied users than (it's a safe guess) ANY other equipment of its kind. Unlike many others, TRS-80 is not just for fun and games; it's professional. It has its own 12" screen — it's not just another add-on to a TV set. And it's available from stock, not just another undeliverable advertising claim. Best of all, you can take it to any AC outlet, plug it in ... and put it to work. Our people can show you its benefits and unprecedented affordability. Please come in to your nearest Radio Shack store. And prepare to be very, very pleasantly surprised!

EVERY TRS-80 SYSTEM INCLUDES:

- *12" Video Monitor*
- *Power Supply*
- *53-Key Keyboard*
- *Realistic® Battery/AC Cassette Recorder*
- *2-Game Cassette*
- *232-page User's Manual*

*$599 system in stock, others may be ordered now.

Order The TRS-80 today at

Radio Shack®

Most items also available at Radio Shack Dealers. Look for the Dealer Sign in your neighborhood. Radio Shack DEALER

A DIVISION OF TANDY CORPORATION

PRICES MAY VARY AT INDIVIDUAL STORES AND DEALERS

signs and banners, catalogs, manuals, software, a memo explaining the "blitz" program, and were told to invite customers to the free seminars to see how easy it was to "hands on" our equipment.

7. Training materials—tapes, handouts, overhead projection lessons—were also planned for Phoenix, for a show that would open in exactly 60 days from then!

I personally laid out and wrote the kickoff newspaper ad, a 3/4 page ad which in reduced size looks small indeed, but you can see how almost every conceivable base was touched. The open area, lower left, was for local addresses.

It's likely that this ad, which ultimately appeared in all of the top 101 major market newspapers, was a first of its kind in the history of mankind.

ADvisory. Since that last figure reveals that we grew our show from its original 50-city to a 101-city plan, it should tell you that Phoenix was successful. We knew it because we *counted* attendance and sales (in fact we measured sales out to eight weeks on a per-store basis); results by medium—TV, newspapers, radio, direct mail invitations, bag stuffers, the works. In advertising, if you don't count you DON'T count as a person interested in knowing what happened to all 100 cents of your marketing dollar.

We blitzed once in March, four times in April, six times in May, seven times in June, eight times in July, seven times in August, and by November we had blitzed 101 times (× two days per blitz = 202 show days). This was the scorecard:

—3138 Radio Shack company stores impacted;
—$2,100,000 spent;
—thousands of computer system sales made in the "blitz" cities and directly attributable to the event;
—hundreds of thousands of people visited the shows, thanks to Radio Shack's expanded local advertising;
—50 "demo" TRS-80s at each blitz were in constant use by visitors (most had never been near a computer); meanwhile . . .

—regular TRS-80 business was soaring, and . . .
—many computer peripherals were being added to the line, including a step-up model (Model II) introduced in 5/79 and given a sendoff at New York's Hotel Pierre.

ADvisory. Radio Shack's ad budget for the year July 1, 1977 through June 30, 1978, had nothing reserved for blitzes or even a heavy media program for TRS-80. And so? So our 63rd Rule of Marketing now goes critical:

---

63 When opportunity knocks in an unusually loud manner, tear a hole in the wall and make it a second door. When your plan for capitalizing on opportunity isn't large enough . . . MAKE it large enough.

Going Public with the TRS-80

Before I reach back for a few more marketing feats, first a bit of candor. Opportunities to pioneer genuine product breakthroughs are only once-in-a-lifetime events and possible for only a few of us. My ADvisories on the care and feeding of this one should be read as the routine seizure of opportunity, NOT as a program good only for breakthroughs.

Radio Shack had just emerged, slightly bruised, from almost another comparable opportunity: Citizens Band Radio.

The Company's first own-make CB transceivers dated back to 1959, but the boom didn't arrive until 1972; a long 13 years had passed between the FCC's gift of this service to the American public and the latter's sudden massive attention to it. Since CB had cantered along at a level of 4%-6% of our growing business, it was one of the quiet, small-scale winners that Radio Shack likes to leave—albeit appreciatively—on the back burner so the scent of something cooking won't attract the competition.

From 1972-1976, our 4% sleepyhead had matured to a vast and treacherous monster: during several quarters of fiscal 1976 and 1977 it had soared to over 20% of our sales, twice to 28%. My "Industry Perspective" in annual report tells of the growth of CB customers rising nationwide from 846,000 in 1972 to 8,200,000 in 1976, but that "by mid-1977 it was obvious something had happened to CB." What had happened, in instant replay, was the coloring in of the other side of Mt. Everest, a "happening" that is typical of what shows up in our country when the public has an unscheduled love affair with a piece of merchandise. The timetable, to mix metaphors, never changes:

Buildup phase. Retailers can't get enough goods to sell. Importers, loft-operators, copiers and traditional suppliers place orders that double in size, redouble, quadruple. By the second year of the boom, the financial periodicals discover it, adding uncertainty and miscalculation to cover their embarrassment at not getting the word sooner; they also identify their choice of probable survivors. Everybody is an advertising genius: every time you dig you strike oil.

Acceptance phase. The big predicters and sorters-out like Arthur D. Little, General Electric, Gallup, Nielsen, graph the boom out to the year 2000, proving that—despite government meddling and eventual filling of the pipelines—CB radio was now a carefully plotted *10 to 14 million set per annum* business, as their research made abundantly clear. Well, not abundantly; you shelled out $800 to $1200 for their data if you were too proud to ask a pal to share his. (But all too soon the conventional wisdom would be back in its rightful place, and you in yours.)

Ad agencies were also striking it rich—convincing proper folks like E. F. Johnson that they should use four-color art on their cartons instead of the usual (cheaper) white, woodgrain or kraft; convincing Hy-Gain that it was smart to get its logo onto an Indy-winning race car; convincing GE that it should pay Howard Cosell to tell the world how GE was CB's heavyweight champion.

Longtime CB dropouts like RCA and Raytheon played with dropping back in. New CB magazines sprouted on the newsstands—all with ads from big hitters like us. We were "brilliant" because, before the boom, we'd gone into the manufacture of CB crystals and antennas, and eventually mobile and walkie talkie radios. Merger-lovers were paying too much, and loving it. The innocent new "Personal Communications" industry was demanding (or anyway getting) its own shows and conventions. And another 32-year-old entrepeneurial genius was born every week.

Disaster phase. Business in this country moves directly from maturity to basket-case the moment apparent oversupply becomes obvious indigestion. It happened in CB. The FCC changed the rules in its not unusual (unfavorable to established companies) manner. The ITC made one of its (later admitted) classic errors of determination. Price points were broken, then pulverized. Radio Shack bought closeouts from competition by the several hundred thousand.

Postscript phase. In subsequent years, CB returned to being a million-set-a-year business or less; many makers and vendors went into bankruptcy; survivors began the slow process of forgetting the lessons they should have learned forever.

If you think these memories aren't fresh on my mind as I tell you how we went public with the personal computer, please think again. Because, yes, sure, we were back in the driver's seat again, starting something over that had killed some of our best friends and left others crippled for life. "Boom to ka-boom," was how I one-lined it during an interview.

But I perceived some crystal clear differences between the fizzling CB and the emerging small computer booms:

1. The TRS-80 and its ilk were serious products, designed not for chit-chat, not for useful short-range communications or S.O.S.-ing but as permanent parts of the permanent process of educational and professional life. For example: the storage, retrieval and manipulation of essential data; the performance of repetitive tasks—tasks like the meeting of payrolls, the printing of mailing list labels, the processing of receipts and invoices.

2. The little computer was faster, cheaper, and more ac-

curate than many "by hand" procedures, but, once built into one's procedural life, such computers needed to remain "up and running" (as they say in computerese, never saying up what). Service had to be almost instantaneous. Fixes had to stay fixed. Bugs—another sample of computerese—had to stay debugged. Spares of everything had to be local and available.

3. The utility of a computer was dependent upon the kind of software developed for it—software being analogous to computers as LP records are to audio systems (the latter, in turn, being analogous to what computer folks call hardware). And it was not enough to talk software; it had to be ready to "up and run," unless you wanted to sell someone a smart new car that runs on unavailable Isogen. (If Isogen is your trademark, just remember who thought of it second.)

4. The price of little computer systems, although low by mainframe and mini-computer standards, was high enough to warrant sobriety on the part of the purchaser, not to mention a generally higher class of mind set. Yes, a computer system was obviously a product designed for longevity rather than for leisure, and would probably expand in cost and complexity. All this morally obliged the original supplier to remain near the farm to furnish seed and fertilizer and guidance.

5. The high built-in parts cost and "clean room" manufacturing environment endemic to computers would serve to fend off most low-ball copycats, leaving the field relatively free of chaps who don't know a peripheral from a periphery. Note: I refer to *business*, not *home* computers.

6. The sale of computers requires something more in selling time and salesman's knowledge than our big time competition—Sears, Wards, Kmart, catalog showrooms—would appreciate. Meanwhile, Radio Shack would, so help us, teach its 8200 shopkeepers how to sell a small computer without over-selling.

Flashback. Before 1978 was over there wasn't a store in the system that hadn't sold a TRS-80!

7. That the computer was a different breed of cat (we always call products cats until they turn out to be dogs), was made apparent by our receipt of letters such as this one from a staff member of Johns Hopkins University's famous Applied Physics Laboratory:

> I want to congratulate you and your Tandy team for the visionary perspective and drive you are bringing to bear on this challenge. The potential of the task you are undertaking—literally taking computing to the masses—is only beginning to be appreciated, even by knowledgeable people in our field. I believe its potential rivals that of some of the great technological developments of our time . . . because you are not only providing an advanced technology to the public, you are actually making possible the tapping of human innovation of an unprecedented scale.

ADvisory. A letter like this would make a believer out of a wooden Indian.

The View from the Podium

We began to be sought after as speakers. At the first Morgan-Stanley conference on microcomputers I noted that the personal computer was already showing up in bedrooms and might replace sex as a leading home entertainment.

At the National Computer Conference in Anaheim I trumpeted how nice it was "to share and debate [the small computer's] potentials with you, and—to be a bit chauvinistic—here in the Far West rather than the Far or Middle East."

At an AMA meeting in Atlanta I told them, "There will be some of you who—due to some failure of marketing communications, ours or yours—do not know what a Radio Shack is," but in spite of that we had done a most notable deed: we had managed to sell somebody over 200,000 computer systems and were shipping at a rate of hundreds a day. (Note that was before we stopped saying how many we were selling . . . and when others started.)

In my presentation of the status quo at an industry

event called "Electro 79" I described how the "price of success" had included enormous quantities of phone calls, correspondence, complaints, requests for delivery dates, questions on computer capability, service, maintenance, offers of help from consultants ("where were you BEFORE we came to market?") and from ad agencies ("we've managed to sell 200,000 without you so we'll probably keep going that way"), and offers from institutions of all types asking for free samples.

Flashback. The year is 1977, the month October, the scene the bathroom of my room at Osaka's Royal Hotel, and it's 7 A.M. Japan time. My bathroom phone rings; I answer it and continue shaving. "This is Mr. Z in Zanesville [to conceal Z's actual identity] and I have a complaint about your computer."

"What's your problem?"

"I need one this week."

"We're filling orders on a first-come first-served basis, and—"

"I know that," he said, "but I'm about two months down on your list."

"So you'll get it in two months," I said, sloshing lather onto the handset. "Save your money and believe me."

"That's not good enough!"

But for me it was. "Look, Mr. Z," I said, "I'm going to give you the name and phone number of my executive vice president in Fort Worth. Call him and see if he's a softer touch than I am. As for me here in Osaka, I'm hanging up."

Now the scene shifts to three days later in the Hotel Okura in Tokyo, where they also have bathroom phones; the time is 7 A.M. and I, creature of habit, am again shaving as the phone rings. "Moshi-moshi," said I, ever anxious to trot out my supply of Japanese.

"This is Z again," said Mr. Z.

"Je-e-sus . . . first Osaka, now Tokyo. I can't imagine why you couldn't call that guy in Texas and save your money."

"I did. And he told me the same as you . . . to wait."

"I can't believe you'd phone me here in Japan just to tell me the obvious," I said. "Is there more?"

There was. He wanted to know the name of our lawyer in Zanesville. Why? To sue us, although for what I couldn't imagine. The judge agreed with me: there was no cause. Even the *lack* of personal computers made history in 1977!

Back now to "Electro 79," where I also told my audience how "late in 1978, we announced plans for a new type of outlet to be called a 'Radio Shack Computer Center,' to be located in the top 50 major markets which encompass roughly 50% of our stores and sales in the U.S.A." Aside from lightening our load at headquarters, the centers would provide classrooms for area store manager training; schools for customers and prospects; places to display the entire TRS-80 line of hard and soft wares and furniture; fast question-answer service; salesmen for large or complex outside sales; servicemen to maintain the product. We met—and then exceeded—that promise.

All 50 were opened by December 1979. And by mid-1982 there were more than 220 Computer Centers in this country alone!

Alone? Yes, but we'd also need centers in Canada, Australia, Japan, England, Belgium, France, Holland, and Germany; by another happy accident, the TRS-80 program had helped turn sobering overseas start-up retailing losses into profits almost the moment the product line hit their shelves! At last we had a reason to merit positioning and more awareness. (In one word? Exclusivity! In three words: exclusive HOT product!)

Of course you know why I'm telling you these mostly very pleasant stories. It's because this chapter is called "Marketing the TRS-80," and I mean to show you that when the good fairy touches you you run to every marketing door: RUN not walk. Radio Shack certainly hadn't properly appreciated the size of a possible microcomputer market when it put TRS-80 into production. In proof of which:

—first production plan was for only 1000 computers;
—second production plan was for 3000 because "if it fails

to sell we can choose between closing it out or putting one in every store to help us control inventory";
—the '77 ad budget didn't include TRS-80 promotions.

What happened? When we saw everything coming up roses, we put on rose-colored glasses . . . that day! We hired new hands, rented new spaces, changed the rules for permissible inventory levels in stores, reserved a page a month for TRS-80 in every flyer, got peripherals made or bought—but anyway onto the shelf—with a minimum of meetings and executive massaging. In fact, everyone with sleeves rolled them up, everyone with hands and heads used them, and somehow we managed to avoid blowing our regular business.

Here's your scorecard for factory people and square footage devoted to TRS-80. Five years after those seven employees and 15,000 square feet went into our first TRS-80 factory, there were 1600 employees, 400,000 square feet, and six factories for the TRS-80 line in America alone . . . plus an acquired high-tech printed circuit board factory in California, a new joint venture factory (Texas Peripherals) with Datapoint. But even that's not the end of the story.

From zero computer sales all the way from 1921 to August 1977 inclusive, in just one recent year TRS-80 category sales soared above $500,000,000. From a zero base! In hard times!

What's it all about? It's about there being something more to marketing than four-color magazine ads, ubiquitous PR stories, $200,000 product display booths at conventions, and clever appearances on prime time television.

Did you get what that "something more" is from reading the TRS-80 marketing story as told by someone who was really there? A good team, a hard charge, 20/20 hindsight (in time!), and a willingness to do whatever it takes to succeed.

TWELVE

Advertising's Articulate Anti's

Among the privileges of a free society, but not necessarily high among them, is the right to advertise one's wares and services for entertainment, education, examination, barter, rent, loan, or sale. Advertising's rating among the privileges is clearly not that of a divine or "free" right, because the societies circumscribe it with regulations aimed at such worthy targets as honesty, decency, physical safety, and matters of law and order—including national security.

Puffery as a Fact of Life

In general (but without documentation), advertising is taken *cum grano salis* by most people in this country who have ever bothered to compare a product bought with the advertising claims made for it.

They are willing to buy a cigarette that promises them "a new world of pleasure," without, on the one hand, actually anticipating receipt of pleasure of that (or any new) magnitude, or, on the other hand, becoming upset by the apparent wide acceptance of such puffery as a "fact of life" because it exists in the real world as picture and printed word.

By the same token, perhaps, the BMW car is only the "ultimate driving machine" if you select a variational meaning of the "ultimate" (= maximum) or are about to die before getting the chance to buy an ultimate (= last) car. Not to forget that an ultimate (= most remote) car is one that costs nothing, has an EPA of 222 mpg, and drives itself.

"Anyone knows," says my imaginary heroine, "that neither Arpege nor Chloe could make me as lovely as the women in their ads, so I guess you can say the perfume and clothing people want to—and are allowed to—show off their goods in the most glamorous, hyperbolic way possible. But I can dream, can't I?" she pleads.

Yes, up to a point you can dream. And up to a point advertisers may spread illusion. But beyond that point—and admitting that we don't always know precisely where the point is at any given time, and who made it, and not necessarily due to mere travesties of taste or truth—you run afoul of nothing less than damnation from pulpit, lectern, microphone, picture tube, and publication. The din against advertising is a deep cry of outrage at least equal in intensity to that leveled at despoilers of the environment. And are minds, souls, spirits and aspirations not components of environment?

In individual instances, the extent of outrage depends upon the products or services advertised, the target audience, and matters of truth, taste and the like, which go far beyond a need for specification. But the seriousness of the situation is broad brush rather than pointillist; in the instance of TV advertising it is the medium itself that is under heavy attack, and from quarters that are as influential as they are articulate.

"Who the hell is Heilbroner?" I muttered while watching William F. Buckley, Jr.'s program "Firing Line" on PBS a while back, having missed his introduction but caught his name in subtitle, when he suddenly said: "May I say something absolutely shocking?" and the following dialog ensued:

MR. BUCKLEY: Sure.

MR. HEILBRONER: I will. If I were asked to name—and in a book that I'm going to write one of these days I will name—the single greatest subversive force in American life—I mean "undermining" . . .

MR. BUCKLEY: Television?

MR. HEILBRONER: Well, that comes close to it. I mean something equivalent to whatever it was that sapped the Roman empire or what have you. It would not be the Communists, and it would not be big government, and it would not be high taxes. [Italics mine.] *It would be advertising.*

That, as the current saying goes, got my attention.

Examining the Critical Pile

It turned out that Heilbroner was Robert Heilbroner, a professor of economics at the New School for Social Research, and that that "something absolutely shocking" wasn't the whole of it by any means. As the transcription of that program reveals, he had previously said:

> Let's imagine that we're back in 1945 [Note: pre-TV] just out of the war . . . and that I could show you all of a sudden . . . what an evening's TV entertainment looks like . . . people singing about flying, and housewives having little dramas about making the floor clean, and banks—these dignified institutions—debasing themselves with antics about what happens to the muddled man who can't get to the head of the line . . . can you imagine the American public being fed this constantly . . . [and what] will be the consequences on American thought, language, moral virtues, things like that. . . . And I think you would say, back in 1945, "God Almighty, God forbid". . . . And it didn't happen because of the government, it happened in the curious way that changes insinuate themselves." [Then followed a brief exchange in respect of the small amount of daytime TV in other countries.]

Flashback. I am reminded of returning from the Solomon Islands on a small ocean liner converted to a troop ship, and hearing my first singing commercial (1945) on the wardroom radio while in the act of telling a fellow Marine of my decision to go into advertising as a career. Far from being entertained by it, I found this form of advertising embarrassing.

Shortly afterwards, on landing in California, I found the war had changed another form of marketing: we were now to buy oranges *by the pound* instead of by the dozen. "All changed, changed utterly," as Yeats said of a "terrible beauty" being born, the change here being toward greater accuracy and away from mere digits which, however accurate, lack the "terrible beauty" of defining the orange by weight—with added intimations of size—as well by quantity.

Again shortly thereafter (pun intended), shorts and other essential male garments were offered in 3-packs, a marketing treat that is not always a trick, since "genius is the capacity to see ten things where the ordinary man sees one." Nevertheless, some critics believe advertising insures the sale of this perception to a bemused public, resulting in the sale of more of an item than needed and no savings concurrently attributable to multi-item packaging.

When I was in Boston in 1981 to receive an honorary degree from Boston University, its president, John R. Silber, gave me a little 32-page hard-covered book of his, entitled *Democracy: Its Counterfeits and Its Promises,* which would turn out to contain some of the most severely adverse comments ever made about advertising, none of which, fortunately, could be said to impinge directly upon Radio Shack practice:

"Once it is agreed that the criterion is pleasure, pleasure becomes its own justification," thunders Dr. Silber, drawing a bead on the television industry which, with its advertisers, has "promoted the pursuit of pleasure . . . as a substitute for the pursuit of *happiness,* [my italics] and is not at all what the Founding Fathers meant by what they wrote into the Constitution immediately following the three words 'life, liberty, and'——."

He speaks of the "ursurpation of moral instruction by cynical television advertisers" from its proper sources—school and church. "Schlitz, a firm with license to brew but none to preach, intones, 'You only go around once in life; therefore, get all the gusto you can!' These are not statements about beer," Silber asserts, "but a theological claim and moral injunction for which no justification has been made. 'When it's right, you know it' [tells the child watching a Schlitz ad with this theme that] ethical decisions—among the most difficult and important that he will ever make—are simple matters of intuition, no more difficult than the assessment of one's delight while drinking a can of beer."

He then takes off on breakfast cereals. "Dedicated to the pursuit of pleasure rather than happiness, television has reduced the pursuit of nutrition to the pursuit of sweetness . . . [via new] trashy concoctions designed to please rather than nourish." And finally: "Television has educated a generation in self-destructive eating habits [and] successfully instilled the idea that the first meal of the day should be dessert."

And another I particularly cherish: "The presence on television of a lovable, racist bigot like Archie Bunker is frequently applauded on the grounds that it does the country good to see itself as it is—even to the point of indecent exposure. . . . In sordid truth, Archie gives us pleasure by indulging gloriously in our vices, and we indulge vicariously through him, with no feeling of guilt: without responsibility or guilt, we achieve no-fault participation." (Of course, there is no-fault advertising before, during, and after.)

How the student perceives advertising, now that we have the academician's viewpoint, may very well be summed up in this excerpt from a young American writer's first major literary publication. "Advertising," says Andrea Lee, "of course, is the glamorous offspring of capitalism and art." But why "of course"? And what, after all, is propaganda?

Pravda Means "Truth"

A wild paradox, wouldn't you agree, that the name of Russia's best-known newspaper, Pravda, means truth in their language! One learns this from reading the memoirs of composer Dmitri Shostakovich who, inasmuch as he was the opposite of sanguine in practically all matters, eventually got around to giving one of my book's chosen professions its due. "Truth and advertising have little in common," he said, as casually as if he were pointing to a fly that had just landed in the borscht.

"A hue and cry in itself doesn't prove a thing," Shostakovich said, and "often is nothing but publicity. I remember that when I was young they used to lure people into side shows with loud patter, but once you got inside it was a total disappointment."

To a sensitive soul like his, such deceit can cause permanent damage; but as noted previously, *most people get hardened to "total disappointment" by registering it as less than total* on their own private balance sheets of Promise and Fulfillment.

After all, yes, there really were tangible freaks in the side shows attended by young Dmitri Shostakovich. The problem was that their freakishness failed miserably to live up either to advertising claims or to satisfactory fleshly manifestations.

If you respond to the advertised request to "give your cold to Contac" with a purchase, you merely slough off some angst onto the pill bottle, trusting in Nature to come again into your life (with a fix in time to save thine!). The product, Contac, is but a minor freak in the side show of harmless illusion. And if such legerdemain were the end-all of our problem of truth and taste in advertising we could—as another idiom says so aptly—"live with it."

We Rolex watch owners suffer not only the illusion that our watches are really worth x-times more than comparable instruments, but also the mortification of being caught in public with a status symbol on the left wrist. Nevertheless, none of this is the fault of Rolex, if you can overlook the allegation that the case is not actually *carved* from a solid block of gold or steel but *machined.* But then along come timepieces called (in an ad) "remarkable replicas, made by another fine Swiss watchmaker"; still okay because the whole world is probably a knock-off of some other world, right?

Consider, however, the headline of a newspaper ad for the replica Rolex, and then you tell me how you'd rate it on a scale of illusion of 10-max to 0-min. It reads: "FOR LOVERS OF CLASSICS WHO DON'T OBJECT TO SAVING $1500-$2000."

How are those savings justified? By the following copy

claim: "The Men's Rolex costs $2100—the Women's model $1600. The price of these men's or women's . . . replicas is just $99." Still okay; we'll ignore the omission of details such as jewel count, underwater capability, craftsmanship, etc., which are presumably not really replicated in the sense of cloning.

But we most certainly will not ignore the line of body copy that states: "And when you can buy both his and hers for a savings of $3502, that's a reason as good as gold." No way!

The time is long gone when you could advertise "savings" as an automatic result of price reduction, not to mention savings that are derived from comparing unlike items!

Years ago retailers consented to agree that List Price as a basis for claims of savings (List Price $49.95, Sale Price $24.95, Save 50%) was a no-no *unless the list price was your actual regular selling price.* We also agreed on the meaning of the word savings. It was to be used only when your own actual regular selling price was reduced to a lower selling price, either temporarily or permanently.

Even in the instance of a special purchase (such as a $20 necktie bought into the store to be sold at $8.88) you were not allowed to claim savings per se. Why? because you were probably going to get your normal gross margin on the sale, and the "reduction" was not from your regular stock's regular price since the item was not *from* your regular stock.

Also, as a condition of "saving" $1500-$2000, your imitation Rolex isn't 14K or 18K gold; they acknowledge it to be gold electroplate. So who's complaining? Kornfeld! Not about the gold electroplate, but because the $1500-$2000 savings *aren't savings* but rather the lure of fool's gold that is one of advertising's many serious problems. (The mere fact that you didn't spend doesn't mean you saved!)

I'm not adverse to the idea of calling it a look-alike Rolex, or to legitimate comparison of real to replica, or even to calling out the price difference (c.f. fake diamond advertising). My opposition is to an overt claim of savings that cannot be justified per the above-cited accepted industry standard.

But let's not let the media off without a hard stare. Is it

not, in fact, the medium's (here the *Wall Street Journal*'s) job to question the admissibility of advertising when the question of propriety is as clear as my example?

Look, all ye advertisers whose loyalty to product or client has incited you to the occasional lapse—see how easy it would have been to re-write the headline:

FOR LOVERS OF CLASSICS—leave unchanged that first line. WHO DON'T OBJECT TO SAVING—change that second line to read WHO DON'T ENJOY SPENDING. And line three—$1500-$2000—is also acceptable as written. Down in the body copy's many lines of salesmanship, there's only that one sentence to change, the one reading, "And when you can buy both his and hers for a savings of $3502, that's a reason that's as good as gold." Why not say—"for $3502 less than the real thing"—and be satisfied? Why not?

Is there some little demon within us salesmen that prods us to the brink of hyperbole and then says, "The next little step is yours, Master," which we then take despite our better instincts?

Earlier, I described Swami Pradhupāda's second basic defect of man . . . remember? It was his susceptibility to being illusioned, where "illusion" means to accept "something which is not." Such acceptance, in turn, implies *a source of illusion,* and, I'm afraid, advertising has come to be looked upon as being precisely that—the wellhead or at least the medium of transmission of "something which is not." And the degree of "something which is not-ness" matters in direct proportion to the fundamental importance of the subject to society.

My example of the Rolex replica, though it calls out one of the least villainous roles played by advertising, at the same time *dramatizes the potential of ONE mis-cast word!* In the fable about the crying of "Wolf!" one time too often, here, too, we have a tale of the abuse of just one small word! And to run history out to its end, the matter of the first two A-bombs may be summed up as a choice among three words: "Drop," or "Scrub mission."

Falsies: Does She or Doesn't She?

An interesting piece in *Fortune* magazine told about a chap named Ken Mason who was "an advertising boy wonder in his 20s, partner at his own thriving agency in his 30s," and then went on to become president of Quaker Oats and—quit. The story was *why*. And my excerpt melds directly into this chapter on advertising.

"Managers, he thinks, do not pay attention to long-term social consequences of actions," says the article's writer in paraphrase of Mr. Mason, "and the results have been contrary to business' best interest. For example [my italics] *the fact that more than half the public now thinks ads are usually misleading* indicates to Mason that management has dulled a valuable business tool."

Ads that mislead, my common sense dictates, are ads that are untrue in one, several, or many respects. How is a layman to interpret such a newspaper headline as this? "FTC judge says Bayer Aspirin's ads deceptive." And the following copy which included such snippets as: "Sterling [does] not have a reasonable basis for claiming that Cope is superior for relieving headache pain caused by nervous tension . . . the ingredients in Bayer, Cope and Midol do not relieve tension, nor do those in Midol relieve depression [my italics] *as claimed in ads*."

How to consider this additional copy? "The commission said ads for Aspercreme are inherently deceptive because they lead consumers to believe the product contains aspirin, which it does not. . . . The case also names Ogilvy & Mather Inc., the New York advertising agency for Aspercreme."

Invariably such news reports include a paragraph which reads like this one from the same story: "Sterling announced immediately that the decision will be appealed to the five-member commission. It maintained that its ads 'appropriately and accurately reflected the scientific data.'"

May heaven help us, and "the public be damned," as W. H. Vanderbilt once said to a reporter, because, owing to our system of appeals beyond appeals and before settlements, we rarely get to the bottom of anything. The first accusation has an impact factor of 75. The first denial has an impact factor of 15. And after that it's downhill and single digits. Nearly 11 years were to pass between the filing of a libel suit by Bose Corporation against Consumers Union (Bose claiming that its speakers were improperly reviewed by CU's *Consumer Reports* magazine) and the court's award of damages to Bose, just to give you one weary example from my own industry and to note that of course (3/82 issue) "Consumers Union will appeal."

Then along comes Gerald F. Cavanagh, S.J., with a column in the *Dallas News* on ethics that drops a few violent depth charges. Roll with this one, if you dare: "Leaders of other American institutions also do not have the trust of the American people, but no group suffers from such a lack of confidence as do the leaders of advertising: [my italics] *they are the least trusted of any major American institution.*"

Is that on the verge of calling us the guys in the black hats? No? Then try to like your image as a sort of Super Pusher, as the cleric quotes a national poll which says (he says) that "more than two-thirds of Americans thought that 'advertising causes people to buy things they don't need.'"

Most awful of all is his Variations on the Key of IF: *"If advertising is more exaggeration than information, more trivial than tasteful, more crude than humane, then we Americans begin to think of business and business people as articulate, clever and smooth, but also insensitive, not trustworthy and perhaps even unprincipled."* [My italics for emphasis.]

The foregoing is quite an indictment! Without TV in the picture, so to speak, I wonder if it would be as serious? Or did something happen in the recent past to make it more true in the eyes of that writer—a teacher in the B-school of the University of Detroit, something that encourages him to believe that while business leaders of "15 years ago" had a confidence factor of over 50%, "this has dropped to less than one quarter (12.5% of the people) having confidence today"? Since that puts high confidence somewhere in the Johnson/Nixon era, Fr. Cavanagh, I would have to disagree that things are worse in advertising or the moral climate today, with the possible exception of sexuality on display and for sale CHEAP.

In the area of defective goods, he observes, "Since advertising's purpose is to sell, it is perhaps unrealistic to expect that product or company defects . . . will be acknowledged. Positive information that is accurate is perhaps the best we can expect from advertising."

America's most famous expert on quality control, since he is believed to have sold "zero defects" to the Japanese at a time when global perception of Japanese industrial goods quality was as low as such things can go, is Dr. W. Edwards Deming. An article in *Nation's Business* magazine has this to say about Deming, defective goods, and thus, by implication, illusory advertising:

"Deming's system begins by determining what quality is acceptable to the consumer of a product. 'Good quality does not necessarily mean high quality,' he says. 'It means a predictable degree of uniformity and dependability, at low cost, with quality suited to the market." This has to do with statistical quality control which, with a bit of planning, not only might be introduced to advertising but *should be,* in order to cut off these Indians at the pass. I will present a simple "laundry list" of AQC (ad quality control) checkpoints a few pages further on.

Surely it's not good enough that *Magazine Age* finish an editorial with these thoughts in reference to the relationship between advertising and freedom of speech: "This is a critical issue since, in some minds, advertising is something sinister and akin to brainwashing. Advertising plays a key role in our economy; it is also an important element in supporting a free and independent press. Considering the major role advertising does play, the view that brands it a public enemy is wrong and short-sighted."

But is it unwholesome to imagine that we could do without much or any advertising in our press and anticipate an even better product, as the *International Herald Tribune* proves with its six thin issues per week? Justification of 300-page Sunday newspapers even on a freedom basis is difficult enough without also trying to sell their lead banker, advertising, as anything more than what it is. And at the moment, its critics have the floor.

"You can't inspect quality into a product," somebody once remarked, and there are a lot of other things you can't do to prevent or repair defects, including talking them away.

On Infecting the Culture

Television's broad reach—broad because the reach of pictures is so much broader than words, especially in respect to children and semi-literate peoples—has made it a communications tool of unmatched power, and all in the short span between the end of WWII and now, a mere two generations. The abuse of such awesome power, whether predictable or not, is beyond dispute but, as we shall see, far from beyond debate.

The same Ken Mason mentioned a few pages back said in the same *Foı tune* story about him that "TV looms very important in infecting this culture with the very diseases businessmen decry: a lack of value on the part of the work force, loss of the work ethic, kids who don't have any ambition."

The dark side of television's nature has come under attack from such ambivalent forces as the Coalition for Better Television, and spokes-reverends such as Donald Wildmon and Jerry Falwell.

Nothing less than quality in programming and the responsibility for program content are at issue, with particular emphasis on what the *New York Times* specifies as "'excessive' sex, violence and profanity," its writers finally warning that those advertisers who ignore the storm signals "risk the same kinds of internal and external disruption they have suffered in the past 15 years from movements that arose from the left" (citing Ralph Nader, Gloria Steinem and Rachael Carson as exemplars).

Boycott is one of the weapons favored these days by social warriors who want to bring big business to heel for its transgressions, particularly those transgressions which I lump under the single heading Taste, even when issues such as saving the white whale or curbing the handgun are at the bar of justice, because if "good taste" is displayed on our boob tubes, at least our babes will not be exposed to "bad taste." I would have said "our boobs" but that would have been post-impressionism in the very real sense, or, since boobs—as a singular plural noun—has acquired a secondary (mammary) meaning, it would also be after-the-fact exposure.

On several memorable occasions, I, as the spokesman for Radio Shack, was offered a choice of boycott or shut up (in the case of taking an unpopular CB position), or boycott no matter what (in the instance of mentioning that among guns, handguns were exceptionally dangerous). No matter how coolly, how civilly one takes these threats, the blood rises to the face and the heart thumps like a kicked drum.

Nor is it always program content that offends. In the issue of the *Wall Street Journal* that was published exactly eight days before my 65th birthday, its marketing column writer found "commercials for pantyhose, designer jeans, bras and girdles, laxatives and feminine hygiene products . . . the most 'disasteful' ads on television," leading a majority of those polled to say they avoid buying them—the brands advertised—for that reason. Documentation followed, indicating that while 70% found feminine hygiene product advertising was in poor taste, only 18% found that to be the case in perfume ads. Only the unreal world has the poetic license to disseminate the stuff of dreams, name generations, and create pauses that refresh!

There are two vigorous censors at work, one wrapped around the other: the National Association of Broadcasters (NAB), and the Television Code Board. Many products banned from TV advertising in the landmark year 1952 have since escaped—I will spare you the details until after dinner—but one was taken to a poll: to ban or not to ban ads which pitch contraceptives.

"Most Americans Would Find Them Embarrassing and Distasteful, Poll Shows" is how the *Journal's* headline writer reduced it to ten words that may or may not shake the world. (Seriously, as it happens, the Planned Parenthood people think contraceptive device advertising is exactly what's needed to curb teenage pregnancies!) Taste or its lack, given the issue at hand, seems to generate "no fury like that of a point of view scorned!" (The dactyls are from an unwritten sonnet.)

To borrow again from columnist Milton Moskowitz, not only are there "always those who claim they know 'The Truth'" but the latter "have this peculiar tendency to want to punish anyone who doesn't see things the way they do." And the seven fundamentalist and conservative groups which created the Coalition for Better Television, says Moskowitz, "recently brought to heel some of the biggest companies in the nation, including Proctor and Gamble (P&G), our most successful marketer of consumer goods. The issue was sex and violence on television."

Infecting the culture via television—plus a heavy assist from its financial planner, advertising—has other implications beyond *loss of the work ethic* (Mason), *shocking the quality out of the American way* (Heilbroner), *creating a bad public image for business and businessmen* (Cavanagh), and *promoting bad taste and the acceptance of hype as "untrue but true enough"* (all critics). Let's return one more time to university president John R. Silber:

"Through television we have prepared ourselves and our children for disaster. We have advocated a system of hedonism, of immediate gratification . . . when natural resources and energy will not sustain our luxurious appetites . . . when television has informed us of merciless want in the rest of the world and in parts of our own country."

We have prepared ourselves for nothing less than the enslavement of mankind by its own swift, cunning, reckless, newly empowered mutant—the communicator. The saying "bad news travels fast and far," was old enough in Plutarch's time to be known as a proverb, but it took miracles of electronics and 1900 more years of spring-winding to build the momentum of communications to the speeds of sound and light.

We are also in confrontation with another "instant" miracle of electronics—the computer—which no longer leads a life of solitary bachelorship but is presently at the altar alongside communications in order to form a more perfect union. Of what? With what? Of *science* with *control*. The same people who brought you the physics for terracide have now brought you the ability to be killed, tallied, and told at approximately the same time.

Meanwhile, all is not lost—for the simple reason that all has not yet happened. Reapplication of the Newtonian law which says that *every action has an equal and opposite reaction* (and which I use to explain anything requiring a reason for being) can work in the following nice way. Just as bright invention has its corresponding dark side, that dark side must in turn have its own light side; something like a ball is a ball is a ball until it--- isn't!

Getting *control of the controls* is the essence of mankind's problem, and before—not after—their visible components "disappear" into integrated circuits, because when "I see" is reduced to "IC," the power of man over destiny will be reduced to the vanishing point: whatever is then "in the machine" will be "the way it is," regardless of whether the machine has a soul, a will, or a program of its own.

I speak of a turning point not less earthshaking than the day, August 6, 1945, when civilization's control went over from "God's mill" to Man's manipulated nuclei. In residual matters of mortal control, the marriage of the computative with the communicative sciences will shortly be seen for what it is—a quite final consummation. Now—now!—is not a microsecond too soon to consider how to prevent being cheapened and manipulated by technology, if not killed outright by the deceptively soft trailing edge of its ingenuity.

If you have survived my thoughts on our most recent and sometimes most revolting technical revolution, you will certainly take in stride an opinion that today's technology is more than ordinarily "ultimate." Previous generations of society have all thought the same thing of their newly exposed layers of the onion, but now, I believe, what has most recently evolved is susceptible only to constant little touches of refinement (cf. French cooking). Computers, television, audio-visual information sharing, and the prickly detritus of macro and micro electronics are paradigms of what is here to stay.

Small wonder that before her division into (sic) multi-bells, Ma Bell had begun advertising herself not as throughput but as a information company. Hers was a mad, frightened, even unseemly dash to become more than America's best-paid hooker (of you to me) and not to be left standing on history's turned corner.

Now It's My Nickel

Surely, as long as we have any communications more cultivated than a blow to the head, we will have advertising. And advertising that merits criticism. And critics . . . who by the very nature of their calling are advertisers!

All advertisers have a duty to clean up their act before it cleans them up (with more veneers of regulation and/or silence). Father Cavanagh himself acknowledges "advertising's purpose is to sell," a fact I reflect on whenever I drive by a church whose illuminated roadside sign sells seventh day high fidelity or the likelihood of Monday starting another septenary of 85% infidelity unless certain remedies are taken.

The way to get more remedies sold and taken is by advertising them to the public sector, a certainty which, in my gusto-saturated "one time around" in life, has involved the spending of perhaps 6/10ths of a billion dollars for the purpose. Time and reflection have encouraged some reforms.

Flashback. In the vicinity of 1960, my quest for things to sell led me to knock on the doors of a famous watch company to select two items for our flyer—an alarm watch and a chronograph that was also a conventional wristwatch. On selecting the models I liked and solving problems of quantity and cost, I asked the salesman what list price I could use. Note: that was before the FTC denied list price as being an acceptable comparator in media.

My vendor pawed through a little box of tickets. "How about $89.95?" he inquired pleasantly, holding up a metallized paper tag with that amount on it.

"That much! Is that the list?" I asked with an equal amount of surprise and innocence. "Can you pick and choose?"

Thus I learned that the watch industry, and maybe even the whole jewelry industry, had list prices that were unrestrainedly optional. The truth was, if truth is the *mot juste,* that the game of "list price" was actually "dealer's choice"; not what the market would bear but what the customer wanted to see in the sense of (a) value, and (b) savings from seen value. (The black-faced chronograph I'm thinking of was flyer-sided in 1960 in this unabashedly culpable manner: EXCLUSIVE! SAVE $50 ON PRECISION CHRONOGRAPH. The story showed a "Mfgrs. List" of $79.50, and a resale price of $29.95 plus tax. Alas, even the $50 savings was 45¢ short!)

I learned another curious lesson about "fair" pricing from Radio Shack's days of selling WWII surplus electronic parts and equipment, and some surplus that was not in the least electronic—as, for example, trench shovels! This particular event involves our displaying a few pieces of an electronic component called, although I may be mistaken, a bolometer, but anyway an item which, having no perceptible value, was priced in the store at 50¢ each. One day a floor salesman came up to our chief merchant with a sample in his hand, asking if we had 500 more of them in stock.

"Oh, we do indeed," said our man, with a shrewd look which said (to me) something like "I can tell when a straight line is off, even by 1/64th of an inch." He then said, *"But our price in lots of 500 is $1 each, not 50 cents."*

After our confused but informed salesman had left, I asked our chief merchant how he could get away with raising the price of a 50¢ item to $1 in the face of a quantity offer, or indeed raising it for any reason.

Followed then his thin tutorial smile and this rationale. "At 50¢ it was an item we didn't know what to do with, but at the 500-piece bid level it was clear we had a customer who did and who also probably knew its cost to the government was $25 or $30." (Note: the customer paid 50¢ each for the three on display, and $1 each for 500 that weren't.)

Most people, I have decided, learn about pricing and

such matters in the dark of the business jungle; there, too, they learn about the thrust of advertising . . . which is SELL THE HELL OUT OF IT. Now enters the "conditioned soul" referred to by his Divine Grace A.C. Bhaktivedanta Swami Prabhupāda, ready to commit the latter's four basic defects which I have spelled out for you in previous chapters:

1. *To commit mistakes.* Our conditioned advertiser does as little research into his claims as possible since he's probably going to be wrong anyway; to err is human.
2. *To be illusioned,* and to spread illusion. These conditions are as natural as rain once you believe that "it's what the customers wants that he buys," whatever the facts.
3. *To cheat* is clearly a human propensity, as we get down to bedrock. If you really start thinking about the different ways you cheat "a little here, a little there," even you can be embarrassed. Especially if your product fails because of defects caused by irresponsible cost-cutting or lack of adequate safety warnings; or if the "gold" is only the color; the "solid leather" is not leather inside and out; the product life is shorter than you dare discuss; the value of your Sunday-special insurance package is a palpable fiction to anyone who understands insurance; your "estate diamonds" ad is not actually an offer of anything other than never-before-sold stones; your vitamin-enriched soap is worthless, as a vitamin product, because only the ad and the soap maker are usefully enriched; your "retire a millionaire" IRA advertising is dependent on many unmentioned conditions and devoid of any commentary on what inflation will do to that million; your money market fund offer is star-studded with asterisked disclaimers, and its largest percent of yield is actually so conditional as to be a fable.
4. *To possess imperfect senses* supports the defect that your senses cannot distinguish between good and bad taste, natural and vulgar sensuality, propriety and impropriety, protection and harm, truth and fiction. Your unique, imperfect senses tell you that your rights to free speech and to satisfy urges are all you need to vindicate any means

you choose to get your product distributed, advertised, and sold.

I hope I can summarize this chapter quickly. There is little less remarkable than the beating of a dead horse—defective advertising and marketing—which refuses to die. So, first to paraphrase Carl Sandburg:

> Look out how you use false words.
> When you let false words go, it is not easy to call them back.
> They wear long boots, hard boots.

He said "proud" where I say "false"; the difference here is not crucial. At the top of his craft in the pre-TV era, he had already anticipated the threat of words and pictures simultaneously heard and seen around the world, and of instant dehydrated news, and of disinformation, and of sectional differences in language and culture and faith that flare and smoulder in the same geopolitical lesion for the hundreds of years.

"Long . . . hard boots" come in many sonorities, too. Why should we merely sit and listen for their sound in the night of our streets? Whatever happens is not "supposed to happen," as some of my friends in Texas—ready for anything except bankruptcy—say when some bit of life's excrescence hits the fan. However little, we can do something about it. My "something" is the dozen-item checklist that follows.

Every ad you produce, authorize, pay for, and disseminate, should at the very least be run by a List of Considerations like this—if not for revision, then simply for the exercise of your senses. If you like to keep score, use the yea/nay system made famous by computers: ONE (1) or ZERO (0).

- □ Is the copy accurate?
- □ Is the copy accurate but likely to mislead someone?
- □ Is the copy "some," "all," or "warts and all?"
- □ Is the picture in good taste?
- □ Is the picture honest or deceptively simulated?
- □ Is the picture meaningful or illusionary?
- □ Is the product or service beneficial? How and why?

- □ Is the product or service socially subversive in any way?
- □ Is the product or service guaranteed? How long? For what?
- □ Are price and terms of purchase fully spelled out?
- □ Is your place of business fully detailed?
- □ Did you forget to disclaim something?

We who are privileged to bring our wares to market, to utilize the many available media, to penetrate collective and individual privacy, have duties as well as privileges.

Because we seek to exchange our form of wealth and productivity for another's, we have a moral (if not altogether legal) obligation to deliver mutually agreeable parity.

Inasmuch as the reach of advertising, using media as carrier, is now so ubiquitous and swift, it now has even more critical obligations to society: to refrain from pushing anti-social goods, ideas, services, to deliver "as advertised."

If we have tended to abuse taste—as, for example, by the post-WWII switch from selling romance to explicit sexuality—we must at least seriously question the cost of not disabusing it.

Since we are promoting the fiction of monks in ecstasy over office products, executives perplexed over such simple matters as getting packages delivered and long distance phone conferences arranged, and hemorrhoids and "brown spots" zapped into near oblivion by unguents, we can at least reexamine the wisdom and effect of self-defeating salesmanship.

Are we saved by ridiculing to death the Federal Trade Commission and agreeing—as a recent FTC chairman (J. C. Miller) is alleged to have said—that today *access to shoddy goods is an inalienable consumer right?* Is caveat emptor really the free market at its most free? The head of a pin isn't designed only for seeing how many angels can fit on it; it's also to prevent the pin from pinning all the way through!

THIRTEEN

Advertising During the Depression

Reprint of *Harvard Business Review* Article, "The Use of Advertising During Depression"

Owing to the sensitivity toward the number 13 of many Americans, I decided that in these "parlous times" it might be good business just to forget about doing a 13th chapter. Fortuitously, the estimable *Harvard Business Review* made it both possible and logical to have one after all when it sent me (as a potential advertiser) a reprint of its article "The Use of Advertising During Depression," written by Roland S. Vaile for HBR's April 1927 issue as pp. 323–330.

What's more, a peek at how our fathers marketed their way out of the economic "pits" might provide some tiny clue for what's left of the once glorious 20th century. Would the people at Harvard let me reprint *their* reprint and save it for posterity's review? Gladly, if only I would give them credit (as I did in the preceding paragraph).

But when I began reading about what I'd hastily assumed was 1929, I suddenly realized it was not 1929's depression, after all, but *the depression of 1920-1922* which had attracted our author's attention; 1929 was still a future date for all concerned.

What had happened in the earliest of the 20s to warrant

investigation? Not really a whole lot by contemporary Wall Street semantics, which uses the word "plunge" to describe the dollar's fall of a few U.S. cents against the pound, and "fell sharply" in speaking of the British pound on a day it actually finished slightly above the previous day's $1.8313.

In the words of historian Samuel Eliot Morison, what happened was "a postwar recession (or minor depression)"; yes, even he shows the academician's familiar disposition to mince economic pies when it comes to describing conditions beyond New England with absolute certainty.

The Dow Jones average of the day does indicate a drop from just over 100 at the start of 1920 to just under 64 in 1921; the Great Depression's low would be 41.2 in 1934. This was followed by a rapid return to the 100-point area by the middle of 1922.

Using rounded figures, the GNP went from (billions) $86 in 1920 to $70 in both 1921 and 1922, which, by the way, is less—that $86—than Belgium's GNP for 1978! Government expenditures in the same three years ran about (billions) $6.5, $5.0, and less than $3.5, respectively, meaning that AT&T's *profits* of 1979–1981 would have surpassed the entire U. S. government's expenditures of 1920–1922. And Harding was elected president.

What DID advertisers do, and what should they consider doing, in the vise of hard times? Good questions.

Most people in charge of marketing today know "depression" in the economic sense only about as well as they know the Grand Canyon—as the Big Daddy of plunges; if a good place to visit, certainly not a good place to live.

> ***ADvisory.*** In that year (1922) *Harvard Business Review*—then a quarterly but now a bimonthly—had a per-copy selling price of $1.25 and there was no frequency discount; by 1982 its newsstand price had soared to a princely $5, but $4.50 to subscribers. Present-day advertisers asked to ante up $5220 for a full page on a one-time rate basis might be glad to learn that—at 225,000 guaranteed net paid circulation—the cost of reaching HBR's "top business executives" readers is *only .0232 cents per individual,* and that the probability of reaching them is on the high side of average.

Today's "penny" postcards cost 13¢ apiece (plus message) for a 1st Class (low class) attack; a 3rd Class mailer such as Radio Shack's flyer will cost you about 50% more.

This is not presented in repayment to the *Review* for its courtesy to me. Mine is, after all, an anecdotal book on advertising and marketing which hopefully will inform executives who habitually approve invoices for advertising promotions they haven't evaluated because—ha!—they're supposed to pay up without looking up. See how easy it can be to examine the facts of demographic life and costs per M of circulation?

Well then, since you're now so keen on such matters, what do you think that the Ford motor car company did in respect to its rivals and its advertising during the 1920–1922 slump?

Why didn't Harvard's author, Mr. Vaile, draw a conclusion on the effect of more or less advertising on net profits in that depression?

Read all about it, and more: HERE! NOW! At NO extra cost! I'll return for a postscript after the *Harvard Business Review* material has been presented here verbatim.

HARVARD BUSINESS REVIEW

VOLUME V NUMBER 3 APRIL 1927 PRICE $1.25 A COPY

No. 80001

HARVARD BUSINESS REVIEW

VOLUME V NUMBER 3

APRIL, 1927

PUBLISHED QUARTERLY

FOR THE GRADUATE SCHOOL OF BUSINESS ADMINISTRATION, HARVARD UNIVERSITY
BY A. W. SHAW COMPANY, CASS, HURON AND ERIE STREETS, CHICAGO

The subscription terms: $5 a year; single copies, $1.25. Entered as second-class matter October 12, 1922, at Chicago, Illinois, under the Act of Congress of March 3, 1879. Acceptance for mailing at special rate of postage provided for in section 1103, Act of October 3, 1917, authorized October 12, 1922. Address editorial correspondence to the Editor, Morgan Hall, Soldiers' Field Station, Boston, Massachusetts.

Communications relating to advertising or subscription should be addressed to the publishers at Chicago. Make checks payable to A. W. Shaw Company.

Copyright, 1927, by A. W. Shaw Company. Entered at Stationers' Hall; copyrighted, 1927, in Great Britain. Printed in the United States of America.

FROM THE CONTRACT BETWEEN HARVARD UNIVERSITY AND A. W. SHAW COMPANY

"Section 5 . . . the Publisher will in each year pay to Harvard all net profits, if any, shown . . . to have been realized by the Publisher . . . Such net profits received by Harvard shall be applied from time to time by the Dean of its Faculty of Business Administration for research in some field of business."

THE USE OF ADVERTISING DURING DEPRESSION

By ROLAND S. VAILE

A COMMON policy among manufacturers has been to gage the amount of their magazine advertising by general business conditions; advertising space has been increased during prosperity and decreased during depression. Professor Crum [1] found that the "major fluctuations in the volume of advertising carried by magazines since the war have taken place slightly in advance of similar movements in general business conditions." The figures which he published also showed that the fluctuations in advertising were somewhat wider than in general sales.

There are numerous departures from this general policy, however, in the case of individual firms. These departures are conspicuous, not alone because of the magnitude of the variations, but equally because of the outstanding character of some of the firms. There are many cases where institutions which appear to be directly competing have evidently used markedly different technique in this part of their sales promotion.

The figures in Table I are illustrative of these differences in policy. They are adapted from the monograph of the Crowell Publishing Company, *National Markets and National Advertising, 1925*. The changes in expenditure for magazine advertising during the five-year period, 1920-1924, are contrasted for individual firms in similar lines of business. The money expended by each firm during 1920 is taken as 100, because Professor Crum's study showed that magazine advertising reached a peak in that year, to be followed by a marked slump. The expenditures for subsequent years are reported as percentages of this year. In each case the two firms contrasted are engaged in similar lines of business and they have been, in general, heavy users of magazine advertising.

Many similar differences appear in almost every line of goods. The illustrations given seem typical and could be multiplied many times over.

Some of the differences portrayed are doubtless accounted for by changes in policy between the use of magazine advertising and other forms of sales promotion, although in several cases personal correspondence with the sales manager of the company indicates that the movement of magazine advertising fairly represents the general sales policy at the time of the 1920-1922 depression. Some of the differences may also be due to a willingness in 1919 and 1920 to spend money extravagantly for advertising rather than pay high corporation taxes. After all allowances are made, however, it seems that a real difference in institutional policy exists in regard to sales promotion during times of depression; some concerns have apparently assumed that advertising is one of the costs which may be reduced during depression, while others have looked upon it as a force for making sales when they are hard to make. Both of these points of view have fre-

[1] Crum, W. L., Harvard Economic Service, *Weekly Letters*, Vol. 3, p. 47.

TABLE I. CHANGES IN MAGAZINE ADVERTISING, 1920–1924
(Expenditures for 1920 = 100)

Firms	Actual Expenditure 1920	Relative Expenditures				
		1920	1921	1922	1923	1924
Clothing						
Hart, Schaffner & Marx	$ 188,500	100	150	155	165	150
Kuppenheimer	240,718	100	50	65	65	45
Foodstuffs						
Postum Cereal Company	375,615	100	120	160	135	330
Quaker Oats	1,390,108	100	40	40	45	40
Soap						
Palmolive	377,150	100	125	150	185	190
Resinol	424,197	100	60	55	70	40
Paint						
Valentine & Company	184,270	100	120	150	225	320
Sherwin-Williams Company	201,815	100	55	50	60	115

quently been defended in articles appearing in *Printer's Ink* and elsewhere, largely on *a priori* grounds. Little factual evidence has been presented in support of either side.

Two questions are suggested by these differences in policy:

1. What is the effect of each policy upon sales?
2. Is the effect the same in the case of all commodities?

In order partially to test these questions, the writer has compiled sales figures for the years 1920 to 1924, inclusive, for about 250 well-known firms. A large portion of these figures were obtained from Poor's *Manual of Industrials—1926*. These were supplemented, however, by direct correspondence with the companies in cases where Poor does not report sales. In a number of cases the request was made that the sales of individual firms be held as confidential, so that no report is made in this paper of sales by firms.

In approaching the first question. the sales records of the firms were sorted into three groups, namely:

1. Firms which did no magazine advertising from 1920 to 1924, inclusive.
2. Firms which increased their magazine advertising from 1920 to 1924.
3. Firms which decreased their magazine advertising from 1920 to 1924.

Some firms, for which sales records were available, were so inconsistent in their advertising policy during these years that they could not be classed in any of the above groups. Such firms were not included in the study, only those with marked trends being retained.

The average (arithmetic mean) sales for the different groups in 1920 were as follows:

Non-advertising firms	$23,000,000
Increased advertising	25,000,000
Decreased advertising	21,000,000

All sizes were represented in each group, with a range from $1,000,000 to nearly $1,000,000,000 in each case. In the same year, 1920, the average expenditure for magazine advertising was $170,000 per firm, both in the group which subsequently increased and in the one which decreased their expenditures. This amount was 0.68% of sales in the first group and 0.81% in the second.

Because of the difference in size of individual firms, the annual dollar sales of each were reduced to relatives. The sales for 1920 were arbitrarily taken as a base in all cases, because it was the first year for which records were available for many of the firms, and because it was generally a year of high sales. Relatives were used rather than dollar sales so that the movement in any one firm might have equal weight with the movement in any other. The writer believes that this gives a more accurate picture of the relation between advertising and sales than would a study of total sales, wherein the movements in the large firms might entirely obscure the movements in the smaller firms. The question may still be raised whether advertising during depression is more effective with firms of one size than with those of another; the present paper makes no attempt to answer this question.

Table II shows some of the characteristics of each group, together with the relative sales associated with each of the magazine-advertising policies.

The sales of the non-advertising firms were 20% lower in 1921 than in 1920. In contrast, the slump was only 12% for the firms which increased their magazine advertising, while it was 26% for the firms which decreased their advertising expenditures. All three groups showed increasing sales from 1921 to 1924, but the increase was most pronounced in the group which increased their advertising, and least pronounced in the non-advertising group.

While the firms which increased their advertising also increased their sales, they did not do so proportionally. Advertising became relatively more costly in this group, while it became relatively less costly in the group which decreased advertising. Just what effect these changes may have had on net profits has not been determined; it seems impracticable to study the movements of net profits without a more intimate knowledge of the accounting methods of individual firms than is given in the published reports.

TABLE II. CHARACTERISTICS OF EACH GROUP, WITH RELATIVE SALES ASSOCIATED WITH EACH OF THE MAGAZINE-ADVERTISING POLICIES

	Year	Firms Not Advertising in Magazines, 1920–1924	Firms Which Increased Advertising in Magazines, 1920–1923	Firms Which Decreased Advertising in Magazines, 1920–1923
Number of firms		105	58	67
Average sales	1920	$23,000,000	$25,000,000	$21,000,000
Relative sales	1920	100	100	100
	1921	80	88	74
	1922	92	107	88
	1923	105	128	103
	1924	108	131	105
Average expenditure for magazine advertising	1920	....	$170,000	$170,000
Relative magazine advertising	1920	....	100	100
	1921	....	138	75
	1922	....	157	50
	1923	....	195	54
	1924	....	242	58
Ratio of magazine advertising to sales	1920	....	0.68%	0.81%
	1921	....	1.04	0.81
	1922	....	1.00	0.46
	1923	....	1.03	0.43
	1924	....	1.25	0.45

TABLE III. RELATIVE MOVEMENT OF SALES ASSOCIATED WITH DIFFERENT ADVERTISING POLICIES

	1920	1921	1922	1923	1924
Increased advertising	100	110	116	121	121
No advertising	100	100	100	100	100
Decreased advertising	100	95	96	98	97

In order to make the contrasts clearer, an attempt was made to eliminate both secular growth and cyclical variation, which might affect all concerns alike regardless of their advertising policies. Because of the short period of time involved, no attempt was made to fit curves which might serve as base lines. Rather, the relative sales of the non-advertising group were taken as the base and counted as 100 for each year, on the assumption that the sales of these firms would give a fair picture of the combined effect of secular and cyclical variations unaffected by the force of advertising. Table III shows the resulting figures. For 1920, all the figures are obviously at 100. The subsequent relatives are measures of the sales associated with changes in advertising policy as contrasted to sales of non-advertising firms. These figures are derived, of course, directly from the preceding table.

Two facts seem to stand out from these data with considerable clarity: First, a definite spread occurs between the sales of firms which increased their advertising and those which decreased it. Where intensive advertising during depression was a part of the sales technique, sales were maintained in better volume than where advertising appropriations were cut. Second, the non-advertising firms fared better, especially in 1921, in volume of sales than did those firms which reduced their advertising. Advertising is a form of sales effort, and its reduction at a time of depression seems to have resulted in a greater loss of sales than was experienced by the firms which constantly depended on other types of distribution. This suggests that personal selling to the trade and dealer good-will may have more lasting importance at such a time than has consumer recognition.

As a further test of the effect of increasing and decreasing advertising during depression, the relative changes of sales of individual concerns from 1920 to 1921 were correlated with the corresponding changes in advertising. Because of the greater range of change in advertising than in sales, a standard deviation was determined for each series, and each item was divided by the deviation of its series. The Pearsonian coefficient for the resulting figures was $.68 \pm 9$. From this it appears that sales of individual firms may often be materially affected by advertising, even during depression.

TABLE IV. RELATIVE ADVERTISING EXPENDITURES

Industry	Firms Which Increased, 1920–1923					Firms Which Decreased, 1920–1923				
	1920	1921	1922	1923	1924	1920	1921	1922	1923	1924
Personal items	100	115	185	180	220	100	60	50	30	35
House furnishings	100	130	160	250	275	100	70	50	70	80
Clothing	100	180	170	290	360	100	70	35	60	50
Automobile equipment	100	125	150	175	280	100	75	50	60	75
Automobiles	100	145	145	185	250	100	75	25	35	60
Groceries	100	115	130	120	135	100	75	90	75	70
Building materials	100	125	160	165	170	100	95	40	50	35

USE OF ADVERTISING DURING DEPRESSION

Turning now to the second question suggested above: "Is the effect the same in the case of all commodities?" The firms for which data are available are divided about equally among seven industries, namely: (1) personal items, such as tobacco, perfumes, and toilet articles; (2) house furnishings, from kitchen ware to pianos; (3) clothing, including men's and women's suits, hats and coats; (4) automobile equipment frequently purchased directly by consumers, such as tires, shock absorbers, chains; (5) automobiles, of which the Ford was the only non-advertising representative; (6) groceries; and (7) building materials.

The sales figures used throughout this study are the total annual sales in dollars, uncorrected for changes in price level. One of the advantages, therefore, of dividing the data into industrial classes is the fact that within these classes price changes are likely to affect one firm much as they do another.

The same methods of comparison were applied to the data for the several industries as were used in analyzing the changes in sales for all the firms together. Tables IV, V, and VI present the summarized data by industries, giving, first, the relative advertising expenditures both for the group which increased and the one which decreased; second, the growth in sales for each of the advertising groups; and, third, the relative movement of sales of the advertising groups as contrasted to the non-advertising firms.

It will be noted from the above data that in every industry there is a measurable spread between the relative sales of the firms which increased their advertising and of those which de-

TABLE V. GROWTH OF SALES ASSOCIATED WITH DIFFERENT ADVERTISING POLICIES

Industry	Number of Firms	Dollar Sales 1920	Relative Sales				
			1920	1921	1922	1923	1924
Personal items							
Increased advertising	10	$34,000,000	100	93	107	112	120
No advertising	12	20,500,000	100	80	83	90	95
Decreased advertising	10	22,000,000	100	73	82	90	93
House furnishings							
Increased advertising	7	19,200,000	100	83	105	120	108
No advertising	11	8,540,000	100	70	84	104	95
Decreased advertising	7	13,000,000	100	71	86	101	90
Clothing							
Increased advertising	8	16,500,000	100	102	112	118	106
No advertising	20	18,800,000	100	86	96	100	96
Decreased advertising	9	13,600,000	100	77	74	73	70
Automobile equipment							
Increased advertising	7	56,000,000	100	77	96	117	120
No advertising	11	58,000,000	100	67	86	107	110
Decreased advertising	14	28,000,000	100	72	80	101	100
Automobiles							
Increased advertising	8	....	100	78	137	184	177
No advertising	1	....	100	95	126	188	187
Decreased advertising	9	....	100	73	124	159	165
Groceries							
Increased advertising	10	22,000,000	100	87	96	103	120
No advertising	38	21,000,000	100	85	100	103	115
Decreased advertising	10	24,000,000	100	77	87	94	102
Building materials							
Increased advertising	9	14,000,000	100	81	90	120	125
No advertising	12	13,500,000	100	75	87	123	117
Decreased advertising	8	15,000,000	100	78	92	118	120

creased. Moreover, in every case except that of building materials, the firms which decreased their advertising suffered a greater reduction of sales than did the firms which were doing no advertising. Thus the general relationship between advertising and sales seems to be consistent in all industries, but there are differences in degree which are worthy of comment.

The spread between the sales of firms which increased their advertising and the sales of those which decreased is much more pronounced in some industries than in others. It is particularly large in the cases of personal items and clothing, and fairly large with automobile equipment and house furnishings, while it is small in the cases of automobiles and groceries, and almost negligible with building materials. This would indicate that magazine advertising is a more potent force in the sale of personal items and clothing than it is in the sale of the other lines. This is further borne out by the fact that the sales of groceries and building materials were only slightly increased by increased advertising, when compared with the sales of the non-advertising firms in these two fields.

The data of this study of advertising force in various industries seem in harmony with other knowledge of consumers' buying habits. Personal items and clothing, as included in this study, are purchased largely by and for men, as are also automobile equipment items. Men are said to be especially susceptible to brand advertising because they

Table VI. Relative Movement of Sales Associated with Different Advertising Policies

Industry	1920	1921	1922	1923	1924	Points Spread Between Firms Which Increased or Decreased Advertising 1921	1922	1923	1924
Personal items									
Increased advertising	100	116	129	125	127				
No advertising	100	100	100	100	100	25	30	25	28
Decreased advertising	100	91	99	100	99				
Clothing									
Increased advertising	100	118	117	118	111				
No advertising	100	100	100	100	100	28	30	35	28
Decreased advertising	100	90	77	73	73				
House furnishings									
Increased advertising	100	118	125	115	115				
No advertising	100	100	100	100	100	16	23	18	20
Decreased advertising	100	102	102	97	95				
Automobile Equipment									
Increased advertising	100	115	112	109	109				
No advertising	100	100	100	100	100	8	19	15	18
Decreased advertising	100	107	93	94	91				
Automobiles									
Increased advertising	100	80	109	98	95				
No advertising	100	100	100	100	100	3	11	13	7
Decreased advertising	100	77	98	85	88				
Groceries									
Increased advertising	100	102	96	100	104				
No advertising	100	100	100	100	100	12	9	9	15
Decreased advertising	100	90	87	91	89				
Building materials									
Increased advertising	100	108	103	98	107				
No advertising	100	100	100	100	100	4	−2	2	5
Decreased advertising	100	104	105	96	102				

USE OF ADVERTISING DURING DEPRESSION

do not care to "shop," and because they are willing to accept the same article time after time. Moreover, there are several instances within these groups where the use is an habitual one—such as smoking—and in these cases the brand name may become associated with the habit.

Groceries, on the other hand, are often bought on the recommendation of the retailer. George Louis, writing in *System, the Magazine of Business,* for June, 1912, reported a study in which it was found that unknown brands of foodstuffs could be substituted for advertised brands with little opposition on the part of the consumer. Groceries are convenience goods; there is little defined character to individual brands, so that the suggestion of the retailer has much to do with the consumer's choice.

Building materials, even though advertised to consumers, are generally

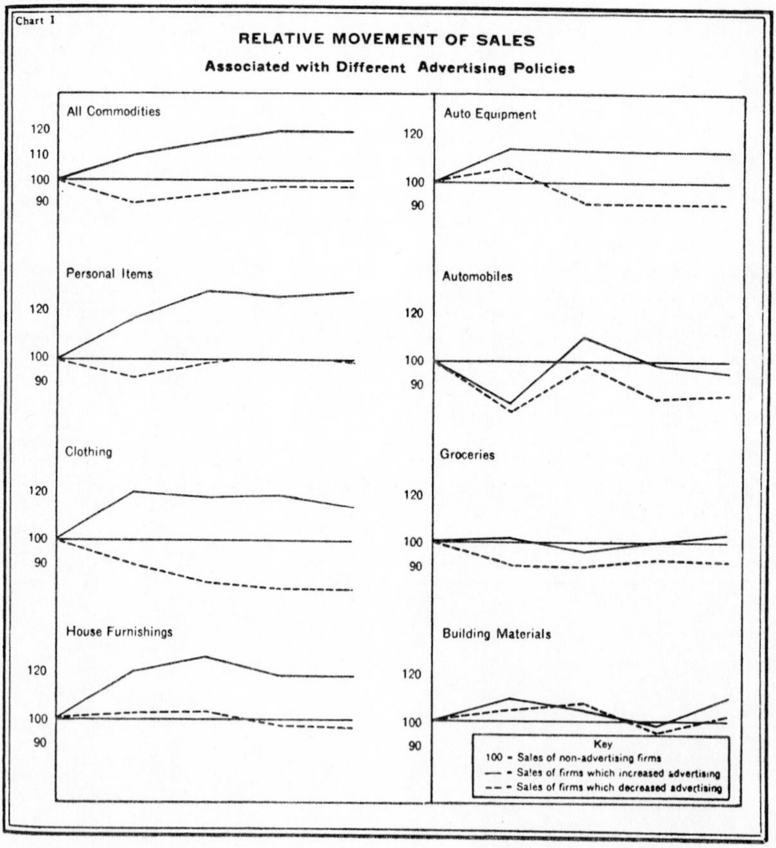

sold to contractors and others who regard them as industrial goods; profit on the transaction rather than immediate enjoyment of the article is a prime consideration. These buyers are likely to be in close touch with the trade so that they do not need the manufacturer's advertising as an aid in purchasing. For these reasons it was to be expected that consumer advertising would not be as important a factor with such commodities as with strictly consumer goods. It is of interest that there is any measurable effect at all from such advertising at a time of depression.

The fact that automobile sales of the companies which increased their magazine advertising fell off in 1921 more than did the sales of the non-advertising firms deserves special comment. The comparison here made is with the Ford car only, and it is well known that the Ford Motor Company has long received large amounts of free publicity; it is hardly fair, therefore, to consider it as a non-advertising concern. Moreover, it was to be expected that there would be a movement towards low-priced cars during the depression, which doubtless helped the Ford sales in comparison with sales of the other groups. The Ford price in 1921 was just about one-half the average price of the cars included in the other groups. The relatively small spread between the sales of the firms which increased their advertising and those which decreased suggests that automobiles are sold to a large extent by personal solicitation, and that advertising is of less importance with them than with certain other commodities.

To summarize the suggestions that grow out of this study, it would seem:

1. That increased magazine advertising during depression generally resulted in an increase in sales relative to the sales of competitors who did not make such increases.

2. That reduction in advertising during depression generally resulted in a greater falling off of sales than occurred with firms which did no consumer advertising.

3. That different classes of commodities respond in different degree to changes in advertising. In general, it may be said that these differences are in keeping with accepted statements concerning consumers' buying habits.

4. If, in some cases, the decrease in magazine advertising has been offset by an increase in the use of newspapers or other mediums, the comparisons indicate that such change of medium has not resulted in larger sales.

5. The increase in sales which apparently accompanies increased advertising during depression does not necessarily indicate an increase in profits; it has been impossible to consider the profit aspect of the problem in this study.

Postscript: More Cheese = More Noise

Would you recommend that your advertising budget be "increased during prosperity and decreased during depression" as Roland S. Vaile observes was "a common policy among manufacturers" in the period just after WWI?

One consideration is that not all businesses recede when times are recessive: in 1982, "The company (IBM) still owns the electric typewriter field, but the future is electronic. There it faces 16 competitors including Xerox and Olivetti."

So says the *New York Times,* and, in my opinion, there's another competitor group which, by virtue of making printers for computers, is so close to being in the game that it may be waiting for typewriting to catch up!

Regardless of what happens in the world of "omics"—Reagan ones or any others—special situations like this will cause vast amounts of marketing, hence advertising outlays. Emerging and transitioning industries will see a multiplying of promotional expenses, not a diminution, even if some of their aging pitchers are lifted with bases loaded in the 4th.

The U.S. auto industry is another pocket of resistance to the slicing back of "cheese" budgets during the problem years of the 1980s. It can't afford to do otherwise, says a Ford honcho: "Marketing money is the last thing we can afford to cut back on. It's our connection to the consumer." Hmmm, where does this leave dealers' connections to the consumer? (Radio Shack's factory-to-you mentality becomes a bit more sound?)

Since Mr. Vaile is more concerned with manufacturers and, in fact, addresses their behavior without regard for retailers, I decided to contract a large retailer and one outside of the electronics industry. I phoned Stanley Roth, Jr., a vice-president at Woolworth/Woolco, who is called "Jimmie" the way I used to be called "Sunny."

"Jimmie," I told Stanley, "I'd like a rundown on what you fellows do in tough economic times. I'm just finishing a book and you can get in it if you answer me today."

"You increase your dollars for advertising first," he said without hesitation. "You fight harder with promotions and increased markdowns. In the fall of 1981, for example, we did that even when we were in a little budget pinch.

"What happened in the recessions of 1972 and 1975 was that people traded down. This didn't happen in 1981: they pulled out of the market completely."

And as for TV versus other media? Stanley Roth joined my vocal majority when he said: "We felt we get more out of newsprint so we chopped TV down." Not down altogether, just down to a size permitting more advertising coverage across the chain via newspaper promotions.

Some straight from the cranium (and heart) experience in doing well when the economy isn't comes from Charles W. Wagner, the recently retired executive vice president for retail operations of the nation's fifth largest retailer, Montgomery Ward and Company.

Charlie Wagner reminds me of our late, mutual friend Charles Tandy: he was born to sell, born to lead, born to succeed, born to win the allegiance of his peer employees, born to revere the business of making sales over all other enterprises; and he started on the sales floor—not in an office.

His first management coup was taking charge of a Montgomery Ward store in Washington (state) in 1944 and converting it from a loser to a +214% sales gainer in 18 months. When he said "214%" he didn't say "about"; and he didn't remind me that it happened a mere 38 years ago.

Long Beach (CA) was badly depressed in 1948–9, and so, naturally, was Ward's. Wagner asked for that store out of ambition (i.e., executive masochism): he wanted to prove that its history of never having made a profit was a "people problem" and not a location problem; he brought it to a +25% sales gain and a profit within a year.

How? Well, that's our story. And it begins, as anyone who has overcome adversity can tell you, with a selection of targets you know can be hit dead center, regardless of conditions in the world outside. These are Charlie Wagner's bull's eyes:

1. Get the store people behind you.
2. Zero in on the likeliest way to build sales.
3. Find an affordable way to increase advertising.

Getting the store people behind him meant the setting up of goals such as improving the store's appearance, service, and presentation of goods—merchandising. Also: improving inventory control to maximize turnover and minimize interest charges. Also: running internal contests with worthwhile prizes for the employee winners, to create that tritest of trite—but goodest of good—"group feeling of personal pride in their accomplishments."

The likeliest way to build sales, Wagner found, was to increase credit sales. Do people on revolving credit and other plans buy more?—only four to five times more! Montgomery Ward at Long Beach, due to heavy pressure on this button, went from 39% of sales in credit purchases to 63%. But credit wasn't just issued to anyone: 72% of applications were approved; 50% of those approved were converted to actual credit customers. All this a short 14 months after Wagner arrived with a voluntary mission to turn things around!

> ***ADvisory.*** That occurred in the 1948 crunch. Today, Wagner says, the approach of beefing up time-pay sales 62% would be unworkable as long as interest stays at its present unprecedently high level.

"It was essential, even with a pitifully small allowable budget, to increase our advertising," Charlie reflects, "so we could better compete with Sears and the others. I went into a program of getting more sales from recent customers . . . it costs less, you know, to bring 'em in by direct mail than to run ads in the newspapers." (I've preached Recent Customer sermons throughout this book . . . remember?)

"The same mailing was sent to actives and inactives—credit customers with no outstanding balance—but the latter got a special offer. The cost of promoting in this way was about 3% in cost of sales, whereas our traditional company figure was 5% and media promotions could run as high as 20%."

The point was: even when you're flat on your keester, you don't just stand there, you *do something*.

> ***ADvisory.*** There's no drinker cheaper to reach than someone who has already been to your well. And there's

no way to reach him unless you've captured his name and address.

The Charles Wagners of the world are people who know the priorities of marketing better than most people know anything. Will he be missed at Montgomery Ward? You bet!—always assuming they're still in business when this book hits the stands. (There are some who think even its parent-by-acquisition, Mobil Corp., can't save it. It takes more than towers of gold chips to keep a retailer in the retail game!)

In summary, when Vaile was doing his scholarly investigating for his article, magazines were more important to advertisers than they appear to be today, and TV didn't even exist. His conclusion, that a "change of medium [did not result] in larger sales," would probably not be true in the light of today's beefy newspapers with their—literally—pounds of news, gossip, entertainment, magazine-type fare, and seemingly limitless numbers of private sector companies and individuals using display space to sell their fellows something TODAY OR TOMORROW: eventually may be too late.

His conclusion, that "the increase which apparently accompanies increased advertising during depression does not necessarily indicate an increase in profits," is right on the mark. What's necessary, during such dismal periods, is that enough cash flow be generated to maintain Ye Olde Outfitters, Ltd.'s biological functions, however feebly.

In a "big get bigger" world—and was there ever another kind?—while it may be true that bleeding can be fatal, there's nothing more certain to terminate the entity than no flow at all. So, do you advertise during depression? When every day might be your last corporate Superbowl?

ADvisory. Just remember what a media executive said in a recent speech to the Washington Metro Cable Club: "Nowhere is it written, 'thou shalt get the Superbowl for nothing.'"

FOURTEEN

Future Schlock

Schlock" is both an adjective (schlock merchandise) and a noun (trashy, poor quality things); I use the word as a genial figure of speech circumscribing the business of marketing—with special emphasis on advertising—and not without affection. I would be a schmo (foolish person) or schnook (easily deceived person) if I failed to recognize that advertising is more commonly associated with "schlock" than, say, "communications with intent to sell." All definitions courtesy of the *Oxford American Dictionary*.

"Future"? That's more like now than later; we are already "up and running." The 1980's electronic revolution is one whose impact upon the way things get done is without precedent in the annals of what another dictionary calls "the taxonomic designation for modern man, the only extant species of the genus Homo." (The best Oxford's writer could do with Homo sapiens was "man regarded as a species," but if you needed an ad copyperson, he would be the easiest to train!)

Converting Isaac Asimov and Me to Word Processing on the TRS-80

Getting things done was on my mind when I began writing this book on my IBM Selectric II typewriter. It had been a small feat to switch from a "regular" electric with rebounding carriage and separate letter strikers, but I finally mastered it. No sooner had I gotten the ball rotating on Chapter 1 than one of our computer people visited my office.

"You're not going to write your book on *that* antique?" he said with a worried frown.

"How else does a writer write?"

"But you of all people . . . the father of TRS-80! Well, it would be embarrassing to have you typewrite it before you gave our word processor a chance," he said.

"I'm too damn old," I said, "and too tired to learn a new skill after banging on one of these for over 45 years." Although I meant it, we finally agreed (1) that he would deliver to my office a Radio Shack TRS-80 Model II computer system with two disk drives, a daisy wheel printer, TRS-80 Scripsit word processing software, and suitable furniture, set up ready to use; (2) that he would instruct me in its use; (3) that he and other specialists would, as needed, respond to my beck and call and solve every problem, because (4) "I'll be damned if I'm going to read that manual."

"When you're not word processing," he suggested, "you can use the TRS-80 as a regular computer and——"

"And you can go lay an egg," I suggested.

"Sorry! I'll set it up tomorrow. You'll be up and running [that phrase again!] and writing on it an hour later."

He did and I was. And—how human!—it was love at first touch! This entire manuscript was inputted ("typed") by me: into the computer and onto its large 12" readout screen.

Although the screen *displays* 22 lines of "type" at any one time, it *holds* ("scrolls") 27 lines of text plus a bottom line of instructions that includes title, page number, line number; it even says what *letter number* you're on, i.e., which of 63 letters you're on, on my selected line width!

There being no engineers reading this, I'll explain how it works: (1) I "type" on the keyboard; (2) typed matter enters central processor, called CPU; (3) at the same time, what I type appears on the screen. All of this, of course, happens simultaneously in point of time if not in fact.

As each page is finished and all obvious errors and desired changes are made, the system is told by me (by a push of two keys) to store that page and to display the next page.

How the system stores (memorizes) the just-entered page is by instantly recording it—via the built-in disk drive—on a "floppy disk." The disk is a soft 8″ diameter circle of magnetic type about the same as a 45 rpm record in size and shape, and materially like the magnetic tape you use in your audio or video tape recorder, but a mite thicker.

When I want a printed paper copy, called "hard copy" in the trade, I simply activate the printer by means of a few more strokes of the keyboard, and presto—*one double-spaced, 27-line, perfect page on regular sized typing paper delivered in the incredible time of 35 seconds!*

Suppose I have ten corrected pages stored in memory (on the disk) and I want all ten printed in sequence without stopping. One more key push lets it all happen, even as I trot out to the coffee machine. In six minutes I'll have ten perfect pages dangling from my printer, no matter where I am located at the time. Only a spent printer-ribbon can interrupt the sequence.

To conclude: the typed manuscript of *To Catch a Mouse, Make a Noise Like a Cheese*—all 420 pages of it—didn't even fill up four (4) of those little disks. Pick up four 45 rpm records, subtract about 33% of the weight, and you have *this entire book,* less cover but suitable for printing out, mailing, or phone-line transfer to another computer—*even in another city*—even to a printer's computerized type-setting equipment.

And here's a laugh: those four little not entirely used-up disks, with less than $30 worth of tape, contain my labor of *five months or writing for six hours a day, six days a week for a total of 120 days!* No wonder you can "dump" a standard four-drawer file cabinet's contents into a handful of floppies . . . or into just one "hard" disk the size of an LP record!

I think you'll agree that the future—at least of letter and book writing—has already arrived. If you are in the business of making typewriters, whether mechanical, electrical, or "smart" electronic, you've got trouble if you don't get some R&D in a hurry. And the same goes for file cabinet makers. And for filing clerks. And maybe---secretaries?

Digesting the Processed Word

Even though I was a bit hard on spokespeople in advertising in an earlier chapter, I mentioned some exceptions, remember? Here's a perfect example of the totally synergistic personality whose use of the product is actual, logical, in no way a put-up job. Since I've been touting word processors as totally ideal high tech for writers, I now drop the name *Isaac Asimov* for your delectation. He is the dean of science fiction writers, but also academician, autobiographer, editor, husband, and who knows what else. He is also an important addition to Radio Shack's small but classy team of spokepersons, recommending the TRS-80 not only as the last word but also as the first word in word processing.

Now read about his introduction to this present and future writing system, detailed in a recent edition of the magazine *Popular Computing,* but condensed by me, using direct quotes where practical:

> MAY 6: "Big boxes . . . each presumably filled wih arcane incunabula came."
>
> MAY 12: After learning how to avoid looking at the boxes, much less opening them, I was visited by a Mr. Schwartz of Radio Shack who opens the boxes and gives out operating instructions. "To me it seemed like a tremendously complex machine. . . . In my diary that night, I wrote, 'I'll *never* learn how to use it.'"
>
> JUNE 4: A visit for more instruction and sympathy.
>
> JUNE 14: "I decided to make one last try. . . . I sat down and started the machine—and suddenly, with no warning whatever, everything worked. It rubbed its head against my leg and purred."
>
> JUNE 17: Commenced really writing. "I whistled while I worked. I called up Radio Shack and told them to 'put it all up, because I have decided I will keep the machine,' I said. 'I may even pay for it.'"

And that's the way it is with word processing in both home and office, where, respectively, Asimov and your correspondent do most of their writing, recruited away from IBM

Selectricks to a technology in which carriage return, paper insertion, print heads, platens, single-sheet feed—and (occasionally) even the need for any paper at all—are stick shifts in an automatic transmission world.

In an earlier article for the same periodical, Asimov had written of his many fulfilled prophecies regarding the development of the computer, made during 36 years and 50 stories "without ever knowing anything about computers in any real sense." Then he added this soon-to-be-contradicted observation: "When someone asks me if I work with computers myself, I shudder and say 'I am a signpost, sir. I point the way. I don't go there.'"

My experience exactly! Having named, defined and marketed the world's first mass-produced personal computer, the TRS-80 Model I, it was enough, I thought erroneously, to settle for pointing the way and blessing the voyage. Now I can safely predict that *you* will have many a hands-on encounter with small computers before you shuffle off this mortal interface.

Oh, yes. I forgot to mention that this book was word-processed (entered into my TRS-80 computer) without a secretary. No dictation. No transcription. No penciled-in corrections, but corrections by the zillion—even including flipping paragraphs between pages like so many dealt cards—all achieved with mess-free electronics and as little real knowledge of the process as I have when I change TV channels by wireless remote control. Did I remember to tell you that a quick Gal Friday types maybe 50 words per minute but my daisy-wheel printer *types 500 words per minute?* That's *ten times swifter* than ten flying fingers. And here's another "plus": inasmuch as typing by printer is *typing from memory,* you get perfect accuracy every time. Once told perfectly, always remembered perfectly! Again againandagainandagainanda. . . .

Memory's Mass-less Mass

Memory seems to have no mass . . . merely capacity. An understanding of the latter is also an act of faith. Ready? The estimated capacity (memory) of a floppy disk is 2,

500,000 characters, almost double the number of characters in a book. (Trivia: one character = 1 letter or digit = 1 byte = 8 bits.)

One unfloppy disk—a hard disk—can store 313,000,000 characters. Think that's a big deal? Try the encyclopedia with 12,500,000,000,000 characters remembered. How about RCA's new video disk? I'm told it's a hefty 7,000,000,000,000 bytes or characters, but don't ask for a refund if I'm wrong.

What's the Fort Knox of memory devices? The human brain! Mine. Yours. Our incredible memory storage capacity in characters is 125,000,000,000,000,000 or 125 *million million!* That is ten times the character count of the entire contents of the National Archives in Fuzzybyte-on-Potomac. Naturally, there's a catch. Capacity is one thing, inventory is another; retrieval, accuracy, and time are also heavily involved.

How do you prepare meals from an enormous empty refrigerator, or fill minds from a full library whose catalog is so random you can't find a book when you need it? What good are Radio Shack's 25 million computerized mailing list names if they can't be "accessed" every month and meanwhile kept current as to recency of purchase and fidelity of spelling and location? "Accessed" is computerese for "getting to and using," and time is always of the essence in a society that will pay for overpopulating itself with a large amount of enslavement to electronics (Big Brother may cometh in eight delicious flavors but . . . he cometh.)

What has all this got to do with Future Schlock? Well, first you have the "chicken" of over—or at least statistically increased—mating. And the egg—*more people,* with concurrent problems of stress, space, and logistics.

First you have the "chicken" of failing supply and/or prohibitively rising cost of energy and distribution. And the "egg"—new ways of energizing and distributing. One of the new ways of distributing will be for the store (theater, arena, bank, school) to come to the customer, not so much by traditional mail order as by untraditional response to untraditional advertising.

Sony's astute chairman Morita has been quoted as saying, "We are convinced video is the medium . . . for a simple reason: as time goes on—with videotext, cable and so on—[my italics] *people are going to be spending more and more time in front of their TV screens.*" At the moment I'm not talking about Sony's new filmless photography but about the store coming to the customer and the customer being either (1) in front of the TV, or (2) at least able to be "accessed" via TV. Sony, you see, has also announced a *color video printer* to go with its Mavica photography system (MA = magnetic, VI = video, CA = camera), and to me this makes it a technology to reckon with. You deserve an explanation.

Sony's printer—to quote the *New York Times*—"operates by use of four dye sheets and a thermal printing head that receives video signals and generates varying levels of heat according to [signal intensity] . . . the dye evaporates from the heat and is then transferred onto paper [with the result that] a print can be made in about five minutes." Clear? Not yet. But how can a home-video color print be called a white elephant if it's a (not CBS, not Zenith) Sony? Were I Kodak, I'd believe darn near anything I read that Morita said.

> ***ADvisory.*** Radio Shack's lead printer, R. R. Donnelley, recently noted the following about its own foray into a colorful electronic tomorrow: "In 1981, we converted for the first time four-color copy into digital storage without the use of film. Layouts and color corrections can now be done electronically, with images displayed on cathode ray tubes, rather than using techniques of dot etching, layout and stripping." Get that?—digital storage, no film, CRT images!

Donnelly's new Digital Group are concentrating on "composition and tone work . . . without the use of hot metal or film." And what's more, they "can transmit such digital information by satellite, and then . . . generate, at the printing plants, the offset plates or the gravure cylinders necessary to run the presses." Not only are our days numbered, but in addition there's a numerical equivalent for anything we intend to drag (kicking) toward the 21st century, privacy included, or it doesn't come!

The Multi-Accessible Homestead

Something called "Pictureware" is now in the demonstration stage. It's a variation of teletext which uses home VCRs (video tape recorders) that are accessed by a publisher or catalog house. Accessed, not just aimed at—a rifle, not a shotgun. A writer for *TV Digest* watched "the equivalent of an 180-page magazine being sent in 16-second bursts" to be "recorded automatically [on home VCR and] played back on demand, through rapid access to any frame." But that merely puts it on tape, and the staying power of rapidly moving taped messages has yet to be proved to publishers and advertisers.

On the other hand, when you add the (also demonstrated) Sony color printer to "Pictureware" or its equivalent, someone like Sears, Neiman-Marcus or Radio Shack can *send customers and prospects part or all of the store in color and in hard copy,* and perhaps even pay you for receiving it. And, as ever, it will be even cheaper and simpler to tell your story in black and white.

You can do a bit of accessing yourself, because there will be cheap, reliable ways to order from those electronically sent publications that don't involve stamps, envelopes, trips to the mail box, or phone calls. If your response is a purchase order, your bank and balance will also and simultaneously be joined to the activity.

Why do you think AT&T has been so hot to trot into what it calls the "Information Age," and not overly depressed by giving up "all facilities used to provide local telephone service"? For one thing, Little Brother, there's a phone line going into wherever you live or work, and AT&T wants to have access to it for many things beyond regular telephony.

In early 1982 "the Department of Justice dropped its antitrust case against the company," which thereby "modifies the 1956 Consent Decree by recognizing the inseparability of current data processing and telecommunications technologies."

If I may oversimplify what all this means, it means Ma Bell at long last can be in computer-related businesses, even down to competing with the likes of the *Washington Post,* the First National (of anywhere) Bank, Compuserve, Radio Shack, IBM, *Time,* Xerox, and Dow Jones.

> ***ADvisory.*** While "about two thirds" of AT&T "has been lopped off" the surviving parent is fighting to keep the grubby old Yellow Pages; as a national medium, they can be even more profitable when dumped into boob tubes, even more competitive with all the other media which had to make it in life the hard way.

Note: All items in quotes (") in the above three paragraphs are from an AT&T ad in the *Wall Street Journal.*

Flashback. To the 1/31/82 *New York Times* and a letter sent it by the then Postmaster General, William F. Bolger.

In sharp contrast to the AT&T position on these matters, at least as seen by me, he said he has "repeatedly attempted to assure members of Congress, the Administration and certainly the telecommunications industry that the Postal Service has no designs on or intentions of participation in the business of electronic transmissions."

Later he added: "Our business, indeed our mandate for the past 206 years, has been the delivery of hard-copy messages," explaining that his "recently inaugurated Electronic Computer-Originated Mail service . . . is a marriage of our universal delivery system with the electronic technology developed and operated by the private sector." Yes, the P.O., unlike AT&T, knows how it got where it is today and respects the mandate.

In at least one of my "Flyer-side Chat" columns I made a remark to the effect that Bell got rich* by being the world's best phone company—and an unusually protected one at that in view of our free market posture—so why not *stay* that way? The telecommunications industry mentioned by Mr. Bolger and personified by the likes of IBM certainly didn't get where it was up through 1981 with regulatory protection.

---

*1981 profits exceeded those of IBM, Mobil, and du Pont *combined!*

Haven't we learned, from the plight of the airlines, that "quickie" deregulation after generations of regulation is a terribly dangerous and disruptive disservice to the enterprise and its employees, customers, investors and lenders alike?

Deregulation should be gradual, painstaking, and fully public. Who needs two tickets for the price of one when the airlines can't afford to keep planes safe, clean, and on time?

The key to domestic multi-accessibility is not only your phone lines. There are some other lines being run into your 17% mortgage, namely those that are called "cables" and designed to feed you a mess of electronic potage *in competition* with phone companies like Bell, and antenna companies like Radio Shack, and wireless companies like NBC-TV.

At the moment, of course, you aren't forced to attach yourself to the new cable company lines being "passed" by your door; today's free TV and radio programs appear adequate to many, just as no TV before 1946, and no TV or radio much before 1920, seemed adequate to those who never could appreciate audio-video messages about sanitary napkins, clogged nasal passages, and crimes of dispassionate violence.

But what will happen when the value of newly added cable and other telecommunications offerings becomes something you just can't live without? You'll sign on, subscribe, somehow find the resources and the time, just as you did with the telephone and the television set. The sum of available electronic services from the mid-1980s and forward will take priority over and be different from whatever you have had available to you from the mid-1980s back to the beginning of time. These changes will be real and irreversible.

To say it more succinctly: more vendors and advertisers will have more ways of reaching you than ever before, and more other sources—news, data, instructional, opinon-forming—will also have more ways of reaching you than ever before.

The Menu Society

When novelist Isaac Asimov wrote about future schlock in an article for *Advertising Age,* his most potent finding, he told me, was that—thanks to computers—advertisers and other "reachers" will be able to avoid waste circulation and achieve pinpoint accuracy by electronically sorting through many-layered computerized mailing lists for the folks out there who precisely fit the model of your ideal customer.

Discussing this with a Radio Shack computer merchandiser, I found that his ideal would be the ability to search through vendor inventories and catalogs "for the closest thing to what I want." For example, a green wool sweater with zipper closure and two pockets that button.

"My God," I said involuntarily, "that's almost *exactly what advertisers don't want*—a parity position that eliminates a shot at selling you a different sweater, or something you'd forgotten you needed or wanted until you happened to see it." (Buying and shopping are two different things!)

Parity is a search for just the right green sweater, not a saunter along Miracle Mile but a peek and poke through Strangelove's Data Bank—the high-tech darkness of a world operating on fact instead of fancy . . . with unenhanced selection, not salesmanship . . .and more by *look-up* than by *look-at*.

I call this the "Menu Society," and for a very good reason: in computerese, the road to access is by what some engineer once (probably smiling around his cancerous pipe stem) called a menu. The word menu implies what?—selection! At almost every step along the way to anything accessed by electronic means, you're shown a menu and asked to choose from it: not just any old thing but any one thing that's presented in multiple-choice form. Each "dish" you "order" leads you to another and yet another dish until, finally, your appetite for getting info or giving instructions is satisfied.

On my TRS-80 Model II, used as a word processor to write this book, when I press a key marked ESC (ESCape!) while I'm writing my text, the following menu appears immediately along the bottom line of my page: D (define text block), W (set window mode), G (get page), S (search), U (document utilities) and H (help). Don't be alarmed; in five months I never used D, W, S or H even once! Nevertheless, it's a nouvelle cuisine menu with six selections.

When I press the ESC key twice, the page I'm working on disappears and is replaced by a list of the chapters I've written onto disk in my TRS-80, under the heading *Directory List.* Under all that—another menu! O (open), C (copy), F1 (create), F2 (delete), N (next), and D (disk utilities). A six-dish menu of which I was inclined to taste only three during all the months spent writing this book.

> **Note:** Once I asked my youngest son how he knew he didn't like kiwis. "I don't like anything I've never tasted," he replied.

Even when artificial intelligence (acronym AI) upgrades and extends what computers do, menus will still be essential. By acting upon various rules, "the computer creates additional data about the problem at hand. Then, it begins to search for another rule that applies to the new set of data. The computer then goes through this operation again and again until it reaches a final conclusion," says an AI article in *Business Week.* Menus by any other name will still be menus.

Later the writer admits, "The only point on which there is agreement is that the key to problem-solving is not a prescribed method of reasoning but the availability of huge banks of knowledge." Menus, I hasten to observe, are merely signposts within the bank—c.f., your choice of men's room or ladies' room; let's not junk up the discussion with too many cognates and cognomens.

Flashback. Once when I was walking the streets of our UK headquarters city (Birmingham) I found myself looking at a Prestel system in a TV store. Talk about menus! Starting with the part of town I wanted to eat in (menu selection), I went (selection) to restaurants (selection) and then to Italian (selection). It took at least one more (selection) push to discover that the Italian restaurant—the one and only—in that part of the city wasn't open that night. Curses! But that was in 1978, when your fingers walked faster through the Yellow Pages than through your central processing unit.

The magazine article I just mentioned quoted a scientist as saying something like this: Artificial intelligence is more ruminative than regular computing in which "binary decision-making [insists] that something is either day or night before you deal with it," meaning, of course, that "when you make a binary decision, you cannot afford to be wrong, because you are 100% wrong."

"Binary" here simply means "two numbers"—the number 1 and the number 0. And when our scientist conceptualizes deeper things than present computers are capable of, I, ever the practical ignoramus, see only larger menus shuffled through more rapidly. The guy doesn't scare me. Where is it written that his 125,000,000,000,000,000 character-storage-capacity brain is bigger than mine? And even though my book holds only a measly 1,300,000 characters, it's not about to perish from cancer of the lung or eating a poison mushroom.

Menus are rather nicely suggested by cable industry expert J. Leonard Reinsch, as summarized in the magazine *Cablevision*. "His vision of how interactive television will be used in a typical suburban house a few years from now," the article says, goes something like this:

"The day would open with the father checking [on TV] airline schedules for a business trip and up-to-date news headlines. . . . His daughter would then finish some last-minute school work on the television, and an hour later mother would use the cable system to order garden supplies, transfer money from the family savings account and confirm time for a zoning meeting. While she is out of the house, the cable signal will regulate the home's hot water heater and air conditioner while all the time acting as a watchdog against fire and theft." All of them are menus, manually or automatically selected, or, for $99.95 more, voice-actuated.

The biggest battle brewing, perhaps, is between the phone line and the cable line. Which will get the most interesting menus to you—the phone company or the cable company? Or traditional wireless media (local and network TV and radio)? Or traditional hard-copy media (mail, newspaper, magazine)? Or the hard seat of a subway train taking you to Yankee Stadium?

And the biggest question brewing, perhaps, is how can

these media get enough advertising dollars to stay in business?

And the biggest paradox brewing, perhaps, is what will be the eventual impact of "pay cable" information and entertainment on the traditional *"pay to go see"* and *"pay to go learn"* industries that have been fundamental bases of social togetherness since it became relatively safe to sit down beside a stranger an age before the Age of Pericles?

Fractional Advertising and "Infomercials"

Future schlock, even if its act gets cleaned up through some unprecedented conversion of its leading edge, the ad agency—from phony ecstasy to intimations of agony—will still have the same old LCD. Not Liquid Crystal Display, but Lowest Common Denominator. In summary the LCD is salesmanship at a rational, budgeted cost of sales, in order to develop a larger customer base and maintain the old one. It will be a lot harder to make advertising decisions in a "Menu Society" in which offerings will be as plentiful as advice and the 600 B.C. to 1980 A.D. media reduced to fractions of their former estate.

Imagine access to (or by) 100 cable channels as opposed to yesterday's 12-channel TV universe! No——not opposed to, but joined to; make that 112 channels. Plus direct satellite reception. Plus computer-access to all the data accumulated since Neanderthal Man (the first guy to say "no" to the first traveling salesman). And other pluses, however negative they may appear. Imagine, then, the difficulty of getting to—of reaching—the buying public, and of getting them to sit still for your memorable message.

Today's 80-million TV homes can, at least in theory, be reached by a mere three major networks if you have shops, shelves, or salespeople all over the country like those of Radio Shack. But tomorrow's 90 million households won't be addressable so easily, not, at least, in the proverbial "one fell swoop." Want to know what I think of that? I think it's perfectly swell. Try selling—selling, I said, not showing—personal computers in 30 seconds (minus 3 for claimers and disclaimers) and you'll appreciate my flippant dismissal of what some folks think sells beer.

I much prefer what my old friend Manning Greenberg of *HFD Retailing Home Furnishings* offers as the result of an interview with someone from the probably little-known company Narrowcast Marketing USA. "We're providing an organized method that will enable (advertisers) to provide "infomercials" of several minutes' duration to explain their product fully," the man said. "People who voluntarily watch a product demonstration of several minutes . . . are much better sales prospects than people who are involuntarily exposed to a 30-second commercial on conventional broadcasts." How true!

Some of us have spent millions of dollars to find this out, and some of us like to believe otherwise. Why? I think it has to do with the thrill of going big time, the belief that the big cost is synonymous with the big result, and —most important—because even at the steep price tag it's affordable. Ask your ad agency—High Yeller, Inc.—if this isn't the truth according to Madison Avenue, but above #575!

Minutes on TV, not seconds, are the way to go. Those minutes will become affordable even to modest companies as the diversity of prime-time options increases. The 12 to 100 extra channels offered by cable systems guarantee that this will indeed happen, a motion seconded by the U.S. Department of Commerce which predicts cable's reach by 1985 will be to 25,000,000 homes—about one-third of our total.

Any advertiser who can't do tricks with a population like that is just plain dumb; the only real trick is learning how to shape messages into the colloquial "different strokes for different folks." At long last—with longer commercials—High Yeller, Inc., will have to do some genuine advertising instead of that half-minute yak with the sub-logo-slogan ("One great idea after another"—Quasar) (ex Motorola) (now Matsushita). For "infomercials" you'll need piss'n'vinegar, not hot air!

What Industry People Say

Here's what some industry people have had to say about it all, sourced from some clippings collected in the Pendaflex file for this chapter:

On buying ads on cable today: Harry Way, media director of Colgate-Palmolive, "compared some cable buys today to dropping a coin in a wishing well and hoping the audience comes through." (*Broadcasting* magazine.)

How television commercials actually work: Jordon Rost, VP sales of Warner Amex Satellite Entertainment Co., "expects more attention and research into the commercials themselves. While cable changes viewing habits, he said, it also will be "opening that Pandora's box about how television commercials actually work!" (Ibid.)

Note: Tell 'em Kornfeld said most of them don't; it was a feature of his box-opening book.

The brave (or chicken) new world: "The world of computers and communications will ultimately meld together . . . it's a question of tons and tons of data coming down that can be selected by the consumer," suggests Arthur Esch, VP of NABU Mfg. Corp., in the same issue cited twice above—nice issue!

Menus galore: "'We have something for everyone,'" said Michael Schwartz of Time Inc., "of the operation that will offer a local dining guide, a list of movies in the area, airline schedules and weather updated four times daily." (Ibid.)

Note: "There are some who can't wait for Tri-XXX-Nitely's dating service and the Saturday Night Special directory," said Kornfeld, with love and hate in mind, but wondering, at the same time, how to advertise hi-fi on 100 different menus.

Multum in parvum (ad astra): "The newest [cable] systems under construction in major cities will feature more than 100 channels. In those cases, two cables are laid side by side, and as many as 54 channels can be transmitted through each one," reveals Tony Schwartz in the *New York Times* which, among other things, offers almost that many menus for consumption (internal) every week.

TV Digest launches electronic daily: not on water but on NewsNet. It offers "instantaneous delivery of (its) daily, independent of mail, via a local telephone call anywhere in the U.S. and in dozens of foreign countries. . . . [It's a very] straightforward operating system that anyone can learn in minutes [with] printout on paper or display on video screen at choice of user." Not in 1990 or 1985, this, but 1982!

Dow Jones launches "your own private newspaper"—in the same time frame as *TV Digest,* too. Billed as "a productivity tool," sub-headed as "delivered electronically through your own word processor, terminal or personal computer."

Note: I can remember when a perfectly sane newspaper editor, referring to the TRS-80 personal computer, asked me to "tell the truth, Kornfeld, who's going to use these things . . . really?" And how well I remember saying to myself, "Not I," but aloud: "Just about everybody we haven't yet sold one to." He rolled his eyes and smiled faintly. My one-liners often do that to people. (My two-liners never quite get finished.)

FCC nixes SATCOM auction: When RCA tried to auction off places on its new Satcom-4 satellite at Sotheby's—actually *after* the auction—the Federal Communications Commission (FCC) torpedoed it, to use *TV Digest's* exciting verb. "At least one auction bidder—Edward Beagan, chmn., Transponder Leasing Corp.—said he had serious questions about propriety of RCA's latest tariff, suggested RCA may be engaging in 'price fixing,'" the story reveals.

> ***ADvisory.*** This is the sort of thing we'll be reading about in the 1990s, but, said one reporter (Kornfeld): "We could have waited until then."

The unassailable logic of a simple teleconference is how a recent *Dun's Business Month* (nee Dun's Review) starts out a data comparison between a phone conference and a "fly-drive" conference. For example: New York to Los Angeles and Washington D.C.—for a one-hour meeting by phone the cost would be $94.60, the personal "fly-drive" cost $1596.32, and the "savings realized" a fat $1491.72. What the chart fails to tell you, however, is that most conferences don't last an hour; they last many hours. And while the fly-drive cost remains fixed for many hours, the phone conference cost keeps on growing and growing. Also, the flying-driver can get you a lot of other things done, so Dun's, consider your logic assailed!

CABLE TV's advantages: "Cable offers sponsor-provided programming [and the] ability to tailor program to audience, splash logos across screen," and "On cable you don't have to go through screening departments and commercials don't cost thousands of dollars," and cable has a "unique ability to serve specialized audiences." These were some of the feelings expressed at the first Cable Advertising Bureau conference attended by more than 1200 advertising executives in New York City in January 1982.

Radio Shack Stores Linked by Computers

Computer Systems link Radio Shack stores, Fort Worth offices is how the company's magazine told its employee readers about putting some 4400 company owned Shacks on line to "convert paper work to computer work" in mid-1982. "Use of the store computer system has already paid off [by helping] all store personnel become more expert on Radio Shack (TRS-80) computers [and] in many cases an identical system has been sold because a customer sees it actually handling store business," the article revealed.

ADvisory. When visitors to your place of business see you confident enough of your product to use it in everyday operations, their confidence closes the credibility gap and they're ready to buy.

Home Box Office (HBO) adds 3,500,00 subscribers says a *New York Times* story, noting its climb from 4 to 7.5 million between the beginning of 1980 to the end of 1981—in two years. And elsewhere it mentions HBO's prediction that "every television household in the nation" will have access to pay television of some kind by 1989." *Author's note:* Let's just stay with 7,500,000 subscribers, for the moment, and imagine the scenario of 20% of them (1,500,000 payers) buying TV tickets to a play, movie, opera, prizefight or other sporting event, in any tight time frame. Instant success or failure! If you're an advertiser, you're drooling; if you're an in-person promoter, you're sweating. With two-way (interactive) systems, what's to prevent an instant, all-electronic, stay-at-home national presidential election next time around, one without need of polling places and voting machines?

It's AT&T time again: "Scene: San Diego, California. A woman in an office glances at her watch, picks up the telephone, keys up her home number, then presses four more buttons. She pauses, then presses four more buttons. She pauses, then presses four buttons again." Why? To get that roast going in her oven, the air conditioner started, and "all through the local telephone exchange." My estimate is at least 19 pressed buttons. I have already imagined GTE's headline on a completing ad: "6 GTE BUTTON-PRESSES DO WHAT 19 DO FOR 'THE OTHER PHONE COMPANY.' WE'RE NOT 3 TIMES AS SMART. . . OR ARE WE?"

Electronic mail is due to begin amid legal war is an actual *Wall Street Journal* headline. It will be useful in any given year up to 2006. So will this follow-on body copy: "The Justice Department argues that the Postal Service can't legally start the new system without first receiving a valid recommendation from the Postal Rate Commission." *Author's note:* A valid recommendation from them is like alimony, the question always being . . . "Who needs it?"

Brainwave Input Comes of Age

Brainwave input may be a "common part of computer technology" in schools, says *Electronic Education* magazine (11/81 issue), citing the work of Dr. Alfred Bork of the University of California at Irvine, who forsees a "heads-on" interactive relationship between computers and students. "By 1990, 60 million computers will be in homes. The home market will determine what happens in the schools," thinks Dr. Bork. (This insures that the future schlock in respect to the sale of microcomputers will be hot and heavy. Also that such things as "local networking, brainwave input, voice input and intelligent videodisks"—to quote the magazine—are the wave of education's future. From flower-child to digit-kid in a single generation!)

New video technology poses perils for some advertisers reads a *Harvard Business Review* headline over a story authored jointly by a marketing prof and an agency account supervisor. "From an advertiser's perspective, the worst aspect of these new communications techniques is undoubtedly the freedom they give viewers to be selective about what they watch." What new techniques?—Cable, Videodisk, Teleprint, and Two-Way interactive cable TV. Quite a full menu for advertisers whose best idea on staying fit is staying slim—budgetwise, that is, and also creative-wise.

Teleselling Begins

Penney, Target said to plan teleselling is how *HFD Retailing Daily* told about these two retailers trying on an in-home electronic shopping service for size (called Teletel, if you're curious). Time and tide wait for no one. There's one of Kornfeld's Rules of Marketing to cover that situation; it's #65 and it observes:

---

65 There's no business like NO business.

Flashback: To remind us of how things change in short periods like ten years, *Forbes'* 3/1/82 issue tracks the progress of the "nifty 50" companies in the decade from 1972 to 1981. Today all have lower P/E ratios! Today 36 have lower stock prices—that's a whopping 72%! "Real success," says *Forbes'* writer, "requires acting against the trend." In the sense of this chapter, that means acting against the notion that computers are only for owl-eyed wizards and that video technology will never lay a glove on Ye Olde Outfitters, Ltd.

Is Programming the Second Literacy?

Programming as the second literary is the key to a bright tomorrow in the mind of at least one articulate educator. "The opportunities offered by the computer and [related] new educational tasks . . . will shorten a child's way to intellectual maturity, increase his activity, improve his preparedness to occupational performance, including an ability to take part in the second industrial revolution precipitated by computers and new automation technologies. In other words, programming is the second literacy."

To find out more about this, either get the November 1981 copy of *Monitor* magazine, put out by the Association for Educational Data Systems, or contact the author, A. P. Ershov, at the Computer Center, USSR Academy of Sciences, Siberian Branch, Novosibirsk 630090, USSR.

You may not have to come in out of the cold to get the rest of the story!

FIFTEEN

Kornfeld's Rules Revisited

Before I started composing *To Catch a Mouse,* I didn't have a single rule on marketing in any form other than as inclusions in 33 years' worth of memoranda about better ways of getting things done better.

Radio Shack's vice-president for computer manufacturing told me just the other day that he still uses one of my memos on product reliability. Written in 1974, it goes like this: "Reliability comes *before anything else* in our business: before price, before appearance, before novelty, before hustling to get a jump on the market. Who needs to go to the trouble of designing, tooling and building something that doesn't work right out of the box and maybe forever after?"

So I guess "Reliability First" was a rule of sorts.

While I was busy processing these words, Radio Shack's executive vice-president for marketing—which includes both advertising and merchandising—dropped in to show me a bunch of old LK memos he had saved and was still distributing for troop guidance. One of them, written in 1960, advises:

"Picture vs. story? Our flyer stories should not use over 40% of the space. Our pictures should use at least 60% of the space. Our pictures should also be prettier. Get the picture?"

So I guess "The Big Picture" was also a rule of sorts.

When C. D. Tandy was alive and kicking, his quiz went: "What do you guys think your jobs are?" then he'd supply his answer without waiting for yours: "You're *teachers,* is what you are. The g- d- highest paid teachers in the country, so you can afford to listen to me."

Teachers have to do more than teach, they have to help students motivate themselves and they have to succeed at both tasks. If too many students flunk or merit only a C, you're adjudged lousy at teaching. I was surprised to learn that when I did some teaching at the University of Denver. But in business, unlike academe, you can afford to pre-screen your scholars; you try not to have dogs and mules in the classroom when you can have more exotic and productive species for the same starting price.

Hindsight or whatever, I guess that *letting your teachers know they're teachers* is also a rule.

Even if they don't always resemble the cleancut, pinstriped six-foot salesmen the big manufacturers were alleged to prefer back when electron tubes were our dominant category, Radio Shack teachers have done rather well in student training. Well enough to fuel rumors that several prestigious office equipment companies (with very short names) sometimes seek to raid the faculty and/or graduating senior class!

As with ad agencies and other consultants, Tandy was philosophically against intra-industry proselyting, also against the employment of what we usually call "head hunters."

His predictable reaction to most help offered from the outside was a proud, gruff, "I know how to get it done." His very decent reaction to the caliber of his staff was this: "Where can you find a better bunch of men than the men on our team?" It applied even when you actually could find some better men; even when "the men" were women, since Radio Shack had two female VPs . . . and you can think again if you're thinking they were token officials. (Lady VPs can be tougher than chicken-fried steak. That, too, may be a rule.)

Perhaps now you have a better understanding of how my Rules of Marketing "just grew" into my text, and of how the further idea of gathering them into this extra chapter began to seem useful. I could have gathered up my innumerable ADvisories as well, but there are limits—even to the amount of recycled paper useful in a world suddenly awakened to the daymare of its own physical depletion.

Recently I read a review of what seemed to the reviewer to be an unusually good book on Personal Financial Planning for the 1990s. It was unusual, the reviewer noted, because it couldn't be summed up—as could so many similar books he'd read—in 25 words or less. For example: "Buy Gold under $300, Improve and Sell Your Home Every 4 Years, Own Swiss Fs and German DMs, Start IRAs Yearly, and Keep Swimming."

Fertilizer like that, the reviewer said with more than a hint of irritation, has been blown up to 400 pages and sold as a brilliant new book 18 times p/a ever since hamburger went over 77¢ a pound.

I hope this book, too, if only because of this chapter, proves to be unlike the dozens of others written on my subjects: shrinkable to 25 words (after being expanded to thousands during six months of hard labor).

If you rule some of my Rules vintage tautology or contentious chaff, there are more of them than you can easily—even safely—ignore. If their collective reproduction here isn't an "incalculable public service," at least it may be regarded as a summary whose value exceeds by several times the price of its wrapper.

And not only is it a summary, it's also the last word!

RULE 1:

Don't fight problems of creating and placing new advertising or product displays if they seem solvable by old answers. Consider repeating, with or without changes, previously used layout, copy, art, or display material.

RULE 2:

Don't place any advertising lacking consumer news value or benefits. Force your buyers and admen to offer you a choice of benefits; select the best. After a few false starts, they'll get to know you mean it when you demand benefits. When the well is dry, seek out and discuss benefits offered by the competition.

RULE 3:

The more you tend to go outside for advice and services in business, the more you tend to lose confidence and control.

RULE 4:

One of the quickest ways of learning what to do in any business situation is first to be able to observe it done incorrectly.

RULE 5:

Surveys undertaken to reinforce the safety of fairly imminent business decisions tend to arrive at the obvious in a time frame that is too late, and in an amount that is too little.

RULE 6:

A direct order is an instruction that is made clear and workable only when your people have revised it so that it becomes their best judgment on what to do next.

RULE 7:

When your advertising asks for the order right out front, with a price and a place to buy and with "NOW" included in the copy, that's hard sell-advertising, and it should invariably be tried before any other kind.

RULE 8:

When ad agencies or in-house ad employees seem inclined to copy trendy ad themes, rely on comparisons, resort to storytelling, or aim toward winning an award for creative excellence rather than toward satisfying the greater need of their client, these inclinations will NOT be deceiving, and the client must fight them with every available weapon.

RULE 9:

Advertising is usually most beautiful when it's least measurable and least productive.

RULE 10:

No one should allow his selling season to be shorter than 365 days in any calendar year, or allow his ad funds to run dry before they have somehow touched each of its 52 weeks.

RULE 11:

Don't let your bookkeepers make book on your marketing decisions.

RULE 12:

Always investigate the amount of waste circulation you have to buy when you buy space or time in a medium; always estimate the value of waste vs. non-waste and see if there's a better way to spend your promotional bucks.

RULE 13:

Never base a business decision or philosophy on information supplied by an industry bureau or association unless your main requirements are bias and optimism.

RULE 14:

You can anticipate that the results of national advertising will be roughly in proportion to the populations of the affected states or localities, except that the results in your "home" area—100-mile radius from address in ad—will be well above this proportion.

RULE 15:

Your customer most likely to become a repeat customer is your most recent customer.

RULE 16:

Never tell a customer or prospect what NOT TO DO unless you immediately tell him WHAT TO DO in the same or next sentence of your message. A negative command is a no-no!

RULE 17:

It takes at least twice as much money to attract a new customer via newspaper or other form of advertising as to re-attract a repeat customer by direct personal contact; budget to spend 33.3% on recent customers, 66.6% on former or non-customers,and 0.1% on cigars.

RULE 18:

Guard against small details which can needlessly downgrade your image: printed materials, use and size of logos, the area around the cash register, doors that bang when they shouldn't, things whose cost would be the same for a rose as for a bramble.

RULE 19:

Don't put any words on your shop's bag except your company name. Put your name on BIG.

RULE 20:

News, plans, moves, changes, guesstimates and rumors about the company must be responded to by DESIGNATED PERSONNEL ONLY, and all other persons contacted must refer their contact to the designated personnel.

RULE 21:

Color yourself yellow when marketing tactics recommend a retreat and basic principles are not endangered.

RULE 22:

In respect of disclaimers, anything in advertising that needs to be disavowed probably should be disallowed.

RULE 23:

When loss of a trademark is threatened due to people's use of it as an ordinary (generic) word, its advertising must always include a REVERSE DISCLAIMER claiming that the product IS WHAT IT IS, as demonstrated by the use of the word "brand" after each use of the trademark.

RULE 24:

Every ad should carry your logo and/or company name in an upper section, preferably at the top, unless your name can be incorporated comfortably within the headline. When the latter is done, use it in headline type, not as a logotype.

RULE 25:

The copy of every ad should be regarded as "survival copy"—the kind of copy on which many employee lives depend. If all you do is pay for it, learn to recognize "survival" copy; it's copy with a lot of "I" and a lot of "me" in it. If it's only your resumé, put your NAME ON TOP of every page; you're not the only one trying to get back in the game!

RULE 26:

Prior to acceptance by the advertiser, the copy proposed for every media ad must be tested for inclusion of these five essential components: (1) Benefits. (2) Empathy. (3) News Value. (4) Truth. (5) Pheromone Factor. If the presented ad lacks any of these five elements, it probably needs revision.

RULE 27:

You should give long, full, earnest consideration to the risks involved in NOT opting to go "all out" in new product sales promotion whenever you get a chance to vote.

RULE 28:

Any advertising is almost always better than no advertising, but when "any advertising" is your best idea on what to do next, spend as little on its execution as you can, not as much as you can afford.

RULE 29:

If your ad is measurable, then the cost-effectiveness of amenities such as more color or larger size can also be measured.

RULE 30:

Each element of a promotional effort needs to be assigned someone's idea of percent of total available space required for it before the promotion is turned over to the people who will process it to its final form.

RULE 31:

In business, the best time to have a post mortem is when the patient still has a chance to remain alive.

RULE 32:

Even with beautifully drawn or photographed cheddar in

your marketing plan, you won't catch a mouse with it if it doesn't make a noise like a cheese.

RULE 33:

There is no way you can please all of the people much of the time in advertising, but you can easily avoid making ads, packages or displays that imply sexism or racism, and thereby avoid displeasing some of the people all of the time.

RULE 34:

Whether an ad starts with a theme (copywriter) looking for a picture (artist) or a picture looking for a theme, the hardest task is to fuse art, copy and product into a positive request for an order for the advertised product or service. Attempts at relevance that are given force-fit elements result in irrelevance, regardless of their individual quality. Theme, copy and art that don't ask for customers ask for trouble.

RULE 35:

Material created for sales promotional purposes—whether painted, printed, photographed, spoken or fabricated—should make few if any assumptions of prior familiarity on the part of the intended audience. Be leery of presenting hard-to-recognize objects unless their use can be presented with extreme clarity. Avoid making the audience guess your message (paradox) or laugh at it (humor). Shun technical specifications if they are obscure to your least-informed customer prospect. Avoid abbreviations; it's a "given" that many words which are commonly abbreviated in your industry will have different meanings in other industries. Consider if unincluded data on product size, weight or color will encourage inaccurate anticipation by the audience. The road to inattention is paved with unwarranted assumptions!

RULE 36:

When you make an exception to a Kornfeld or any other Rule of Marketing, make your exception EXCEPTIONAL!

RULE 37:

Everything you have to say about and be wary of in respect

to commercial art directors, you can also say about plumbers, interior decorators, and architects.

RULE 38:

When facing any marketing problem, face to the rear first because it's the end result that matters. Once you have honestly and fearlessly determined the desired effect—more business, improved awareness, better positioning, new converts, greater visibility—then face forward and determine how to initiate a process for achieving it.

RULE 39:

In matters between the client and the agency, the client is at fault when fault is found.

RULE 40:

The headline of every ad must challenge or lure the reader into reading further, or risk his skipping to the next headline written by the next advertiser.

RULE 41:

The point made by the main headline of every ad must always be reinforced in the first line of the body copy.

RULE 42:

Unless redundancy is seen to be an essential repetition of what's already been said, ad copy should proceed directly to its next new point—that is, from made Point A to new Point B.

RULE 43:

When advertising copy says something WON'T DO, it must quickly say either WHY IT WON'T DO, or WHAT WILL DO, or preferably both.

RULE 44:

Never say "maybe" in an ad—say "Yes" or "No."

RULE 45:

When making analogies and claims in advertising, clarity of intention is even more urgent than relevance or accuracy.

RULE 46:

Kill a coy ad before it gets to print if you can catch it. Few readers will be entertained or appreciative; a majority won't stay with it long enough to get the point.

RULE 47:

Advertisers who belittle themselves or their products in their advertising, whether seriously or in jest, can expect little result.

RULE 48:

Never mention competitors by name or industry in your advertising unless your intention is positioning for parity or better status, or for adversary purposes.

RULE 49:

No one should be put in charge of corporate identity except in a review capacity, and never full time, and never with a title.

RULE 50:

Since the addition of even one color to a black and white ad costs money, don't buy even one extra color unless you perceive an overwhelming justification for it. If perceived, then execute it brilliantly.

RULE 51:

If your company needs a spokesperson, it's probable the idea came from your ad agency, reinforced by your Yes Man of advertising, and that the person selected will be unsuitable, possibly a large stockholder, probably the Chairman or CEO; and it's certain that a favorable effect of this on your business will be undetectable.

RULE 52:

Before employing a spokesperson as salesperson in media ads, first you should have examined and discarded all other selling techniques. Try to resist using either the boss or other executive as your spokesperson as it causes internal resentment among those who actually do the work. And always be believable.

RULE 53:

Religion and religious figures in secular product advertising should be faithfully observed by 100% omission.

RULE 54:

When positioning your product or plan, identify other similar products or plans with which you'd like yours to be judged in the sense of parity or better, then tilt your advertising and PR implacably in that direction.

RULE 55:

Even if you elect to show your positioned or repositioned product in a more favorable manner than your competitor's, or as being technically superior, use carefully selected specifics and avoid aggressive adversary advertising.

RULE 56:

Don't give the keys to your kingdom to ANYONE inside or outside the company unless you know for sure that a preemptive nuclear strike is now in progress and it's D+10 minutes.

RULE 57:

If the position of your product is seen as parity with others on the market, repeat "vive la différence" aloud until you've worked out a strategy for making it higher and less vulnerable. It's not good enough to be Just As Good.

RULE 58:

A commodity is a product whose retail value is reduced to its lowest common denominator by having that value known and agreed on and changed at the whim of the Market. To make your product a product instead of a commodity, ADD VALUE TO IT, and CHARGE FULLY for the value added.

RULE 59:

After thorough discussion by management, including observation of what others do, your company should prepare and disseminate its own PR in-house, accepting PR as important positional advertising; even if unmeasurable, it is worth doing well.

RULE 60:

If an event has occurred within your company which you think the world should know about, decide how to tell it, who should tell it, what should be told, make it an in-house project. Stick to the central and hopefully only point. Choose your media and adressees carefully. And then let it fly . . . *first*!

RULE 61:

If there is too much discrepancy between the commercial housing of your officers and your troops, don't be surprised when the corporals don't behave like captains and if you are occasionally referred to as some kind of fink (because in a lot of ways you are).

RULE 62:

If you can create advertising that is adversary in the sense of offering to sell something outrageously expensive, but complimentary in the sense of being an intelligent purchase, don't hesitate to be frank and hurt a few feelings. The "hurtable" individual is a person who is much easier to convert into a customer than one whose basic response is "show me."

RULE 63:

When opportunity knocks in an unusually loud manner, tear a hole in the wall and make it a second door. When your plan for capitalizing on your opportunity isn't large enough . . . MAKE it large enough.

RULE 64:

More is always more than less. And more is usually better than less.

RULE 65:

There's no business like NO business.

INDEX

A

OTHER RADIO SHACK PUBLICATIONS

BOOKS IN 1983 CATALOG

COMPUTER TECHNOLOGY

62-1383	Understanding Computer Science
2010	Understanding Digital Electronics
2017	Understanding Microprocessors
2066	Programming the Z80
2003	Beginners Guide to Computers

BOOKS FOR TRS 80

62-2006	TRS 80 Assembly Language Programming
2015	Basic Computer Programming
2016	Basic Computer Language
2061	Level II Basic
2067	Programming in Style
2068	Basic Computer Games
2069	Basic Computer Programs for Home
2073	Intro TRS 80 Graphics
2072	Advanced Level II Basic
2062	Programming Techniques for Level II
2086	Pocket Computer Programs
2079	TRS 80 Business Programs
1002	Basic Faster & Better
2076	Color Computer Graphics
2087	Graphics for Model I/III
2312	Problem Solving on Pocket Computer

2085 TRS 80 Data File Programming
2088 Basic Conversion Handbook
26-3191 Getting Started w/Color Basic
3192 Going Ahead with Extended Basic
3193 Color Computer Reference Manual
2107 Getting Started with TRS 80 Basic
2109 Mod III Tech Reference Manual
2111 Mod III Disc Sys. Owners Manual
2112 Mod III Reference Manual

COMMUNICATIONS

62-2018 Understanding Communications Systems
2051 Antennas

SERVICING

62-2030 Tube Substitution Handbook
2040 Electronics Data Handbook
2047 Dictionary of Electronics Terms
2057 Math for the Electronics Student

GENERAL ELECTRONICS

62-2029 Guide to Stereo HiFi
2035 Understanding Solid-State Electronics
2039 Guide to VOM's & VTVM's
2309 Building Speaker Enclosures
1384 Understanding Optronics
1385 Understanding Automotive Electronics
1386 Understanding Energy Control
2310 Modern Dict of Electronic Terms
2311 Microcomputer Dictionary
2021 Basic AC Circuits Vol. I
2022 Basic AC Circuits Vol. 2
2019 Basic DC Circuits Vol. 1
2020 Basic DC Circuits Vol. 2
1080 Computer Demonstrator